DIET&EXERCISE GUIDE

By MARY MILO
Beauty Editor

and FAMILY CIRCLE FOOD STAFF

Created by Family Circle Magazine and published 1978 by Arno Press Inc., a subsidiary of The New York Times Company. Copyright © 1972, 1966, 1965,1964, 1963, 1962, 1961 by The Family Circle, Inc. All rights reserved. Protected under Berne and other international copyright conventions. Title and Trademark FAMILY CIRCLE registered U. S. Patent and Trademark Office, Canada, Great Britain, Australia, New Zealand, Japan and other countries. Marca Registrada. This volume may not be reproduced in whole or in part in any form without written permission from the publisher. Printed in U. S. A. Library of Congress Catalog Card Number 73-11787. ISBN 0-405-09844-8.

CONTENTS

A luxury in good eating for a bargain in calories—that's this inviting diet meal with Asparagus Roulade (recipe on page 131) as its star. Delicate omeletlike roll is baked, filled with asparagus, and topped with a creamy Swiss-cheese sauce. Parslied Carrots (recipe on page 133) make a colorful, good-for-you platemate

Total calories per serving: 364

4

Be glad
you're a dieter

Can you go on a diet and stay with it till you reach the weight you want? Can you control weight gains—not just this week or next but for years ahead? Yes, you can. Weight-watching, as you know, means better health, a better figure, a more active and satisfying life, greater self-esteem. Look at the tempting meals and dishes that will be part of your reducing plan—and will also keep your family happy and well fed. Try the easy and effective exercises—designed especially for the female figure. These figure firmers will help you slim while they improve your posture, even your morale. Find out how much you should weigh, how activity helps weight loss, how the food needs of your family members differ, and how their varying needs can be supplied. All recipes have been prepared and tested by FAMILY CIRCLE's Test Kitchens—and all are calorie-counted to help you fit your diet menus into your family's daily eating plan. Here is a sound and taste-satisfying approach to diet and weight loss —the kind of service information that more than 8,000,000 women find each issue in the pages of FAMILY CIRCLE. Weight-watching can become a lifetime good habit. This guide gets you started right—and it will keep you on the path of sensible weight control within the pattern of your family's good-eating habits. It will stand by you till—and even after— you reach your goal of a trim and attractive figure.

THE EDITORS

WHYS AND WAYS OF LOSING WEIGHT

YOU will find it helpful, if you are to control your weight successfully, to understand as much as you can about your own particular problem. Think about yourself a little. Why did you gain? When did you gain? How long has it taken those creeping ounces to become pounds? How much should you weigh? How can you lose? How can you reach the weight you want and keep it? If your other diet attempts have failed, what can make this one work?

Are you overeating?

Start by accepting the fact that one natural law of weight control applies to you and to everyone else:

If more fuel than the body can use for energy is consistently taken in, the excess will be stored as fat and weight will be gained. If consistently the body gets less fuel than it needs for activity and to keep itself going, body fat will be burned and weight will be lost.

If you can firmly believe that this is true, the knowledge will stand by you steadfastly while you work at your own weight-control program. This principle helps as well in understanding your weight problem:

If you gain weight, you are somehow eating too much or burning up too little fuel.

What makes you overeat?

Few of us eat too much on purpose. There are other factors at work—and paying some attention to them can in many cases help us stop gaining and even let us start to lose. Ask yourself some questions:

▶ *Is relaxation my downfall?* Relaxation encourages eating. Even an extra 25 calories (a few peanuts, for example) a day can cause a person to gain up to two pounds a year.

▶ *Do I overeat when I'm tense?* In times of stress it's natural to turn to food as a tranquilizer or a pacifier.

▶ *Do I snack when I'm bored?* Sometimes it seems easier to eat than to act. Both eating and lassitude can contribute to overweight.

▶ *Have I maintained food intake as I've added birthdays?* After age 25 (the time when the body is fully developed) calorie needs diminish *(see table, page 10)*. If food intake remains the same, and particularly if activity slackens, added years mean added pounds.

▶ *Do I simply enjoy good food?* If you're a good cook and enjoy cooking and eating, you can overeat simply out of pleasure. With good food abundant and easy to prepare, temptation surrounds us.

▶ *Do I eat when I feel tired?* We can mistake for hunger pangs the body's need for rest, for a change of pace, for exercise.

▶ *Am I from a "fat" family?* There is some evidence that heredity can play a part in a tendency of some persons to gain weight. In other "fat" families there simply is a tradition of overeating. In either case, you as an individual can control your weight with careful dieting and exercise.

▶ *Do I have a health problem?* Weight gain is associated with a number of health problems; a checkup by your doctor to find out your health status should be the starting point of your weight-control program.

▶ *Do I eat the right things?* You may overeat without

getting all the nutrients your body needs to be well-fed. A weight-control diet should supply all your daily food needs except calories. Good nutrition *(see pages 79-87)* will help appease your appetite.

▶ *Have I decreased my activity?* Count up your household conveniences—each one saves body fuel. If you slack off on activity, you should also slack off on food intake. Stepping up your activity can on the other hand help you control your weight.

▶ *Has poor posture filled me out?* Correct body alignment *(see pages 19-21)* can trim you before you lose a pound.

When did you gain?

Some women will say they've always been overweight. Others know they gained at a specific time. Understanding the circumstances in which you gained any extra weight may help get you back in control.

▶ *Are you gaining now?* If you look at the chart on page 11, you will see that weight of women takes a big leap upward at about age 35 and again after age 55. If you are in the 25-to-35 or the 55-to-65 age bracket, it may help to be aware that these are danger zones in weight control. Take into account that, as your daily calorie needs are diminishing *(see table, page 10)*, you are perhaps less active than you once were. Cut your food intake accordingly. Just giving up little extras— cream and sugar in coffee, for example—helps, but may not be enough. Watching your calorie intake and cutting out second helpings can stop the steady weight gains that could one day add up to obesity.

▶ *Did you gain when you got married?* Cooking for a husband has made many a slim bride fat. The pitfalls are tasting too much as you cook (if you follow a tested recipe carefully, you can cut down on tasting), eating leftovers just because they're there, eating to encourage others to eat, or appreciation of your cooking.

▶ *Did you gain with a pregnancy?* Many women gain when they're having a baby and never seem able to get rid of those extra pounds. Sometimes, however, a pregnancy masks creeping overweight that is recognized only when it doesn't dissolve after the baby comes. Doctors today encourage women to hold to a minimum any weight gain during pregnancy and to get back into their prepregnancy clothes within a month or so after delivery.

▶ *Did you gain as a teen-ager?* During adolescence a girl often puts on pounds. Usually doctors take this rounding out matter-of-factly, because a girl usually slims down again as she reaches her full height and her body adjusts into womanhood. Sometimes, however, the extra roundness stays. In your early 20s you should be at your normal—your best—weight.

▶ *Have you always been overweight?* If so, you probably are accustomed to overeating and underexercising. Habitual overeating—or heredity or some health factor —may have set your appetite-governor too high. Long-term diet control can help you adjust it to a lower food demand.

What's your ideal figure?

Ideal weight for you has much to do with the way you want to look and the way you feel most comfortable.

DESIRABLE WEIGHTS FOR WOMEN AGE 25 AND OVER
weight in pounds according to frame (in indoor clothing)

HEIGHT in 2-inch heels		SMALL FRAME	MEDIUM FRAME	LARGE FRAME
FEET	INCHES			
4	10	92— 98	96—107	104—119
	11	94—101	98—110	106—122
5	0	96—104	101—113	109—125
	1	99—107	104—116	112—128
	2	102—110	107—119	115—131
	3	105—113	110—122	118—134
	4	108—116	113—126	121—138
	5	111—119	116—130	125—142
	6	114—123	120—135	129—146
	7	118—127	124—139	133—150
	8	122—131	128—143	137—154
	9	126—135	132—147	141—158
	10	130—140	136—151	145—163
	11	134—144	140—155	149—168
6	0	138—148	144—159	153—173

Desirable weights and average weights courtesy of Metropolitan Life Insurance Company

AVERAGE WEIGHTS FOR WOMEN
weight in pounds in indoor clothing

HEIGHT in 2-inch heels FEET INCHES		AGE 20-24	AGE 25-29	AGE 30-39	AGE 40-49	AGE 50-59	AGE 60-69
4	10	102	107	115	122	125	127
	11	105	110	117	124	127	129
5	0	108	113	120	127	130	131
	1	112	116	123	130	133	134
	2	115	119	126	133	136	137
	3	118	122	129	136	140	141
	4	121	125	132	140	144	145
	5	125	129	135	143	148	149
	6	129	133	139	147	152	153
	7	132	136	142	151	156	157
	8	136	140	146	155	160	161
	9	140	144	150	159	164	165
	10	144	148	154	164	169	
	11	149	153	159	169	174	
6	0	154	158	164	174	180	

Your weight is right for you when it satisfies your idea of what you want to weigh, when you can wear the dress size that suits you perfectly, when you are pleased with the picture you get when you see yourself sideways in a full-length mirror, and when your figure approaches the standard set by your social circle.

Weight loss alone may not give you the figure you want. The way you stand and move, the firmness of your muscles, your feeling of vitality also play a part. The firmer your muscles and the more truly your body is aligned the better you can carry any added weight. This is why figure-firming and posture control should go right along with weight loss. In fact, it is often better to judge your progress in figure control with a tape measure round your waist than by pound variation on the bathroom scale.

How to measure yourself

Body weight is made up of bones, muscles, various organs, body fluids, and the contents of the digestive tract as well as of fat. You know that the taller you are the more you can weigh without being overweight. Again, if your muscles are well-developed or if you have large bones, you can, without having too much fat, weigh more than a soft-muscled or a small-boned person. A man's better-developed muscles and his larger bone structure make normal weight for him higher than that for a woman of the same height.

To evaluate your ideal weight you should know your height accurately and have a fair idea of your frame size.

Have your doctor or someone else measure your height in feet and fraction of inches. And be measured two ways—in your usual stance and when you have drawn yourself into good alignment and to your full height. Any difference will be important in disclosing that poor posture is a factor in your figure problem.

Keep a record of your height to the nearest eighth of an inch—you may "grow" with good posture.

Evaluating your frame size may be difficult. If you have very tiny or obviously large wrists and ankles, they indicate whether your frame is small or large. Otherwise, your glove size may be a clue to whether you are of a small, medium, or large frame. If your glove size is between size 6 and size 7, you probably have a medium frame; if glove size is under size 6, you are probably small; if over 7, you probably have a large frame.

Keep a record, too, of changing measurements. The places to measure are the smallest part of the waist, the largest part of the hips and the bust, the upper thigh at its fullest part, the calf at its fullest part, the ankle at its smallest part, the upper arm at its fullest part, and the neck at its smallest part.

How much should you weigh?

With your height and frame size as a guide, look at the table on page 8. Here you can get an idea of what is considered normal for your height and body build. As you will see, there is no added pound allowance for years over age 25.

The reason? Even though full height is reached earlier, the body continues to develop up to about age 25. Between age 18 and age 25 it is considered normal to add about a pound a year. At age 25, your weight should become stable, and it is considered unhealthful to add pounds after this age. In fact, you should lose. (As you can see from the average-weight tables on pages 9 and 11, after age 25 women have a weight problem.)

Are you overweight?

If you felt that your weight was about right at age 25, you can consider this the desirable weight for you. Compare the figure, however, with the figures given in the table to be sure this weight is within reasonable range.

Next, find out what you weigh now. Again, the weight on your doctor's scale should be your official poundage. For your own checkups the best guide is a bathroom scale on which you can weigh yourself regularly at the same time of day.

If your present weight is 10% or more above normal weight for your height, you can consider yourself uncomfortably *overweight*. If you are 20% or more above normal weight, you are considered *obese*. Obesity is a serious health problem, and you should undertake any weight-control program only under a doctor's supervision.

How can you lose?

Ideally, about 19% of a woman's body weight should be made up of fat. You need this fat to support the body organs, to cushion the muscles, and to fill out the skin. Any excess is a fuel reserve that your body draws upon in emergencies. When you diet, you create such an emergency—the body draws upon its fuel reserve and burns up stored fat. And this is the only way short of surgery that fat can be made to disappear—by inducing the body to use up its own reserves. If you step up your activity at the same time that you shorten the fuel supply, you increase the amount of reserve fuel that's used. You lose weight faster.

A pound a week is considered a reasonable weight loss. If you have only a few pounds to take off, you needn't lose that fast. For the dieter the longest way round may be the shortest way home; if you lose your weight at a reasonable pace over a fairly long period of time, your tastes become adjusted, your body accepts a new regime, a new individual weight level is established, and you are less likely to lapse into old habits that restore lost pounds.

To lose a pound a week you have to cut 500 calories a day from your weight-maintenance diet—the calorie allowance that would be right for you if you were of normal weight (*see table, page 8,* or use the 1,500-calorie weight-maintenance diet, *page 106,* as a base). Or you can cut 250 calories from your weight-maintenance diet and increase your activity to use up another 250 calories (*see tables, pages 15 and 76*)

How do you get started?

Your weight-control program should be something you

PREDICTED DAILY CALORIE NEEDS FOR WOMEN OF NORMAL WEIGHT

HEIGHT FEET	INCHES	AGE 15-19	AGE 20-29	AGE 30-39	AGE 40-49	AGE 50-59	AGE 60-69	AGE 70-79
4	9	2080	1890	1810	1760	1710	1480	1370
4	10	2110	1920	1840	1790	1740	1510	1400
4	11	2140	1950	1870	1820	1770	1530	1430
5	0	2190	1980	1900	1850	1800	1550	1450
5	1	2240	2020	1940	1890	1850	1590	1480
5	2	2290	2060	1980	1950	1900	1640	1510
5	3	2350	2100	2030	2000	1950	1690	1550
5	4	2400	2150	2080	2040	2000	1740	1590
5	5	2460	2200	2140	2080	2050	1780	1640
5	6	2520	2250	2190	2120	2100	1820	1690
5	7	2570	2300	2240	2160	2150	1860	1730
5	8	2620	2350	2290	2220	2200	1910	1770
5	9	2680	2400	2340	2260	2250	1950	1800
5	10	2740	2450	2400	2310	2300	1990	1830
5	11	2800	2500	2450	2360	2350	2040	1880
6	0	2860	2550	2500	2410	2400	2090	1930

Courtesy of Department of Health, City of New York.

RELATIVE CHANGE IN WEIGHT WITH AGE
over the mean for ages 18-24 years

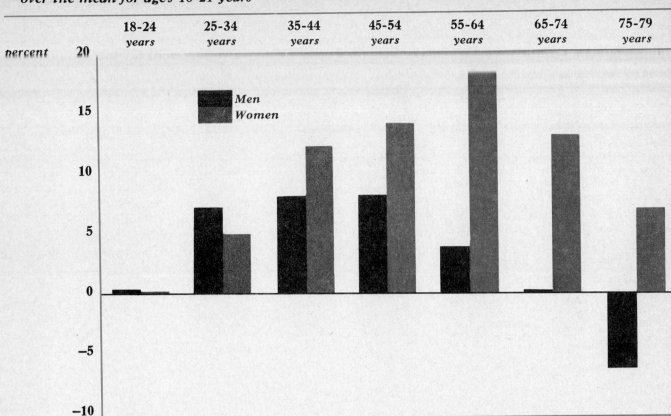

Courtesy United States Department of Health, Education and Welfare.

can live with—and will want to live with. The goal should be to bring your weight down to the level you approve and to keep it at this level long enough for your body to accept the new weight as a comfortable one.

Your program should include a calorie-deficient diet so that body fat will be used up . . . good nutrition so you won't feel hungry and won't endanger your health . . . figure-firming exercises to prevent flabbiness . . . increased activity to overcome boredom and to use extra fuel . . . and posture improvement to smooth out bumps.

Any plan for weight loss should start with a physical checkup by your doctor and should be carried out with his advice and approval. This is particularly important even for a healthy person if you are 10% or more overweight and if you are starting a new exercise program along with a reducing diet. If you have any health problem or if you are pregnant or a new mother, put your weight-control problem under your doctor's supervision.

It's also generally accepted by those medically interested in weight loss that you won't be able to control your weight unless you really want to:

▶ *Start by weighing yourself.* If you are over age 25 and are even a pound or two overweight now, you should face the fact that you will probably go on gaining unless you make an effort at weight control.

▶ *Look at yourself in a three-way mirror.* Figure faults become exaggerated with time unless an effort is made to correct them. Ask yourself how you will look 10 years from now.

▶ *Accept what you have to do.* Look at the weight-main-

tenance diet on page 106 and compare it with your normal daily food intake. Are you getting all the necessary nutrients in what you now eat? What items can you cut from your present diet to bring your daily food intake into line? How can you fit your diet into the family menu plan?

▶ *Work out a menu plan.* A diet works best when it is planned ahead; you can save yourself from temptation by knowing what you're going to eat and when and how your diet can be fitted into family meals.

▶ *Pick a good time to start.* A diet is best begun at a time when you have a good opportunity to control what you eat.

▶ *Allow yourself enough time for your program to take hold.* Avoid crash diets that promise to reduce you in a week or two.

▶ *Bolster your determination.* Bringing your weight under control will improve your appearance—and it will also bolster your self-esteem. Realize that a slim figure is a social asset—at normal weight you will look better and feel better and you will also find yourself free and eager to take part in activities that overweight discourages. Normal weight means increased vitality—it helps keep you young. It also makes you less prone to debilitating ailments; if you are lean, there is less wear on your heart, your muscles, your joints, your digestive system.

▶ *Increase your activity along with your calorie cut.* A weight-control program that fails to include increased activity will bog down in boredom and depression.

ACTIVITY AND WEIGHT CONTROL

YOUR body needs activity just as it needs food. If you can activate yourself on a number of levels, you can make your reducing program more effective and easier—activity contributes many benefits that you would miss by trying to reduce by calorie-cutting alone. For example, one of your goals in achieving normal weight should be the prospect of using your body effectively and pleasurably in your daily activities, of keeping it active—youthful, too.

Inactivity adds pounds

Underactivity as well as overeating has probably played a part in your putting on unwanted pounds. The overweight person tends to be less active—and to burn up comparatively less fuel—than the lean one, even when engaged in the same occupations.

Our energy output has also diminished. Minor conveniences such as the electric can opener and juicer in the home, the electric typewriter and pencil sharpener in the office, use up less energy than the old hand methods. Small items such as these can put pounds on us. Consider how much more body fuel we save by using automobiles, escalators, elevators, power mowers, electric sewing machines, vacuum cleaners, and so on.

Increasing your daily activity can use up some of these saved calories. The activity-calorie table on page 15 will show what you have to do in the way of exercise if you want to eat an extra apple or a piece of cake. Look at it this way—a three-mile walk is worth a hamburger sandwich at the calorie bank.

How to figure your calorie expenditure

If you are to use activity as part of your daily calorie-reduction quota, the exercise must be regular, it must be vigorous, and you must not follow it with an eating splurge.

We use calories, of course, even when at rest. A 154-pound individual will use 1.3 calories a minute even while lying down. This rises to 5.2 a minute for walking briskly; 8.2 calories while biking; 11.2 calories a minute while swimming; 19.4 while running.

The number of calories you will use per minute while resting or working depends on your body weight. It takes fewer calories per day to operate a 120-pound body than a 150-pound physique. It takes more energy—and calorie expenditure—to move a 150-pound body around the house in doing the daily work than to move one that weighs less. The less you weigh the less will be your calorie-expenditure both in rest and in activity; you will have to shave off a few calories per minute on the calorie-activity allotment *(page 15)* if you are under 154 pounds. For calorie-expenditure balance you should also gradually increase your daily activity as you lose weight.

Won't exercise make you eat more?

Active sport may make you hungry, but does mild exercise? Not necessarily. If you exercise regularly and don't eat at once, you may find that those after-exercise hunger pangs diminish or disappear entirely—or may be appeased by a glass of water.

Exercise may in itself become an appetite appeaser. It sets the blood to circulating more rapidly, makes us breathe more deeply, and has a good effect on body tone. If you normally exercise regularly, you will find that, deprived of activity, your body will crave it. If you get into the habit of responding to this need for action with activity rather than with food—if you substitute any other action for running to the refrigerator—you will soon find that your diet plan is working better.

Activity is helpful in keeping you to your weight-control plan in other ways:

▶ It makes you feel better and improves your outlook.
▶ It overcomes much of the boredom that leads to eating.
▶ Depression and the everyday tensions are better relieved with exercise than with either food or medication.

The more you put your body into action the more you do to make your weight-control program effective.

How exercise improves your outlook

Activity need not all be exercise—active sports or walking. Participating in community activities, family outings, and in hobbies is a part of your weight-control program, too. Valuable here is your having something to think about besides food. The more you are doing the easier it is to forget about eating.

Activity helps you to sleep well at night and, remarkably, relieves daytime fatigue. Fatigue alone often tempts us to overeat. Moderate or vigorous exercise or any change of activity can be a wonderful way to overcome tiredness.

Exercise also relieves tension. Tension is a desire of the body to take action—to flee from a situation or to fight back at a frustration. When we exercise to overcome tension, the muscles respond in a wholesome way to the brain's direction to go into action. We end up relaxed and with an improved disposition.

Exercise also keeps us youthful. Our body is designed for activity. Many common disabilities of age, middle age, and young adulthood can be averted by regular exercise.

Can you exercise safely?

Today it is accepted that almost everyone needs some form of mild exercise daily and some vigorous exercise four or five times a week. The body needs mild exercise, walking for example, to keep up its general tone; it needs vigorous exercise—active sport or calisthenics—to keep it ready to respond to emergencies that may someday take place.

Rarely today does a doctor forbid a patient to exercise. But should you have a health problem of any kind or if you have long been leading an inactive life, check with your doctor before starting a new exercise program.

What about exercise in pregnancy?

Doctors often prescribe special exercises for a mother-to-be to do during her pregnancy and for a new mother to do after delivery to regain her figure. If you have no special problems, your doctor probably will not greatly restrict activity during the first six months of pregnancy. Most sports are not restricted—and walking is usually encouraged.

How much should you do?

If you have been inactive for a long time, any exercise program should start slowly. Get yourself started with walking—a few blocks to begin; then perhaps a mile and eventually three miles (an hour's walk at a reasonable pace). At the same time introduce some of the milder muscle-toning exercises. As your body regains tone, you can go along to more vigorous exercises and perhaps graduate from walking to an active sport—tennis, bicycling, swimming, or golf. Any of these pursuits can be followed throughout your lifetime if you remain in good health.

And practice these simple daily routines:
▶ Take stairs, when possible, instead of elevators and escalators.
▶ Walk, do not take the car, as often as you can.
▶ Revive former enjoyments — bicycling, swimming, hiking, bowling, croquet.
▶ Seek out recreation resources. Your local Y or school may offer an opportunity for daily or weekly gym work, dancing, or swimming.
▶ Don't feel imposed upon if you have to walk the length of the house to answer the telephone.
▶ At parties, don't just sit—circulate.
▶ Plan to walk or bike regularly and set yourself a certain distance to go to and to return from. Such a plan helps you fill your allotted exercise time and encourages fulfillment of your mileage quota.
▶ Take care of your feet. If you have foot problems, see a foot doctor and get back into action. Never buy a pair of shoes that isn't comfortable to walk in.
▶ Look about for an active friend or acquaintance and join her in her activities.
▶ Make your exercise program regular but simple to start. Demanding too much can lead to defeat.
▶ Don't make your exercise program overlong. Fifteen —or even five to 10—minutes in the morning is a good beginning. Add, if you like, a five- to 10-minute revival program in the afternoon. Remember that a brief exercise period relaxes you and renews your vitality.
▶ Don't give up. You may at some time bog down in your exercise program as you may in your diet. But don't abandon it. Start gradually again with short exercise periods, and your enthusiasm will return.

What shape are you in?

How well are you able to use your body right now? On pages 16 and 17 there is a physical-fitness test from the National Board of the Young Women's Christian Association. It gives you an idea of what shape you are in right now; use it periodically as well to evaluate your progress. Add to the tests shown on pages 16 and 17 this simple test of your endurance:
▶ Walk a mile in 15 minutes.

CALORIE EQUIVALENTS OF ACTIVITIES
Minutes required at the exercises listed to expend calories in the foods

FOOD	CALORIES	ACTIVITY				
		Walking	Stepping	Bicycling	Jogging	Swimming
		minutes	minutes	minutes	minutes	minutes
Apple, 1 medium	87	17	12	11	9	8
Bacon, crisp, 2 slices	96	19	13	12	10	9
Banana, 1 medium	127	24	17	16	13	11
Beans, green, ½ cup cooked	15	3	2	2	2	1
Beer, 8-ounce glass	115	22	15	14	12	10
Bread and butter, 1 slice	96	18	13	12	10	9
Cake, white layer, 1/16 of 9″ cake	250	48	33	31	25	22
Carrot, raw, 1 large	42	8	6	5	4	4
Cereal, dry, 1 cup, with milk and sugar	212	41	28	26	21	19
Cheese, American, 1-ounce slice	112	22	15	14	11	10
Cheese, cottage, 1 rounded tablespoon	30	6	4	4	3	3
Chicken, fried, ½ breast	232	45	31	28	23	21
Chicken, TV dinner	542	104	72	66	54	48
Cola beverage, 8-ounce glass	105	20	14	13	11	9
Cooky, chocolate chip, 1 average	50	10	7	6	5	5
Cooky, vanilla wafer, 1 average	15	3	2	2	2	1
Doughnut, 1 average	125	24	17	15	13	11
Egg, boiled or poached, 1 medium	78	15	10	10	8	7
Egg, fried or scrambled, 1 medium	108	21	14	13	11	10
French dressing, 1 tablespoon	57	11	8	7	6	5
Gelatin, with cream, 1 serving	117	23	16	14	12	10
Halibut, broiled, 1 serving	214	41	28	26	21	19
Ham, fresh, 2 slices cooked	254	49	34	31	25	23
Ice cream, ⅔ cup	186	36	25	23	19	17
Ice-cream soda, 1 regular	255	49	34	31	26	23
Ice milk, ⅔ cup	137	26	18	17	14	12
Malted milk, 8-ounce glass	500	96	67	61	50	45
Mayonnaise, 1 tablespoon	100	19	13	12	10	9
Milk, skim, 8-ounce glass	88	17	12	11	9	8
Milk, whole, 8-ounce glass	160	36	21	20	16	14
Milk shake, 8-ounce glass	420	81	56	51	42	38
Orange, 1 medium	73	14	10	9	7	7
Orange juice, 4-ounce glass	54	10	7	7	5	5
Pancake, 1, with 2 tablespoons syrup	204	39	27	25	20	18
Peach, 1 medium	38	7	5	5	4	3
Peach shortcake, 1 biscuit and 1 peach	266	51	35	32	27	24
Peas, green, ½ cup cooked	58	11	8	7	6	5
Pie, fruit, 1/6 of 9″ pie	400	77	53	49	40	36
Pie, pecan, 1/6 of 9″ pie.	670	129	89	82	67	60
Pizza, cheese, 1/8 of 14″ pie	185	36	25	23	19	17
Pork chop, 6 ounces raw	314	60	42	38	31	28
Potato chips, five 2″ chips	54	10	7	7	5	5
Sandwiches						
Club (bacon, chicken, tomato)	590	114	78	72	59	53
Hamburger	350	67	47	43	35	31
Roast beef with gravy	430	83	57	52	43	38
Tuna Salad	278	54	37	34	28	25
Sherbet, orange, ⅔ cup	120	23	16	15	12	11
Shrimp, French-fried, 3½ ounces	225	43	30	27	23	20
Spaghetti, meat sauce, 1 serving	396	76	53	48	40	35
Steak, T-bone, ½ pound raw	235	45	31	29	24	21

ENERGY COST FOR 154-POUND INDIVIDUAL

WALKING briskly at 3.5 to 4.0 miles per hour consumes on the average 5.2 calories per minute.

STEPPING 25 up and down steps per minute facing in the same direction consumes an average of 7.5 calories per minute.

BICYCLING consumes around 8.2 calories per minute.

JOGGING alternated with walking (5 minutes each jogging, walking, jogging, etc.) consumes around 10.0 calories per minute.

SWIMMING with average skill consumes approximately 11.2 calories per minute.

Courtesy of Dr. Frank Konishi, Chairman, Department of Food and Nutrition, Southern Illinois University

Physical-fitness test

Stork test for balance

To test balance, stand on one foot with other foot touching inside of knee. With eyes closed, hold this position for 15 seconds.

Fingers touching behind back

With right hand over right shoulder, touch fingers of right and left hand behind the back; then touch fingers with left hand over left shoulder.

Wall test for back curve

Standing against a wall with heels touching the baseboard, flatten back close to wall. Test is passed if only the fingertips can slip between back and wall; but test is failed if the whole hand can slide between.

Flexibility

Standing, bend to touch fingers to toes.

Back-muscle test

Lying prone on floor, alternately raise opposite arm and leg. For the younger group, 30 times a minute; 20 for the older group.

Pushups

Lie, face down, and push torso up with hands while knees remain on floor. The 35-year-old-plus should be able to do 10 pushups a minute; those 20 to 35, 20 a minute; teen-agers, 30.

Standing broad jump

Jump a distance equal to your body height.

Sit-ups

Lie on back and then sit up so that hands touch knees. For the younger group (under 35), 30 sit-ups a minute; 20 for the older group.

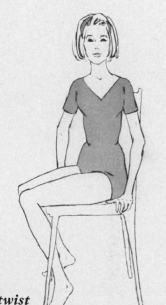

The 90° twist

Sitting in straight chair with feet caught around chair legs, twist body 90° without moving hips.

Knee to forehead

Lying on back, touch forehead with one knee and then with the other.

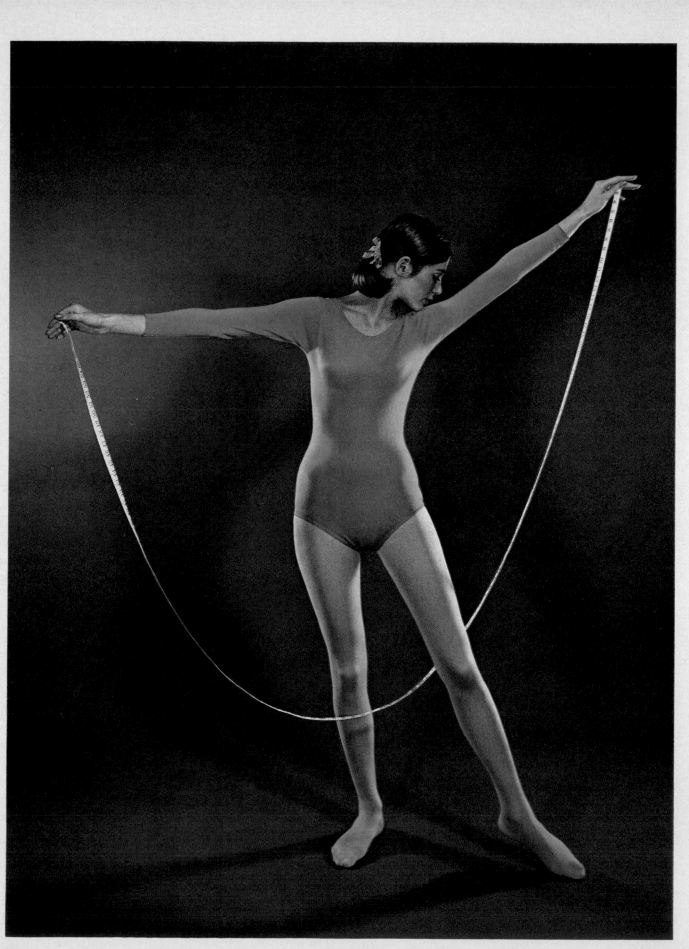

SLIM DOWN WITH GOOD POSTURE

PROPERLY aligned, the body becomes a thing of grace and beauty—there is a free flow of movement without tension or strain. The deep muscles that maintain erect alignment can be developed by use. But any muscle development that does not *evenly* increase the basic support of the spine will throw it out of plumb, with unbeautiful and unhealthful results.

Good alignment helps you lose inches instantly. You can prove it on the tape measure. It also restores the height you have lost through slumping. There are other advantages too. You will feel greater vitality. It is a feeling of vitality that makes a weight-control program easy to live with.

Here—from Sara Mildred Strauss, authority on body alignment and figure control—is the basic alignment you should assume for the exercises on pages 22-23 and 26-39. Practice this alignment as well throughout your waking hours for easy and graceful movement and to control fatigue. *(For illustrations, see pages 20-21.)*

Feet

Heels and toes touch, with most of the weight on the outside of the feet. Toes are slightly curled to lift the inside arch and to make you aware of the strength of your feet. The feet are the foundation upon which the whole body rests in standing and in movement. They must be made strong and flexible.

Knees

Keep the inside of the knees close together, but pull the kneecaps outward slightly so that knees and legs are facing straight ahead. In this position you are developing the muscles of calf and thigh and making it possible to tip the buttocks forward.

Buttocks and lower back

Tip buttocks forward and upward and press down through the thighs and into the knees. This movement straightens the curve of the lower back and gives a firm base for the whole torso—and also controls the muscles of the abdomen, flattens it, and permits the abdominal organs to be held in natural position.

Ribs and chest

Lift ribs high, but do not pull shoulder blades back. Instead, spread them wide and pull them down by firming the muscles beneath the shoulder blades and under the arms. Keep the elbows flexed and rest hands upon thighs. When ribs and chest are lifted and held high, there is ample room for the lungs to expand. Tension at the base of the neck is released, and unnatural pressure is removed from the stomach and the heart.

Neck and head

Hold the neck long and straight, pressing the chin in slightly so that the head rests on top of the spine. When the head is held high in this manner, tension is released in the back of the neck and circulation is stimulated throughout the body. You will also have the feeling of beauty and of confidence.

Correct alignment

Check sitting and standing alignment *(right)* before you begin an exercise:
▶ Feet together, pointed straight ahead; toes curled; weight on outside of feet.
▶ Knees deeply bent; thighs firmly together; buttocks tipped upward; pelvic area firmed.
▶ Lower back straight; torso lifted from waistline so that the waist is slimmed.
▶ Rib cage lifted high.
▶ Shoulder blades down and spread wide.
▶ Chest high.
▶ Shoulder caps down.
▶ Head on top of spine; neck long; chin in slightly.

Exercises to improve your walk

Point feet straight ahead, heels and big toes touching.
▶ Curl toes down so that inner arch is lifted and ankle bones are kept apart.

Practice alignment often to train your feet to remain pointed straight ahead when you walk or stand.

To strengthen inner and outer arches, to develop alignment of feet

Stand with feet in correct alignment, steadying yourself with one hand on back of a chair.
▶ Bend knees deeply.
▶ Cross one foot over the other, little toes touching and both feet pointing straight ahead.
▶ Rise on the flat of the toes of both feet and then return whole foot to the floor.

Repeat 10 times; change feet and repeat.

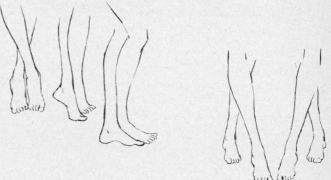

Stand with the feet in correct alignment to start.
▶ Bring right foot forward and straight ahead, crossing it over left foot.
▶ Advance left foot, pointing it straight ahead, and cross it over right foot.

Walk slowly forward in this way for 10 steps; then more rapidly for 20 steps.

To strengthen toes, arches, ankles and calves

Sit on edge of straight chair, feet in correct alignment.
▶ Curl toes firmly down.
▶ Bend toes upward as far as you can, spreading them wide.

Repeat slowly 12 times; increase to 24.

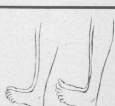

Sit on edge of chair, feet forward slightly, heels resting on floor. Bend feet up acutely and hold this position throughout.
▶ Curl toes firmly.
▶ Then bend toes upward and spread them wide.

Repeat 12 to 24 times.

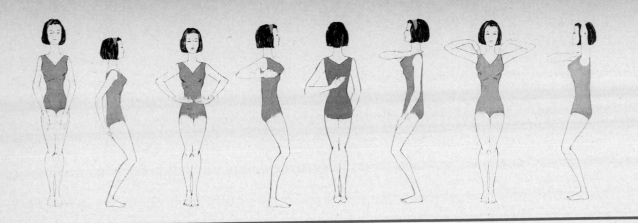

To strengthen arches, to develop and to slim calves and ankles

Stand with feet in correct alignment.
▶ Bend knees slightly and walk slowly forward on heels with rest of foot raised and pointed straight ahead.

Walk ahead in this way for 10 steps.

Stand with feet in correct alignment.
▶ Bend knees slightly and advance right foot with weight on the outside edge of foot.
▶ Advance left foot in same manner.

Walk ahead in this way for 10 steps.

To strengthen entire foot, to develop full ankle action

Sit on edge of straight chair, feet in correct alignment.
▶ Now, with heel of one foot on floor, raise the foot acutely at the ankle.
▶ Raise high the heel of the other foot, with toes pointing down to touch the floor.
▶ Alternate foot position, slowly at first and then more rapidly.

Repeat 12 to 24 times.

Stand with feet in correct alignment.
▶ Bend knees slightly and walk forward on the flat of the toes with the feet pointing straight ahead.

Walk ahead in this way for 10 steps.

Stand with feet in correct alignment, bend knees slightly, and combine the last three exercises.
▶ Walk forward two steps on heels.
▶ Walk two steps forward on outer edge of feet.
▶ Walk two steps forward on the flat of the toes.
▶ As you walk, say to yourself, "Heel . . . outer arch . . . toe."

This is the formula for correct walking.

Smooth, effortless, and easy walking

On the forward foot, weight is first on the heel and shifts through outer arch, ball, toes.
▶ Feet are always parallel and directed straight ahead.
▶ Knees are flexed and face straight ahead.
▶ Arms swing freely at sides.
▶ Buttocks are held firmly, and there is no side movement of hips.
▶ The body is controlled and co-ordinated through the deep muscles; it is supported by the natural girdle.

21

Exercises to help you move correctly

Getting up

Sit on the edge of the bed, feet together on the floor; keep back and neck erect, hold chest high.
▶ Breathe deeply.

Brushing your teeth

Stand in correct alignment and, when you bend over the washbowl, keep this alignment. Don't slouch.
▶ When lifting the brush to your mouth, be sure that you keep your shoulders down, shoulder blades spread.

Combing your hair

Stand or sit in correct alignment.
▶ When you lift and use the comb or brush, keep the shoulders down and let the movement come from the back.
▶ The arms, when lifted, should be held high with elbows wide.

Putting on shorts or a girdle

Bend over to keep the torso, neck, and head in correct alignment.
▶ Pull the garment up without hunching the shoulders.

Putting on stockings

Sit in correct alignment.

▶ Bring knee to chest and bend slightly forward.
▶ As you draw the stocking up, keep your shoulders down.

Carrying

Maintain correct alignment.

▶ Keep the shoulders down and elbows bent.
▶ Carry the weight from back muscles so shoulders stay down.
▶ Keep knees flexed and walk with an easy full stride.

Lifting

First stand in correct alignment.

▶ Place one foot ahead of the other.
▶ Bend over, keeping chest high, and then bend both knees deeply.
▶ Lift the object with strength coming from lower back muscles, keeping shoulders down, elbows flexed.

Using the vacuum cleaner

Stand and walk in correct alignment.

▶ Do not lift the shoulders as you move the cleaner.
▶ Push and pull the vacuum cleaner from the back muscles.
▶ Keep elbows flexed at all times.

FIGURE-FIRMING EXERCISES

WHEN women lose weight, they fear that the weight loss will "show up in the face," that breasts will become slack, and that the flesh of the upper arms and the hips and thighs will become flabby. The figure-firming exercises by Sara Mildred Strauss *(pages 26-39)* can do much to help this problem. They also help you to hold the correct alignment that makes you look slimmer instantly and that helps you move correctly.

Firming the natural girdle

Easy to do and effective at the start are exercises to firm the "natural girdle"—the long muscles that control alignment and that we use to move our body in our work and other activities. When these muscles are firm and are acting efficiently, your figure "takes shape"—comes under control. Bulges in the thighs, too much curvature of the spine, wrong use of the muscles of the back and of the neck are gradually corrected. You seem to slim without effort.

Breasts and upper arms

The breasts are chiefly fatty tissue. There is little muscle and no bone in the breast tissue, and so the breasts have little natural support. If you have long been overweight, the breasts have probably become heavy, and their weight alone may have caused them to stretch. Weight drag is also a problem in the upper arms.

When you lose weight, fat is lost from the breasts as well as from the rest of the body. Because the fat here is "soft," it may well seem that the breasts are the first body part to lose.

Exercises to firm the bosom actually tone the muscles of the chest and shoulders that support the breasts. The upper-arm muscles will be strengthened, too, if the exercises are done correctly. Firming these muscles will need patience, and the exercises should be done while in proper alignment to make the movements effective.

Face-firming exercises

Exercises for the face strengthen the muscles that give support to the skin. To do these exercises correctly use the facial *muscles*—don't just move the skin. Start slowly so that you learn how to bring the muscles into action. In some of the exercises it may be difficult.

These exercises can be done in the few odd moments of the day when you are sitting alone. Be sure, however, you sit in good alignment *(see page 20)* while you are doing them.

Allover exercises

These figure-firming exercises will help you move beautifully and will create a sense of energy and vitality as you do them. Such everyday actions as sitting, standing, lying down, or moving quickly from place to place become more graceful when your muscles are firmed.

Energy boosters

A well-balanced figure—one that moves with grace, that looks slim, and carries itself beautifully—should be part of your goal in weight control. Although you may find some of these exercises difficult at the start, you will eventually discover that you enjoy body movements that get you "off the ground"—that require vigor and a sense of rhythm. When you have mastered the basics, start doing these exercises to dance music.

Exercises
to firm your
natural girdle

To firm and trim hips, thighs, and legs, and to strengthen feet

Stand in proper alignment, with the fingertips resting upon the back of a straight chair.
▸ Bend deeply at the knees.
▸ Rise to toes, firming buttocks and pressing still more deeply down into the knees.
▸ Hold this position for a moment.
▸ Come down again onto the whole foot and back once more into proper standing alignment.

Repeat four times to start; increase gradually to eight times.

To expand and strengthen rib and chest muscles, and to reduce waistline

Stand in proper alignment.
▸ Place thumbs and fingers of each hand together.
▸ Place hand high below armpits, with elbows held wide.
▸ Lift entire rib section as high as you can, but do not lift shoulders and do not bend forward. Breathe deeply.
▸ Lift elbows and ribs high on one side; lower elbows and rib cage; lift to other side; lower.

Repeat lifts slowly on alternate sides, 10 times to start; increase gradually to 20 times.

To reduce ankles, thighs, and buttocks

Sit on the edge of a straight-back chair, hands (palms down) on thighs, torso in correct alignment.
▶ Keeping heels raised, point feet downward and slightly forward with toes resting on the floor.
▶ Now, alternating feet, touch heels to the floor, lifting whole foot acutely, bending and straightening ankles. Feel the movement as coming from the lower back and the buttocks.

Repeat, alternating feet, 12 times at first; increase to 24 times.

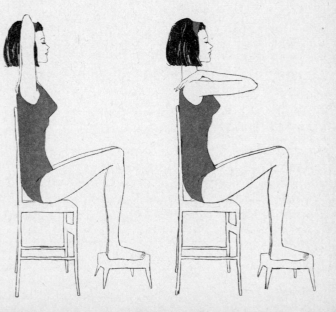

To reduce and strengthen ankles, thighs, hips, and buttocks

Sit on edge of a straight-back chair, keeping torso in correct alignment. Point feet straight down, with toes touching the floor.
▶ Bring one knee upward slowly as high as you can, toes pointed down.
▶ Lower this knee to first position and raise other knee, keeping toes pointed straight down.
▶ Continue raising knees and lowering them alternately. Movement should be slow.

Repeat six times; increase to 12 times.

To slim waistline, strengthen upper torso, ease tension in neck

Sit in a straight chair, torso aligned, and press lower back against chair back; feet together on eight-inch-high stool.
▶ Place thumbs on collarbones and raise elbows overhead. Then allow the fingers of each hand to point down and place them flat against upper back. Be sure hands do not touch head or neck.
▶ Slowly bring elbows down . . . out . . . forward at shoulder height . . . and then up.
▶ During movement, keep ribs raised and shoulder blades down, pelvis tipped upward. Breathe deeply.

Repeat six times to start; increase to 12 times.

To reduce hips, thighs, and abdomen; to straighten and to strengthen the torso

Place side of hands (thumb held backward, index finger forward) at pelvic joint, and raise the entire torso upward as high as possible. Keep knees slightly bent and breathe deeply.

▶ Bend forward slowly at pelvic joint, keeping torso stretched and straight.

▶ Bending knees deeply, slowly straighten again to standing alignment, lifting the whole torso from the lower back, the buttocks, and the thighs.

Repeat four times to start; gradually increase to eight times.

To slim and strengthen back, abdomen, thighs, and ankles

Lie on back in correct alignment. Bring knees up till lower legs make a 45° angle; press heels against the floor.

▶ Keeping feet and knees together, firm the buttocks so that the pelvis is tipped upward. Press lower back against floor to release tension in abdomen.

▶ Keeping ribs raised high and shoulder blades wide, stretch the neck long and flat in the back.

▶ Hands on abdomen, bend elbows wide; rest upper arms on floor. Breathe deeply.

▶ Now bend one knee back as far as you can toward the chest and then lower this knee slowly to its former position.

▶ Repeat with other knee.

Repeat six times; increase to 12.

To slim and strengthen ankles, calves, thighs, and buttocks

Lie on back as in exercise above and repeat action until knee is to be bent back. Instead:

▶ Point toes to touch the floor and then bring first one foot and then the other as far back as you can, pressing the buttocks upward to lift the pelvis and the torso.

▶ Slowly press lower back against the floor to bring the buttocks gradually down again.

Repeat this exercise slowly four times to start; increase it gradually to eight times.

To reduce and strengthen thighs and buttocks, to stretch ankles and arches

In correct alignment, rise on toes; slowly press buttocks and thighs forward till you sink into a kneeling position; keep the torso straight and the hands easy and without tension on front of thighs.
▶ Flatten top of feet against the floor, keeping feet straight and together; now slowly sit back upon heels, pressing buttocks forward and upward and keeping correct alignment in torso. Breathe deeply.
▶ With the same control, return to first kneeling position.

Repeat slowly three times to start; gradually increase to six times.

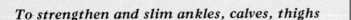

To strengthen and slim ankles, calves, thighs

Take correct standing-alignment position but bend deeper at knees; hands on the front of the thighs.
▶ Lift heel of one foot, pointing toes; return to first position, keeping correct alignment.
▶ Repeat, alternating feet, keeping knees bent but facing ahead and together. Do not move hips, torso, or other body parts as you lift feet.

Start this movement slowly and then make action rapid and at last move forward into a small easy run.

To slim, strengthen every part of the legs

From standing alignment, take a long step forward, feet and knees directed straight ahead.
▶ Bend knees deeply, pressing buttocks forward into the thighs. Keep weight on the outside of the feet.
▶ As you move forward, keep the knees deeply bent and keep the torso in proper alignment at all times.

Go into this movement gradually—do not tire yourself.

Bosom firmers

Stand in correct alignment.
▶ Raise arms at front; hands, palms up, at chest height; fingers together and pointed straight ahead. Elbows are bent and spread wide.
▶ Imagine that an object the size and weight of a large book is resting on your hands.
▶ As if raising this weight, slowly lift the arms about two inches. Feel the movement coming from lower back and chest muscles.
▶ Lower the arms slowly to the first position.

Repeat 10 times.

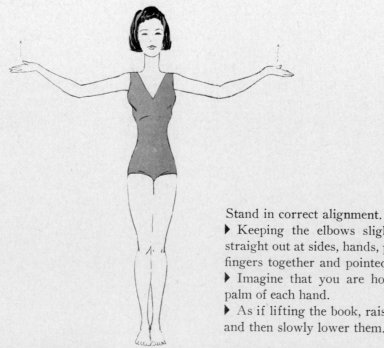

Stand in correct alignment.
▶ Keeping the elbows slightly flexed, raise the arms straight out at sides, hands, palms up, at shoulder height, fingers together and pointed straight out to sides.
▶ Imagine that you are holding a heavy book on the palm of each hand.
▶ As if lifting the book, raise the arms about two inches and then slowly lower them.

Repeat 10 times.

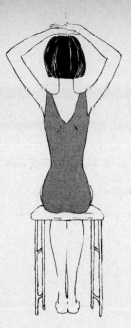

Sit, keeping the chest high, shoulder blades down and wide, and bring the arms out in front of you at a slight angle, elbows flexed, hands at shoulder height, palms down, fingers stretched wide.
▶ In a quick sharp movement that produces an acute movement of the muscles underneath breasts, turn hands so that the palms are up.
▶ Return to palm-down position.

Repeat 10 to 20 times

Sit, keeping the chest high and the shoulder blades down, and put the hands—one upon the other, palm up—on top of the head.
▶ With the imagined weight of a large book resting upon the palm of the top hand, slowly raise both palms four inches. Feel the movement coming from lower back and chest muscles.
▶ Slowly lower the hands to top of head.

Repeat 10 times.

Lie on floor with legs long, knees slightly bent, the back of the heels pressed to the floor and the toes curved downward.
▶ Bring the arms straight out to the sides with the hands, palms up, at shoulder level, fingers together and pointed straight out.
▶ Imagine that a book rests on each palm.
▶ Holding this position, slowly raise the arms as if they were lifting a heavy book about two inches off the floor.
▶ Slowly lower hands to the original position.

Repeat 10 times.

Lie on floor with the knees bent so that lower legs are perpendicular to the floor and feet are flat on floor, the arms resting at an angle to the body.
▶ Bend arms at elbows so that lower arms are perpendicular to the floor, palms of hands up, fingers parallel to the body.
▶ Imagine that a large book rests on the palm of each hand and slowly raise both hands about four inches.
▶ Lower hands slowly four inches.

Repeat 10 times.

Face firmers

To defer lines and wrinkles on the forehead and between the brows; to stimulate muscles of the scalp

Hold head still; look straight ahead.
▶ Raise eyebrows and forehead skin as high as you can so that you feel the movement of the scalp and the muscles around the ears; then bring the brows down as far as possible into a deep frown.
▶ Repeat energetically—up and down, so that you feel the scalp muscles move.

At start, 10 times; increase to 20 times.

To strengthen and firm muscles of mouth, chin, cheeks and to stimulate skin circulation

Keep chin in, head still.
▶ Stretch mouth open as widely as you can—as if you were ready to cheer—and then bring lips back together in a tight pucker.
▶ Alternate the movements slowly at first, using all the muscles round mouth, cheek, and chin as deeply and fully as you can.

Repeat 10 times to start and increase to as many times as you choose.

To strengthen and firm muscles round nose, chin, cheeks, and mouth and to stimulate circulation

Keep mouth closed.
▶ Draw lips and nostrils upward as far as you can, wrinkling the nose in an enormous sniff.
▶ Then pull mouth down, still keeping it closed, to make the nose as long as possible. Do this slowly at first till you feel that you are using all the muscles in and around the nose.

Start with 10 and increase to as many times as are comfortable.

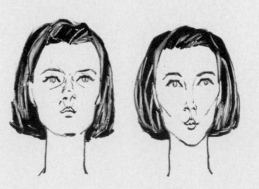

To strengthen muscles behind the eyes and to reduce lines and wrinkles around the eyes

Keep head still, face without tension.
▶ Look straight up; then down.
▶ Look far to right; then to left.
▶ Make a slow circle with the eyes, starting from right —up, left, and down; reverse, start from left.

Do this exercise only a few times to start so as not to tire eye muscles; slowly increase to 10 times.

To strengthen and firm the cheek muscles and to stimulate circulation in the facial skin

Hold head still; face without tension.
▶ Raise mouth and cheek of right side so high that right eye closes. Repeat to left.
▶ Do this strenuously so that you will be using as many muscles as you can in your huge "winks." At first these muscles may not be responsive, but gradually they will "come alive."

Do 10 winks to start; increase to as many winks as you like.

To tighten and firm up the flesh beneath the chin; to strengthen muscles of mouth, chin, and the lower cheeks

Bring lips together in a tight pucker.
▶ Slowly circle this "kiss" to the right.
▶ Stop and then circle to the left. Make these movements vigorous (may be difficult at start).

Try eight chin firmers and increase gradually as the muscles strengthen.

To release the face from tension

Tip up the corners of your mouth a bit, look cheerful, feel a smile inside yourself.
▶ Make this lip lift a habit—check your expression during your daily activities.
▶ If your face feels stiff and tense, smile—and feel the tension go.

Allover body exercises

To shape hips and thighs

Sit on the edge of a straight chair in correct alignment.
▶ Tip the buttocks forward and, with knees flexed, extend the legs forward as far as you can and point the toes.
▶ With elbows wide, place the hands at the sides of the pelvic joint, and keep them there throughout the exercise.
▶ Keeping the ribs high, back straight, and head in line with the spine, bend the torso forward as far as you can.
▶ Slowly return to erect sitting position.

Slowly repeat movements four times to start; gradually increase to eight times.

To shape ankles and legs

Sit in correct alignment on the edge of a straight chair.
▶ Tip buttocks forward and rest hands lightly on thighs, just above the knees.
▶ With knees together and slightly flexed, extend the legs forward as far as you can and point the toes.
▶ Cross the left foot over the right ankle, extending the left leg and pointing the left foot as much as possible. Feel the stretch and pull from the lower back through the buttocks, thigh, calf, and foot.
▶ Uncross the feet and then cross the right foot over the left ankle. Repeat.

Repeat slowly six times; increase to 12 times.

To shape knees and ankles

Stand in correct alignment lightly resting one hand on the back of a chair.
▶ Rise up on the flat of your toes.
▶ With knees pressed together, tip the buttocks forward and bend deeply at the knees.
▶ Now, without moving the hips, slowly turn the knees to the right, then to the left.

Repeat slowly six times; then, more quickly, 12 times.

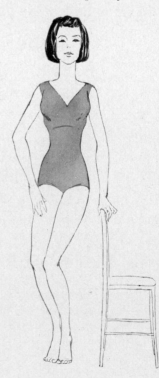

To slim waist and firm thighs

Stand in good alignment, legs spread on a broad base.
▶ Place the side of the hands at the pelvic joint, thumbs back and fingers forward.
▶ Shift weight to left foot and then bend the upper torso to the left, keeping the ribs up and shoulders down and keeping a long straight line along the right side of the body from the torso to the toes.
▶ Shift back to the first position and then to the right.

Slowly repeat all movements five times; then increase to 10 times.

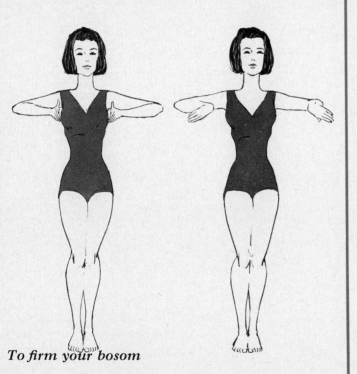

To firm your bosom

Stand in correct alignment.
▶ Raise the arms shoulder high, holding them straight out from the sides of the body. Bend your arms acutely at the elbows and at the wrists so that the palms of the hands turn outward.
▶ Now push outward with the palms as if against a heavy weight, slowly, till the arms are almost fully stretched out to the sides.
▶ Now turn the palms in and push the "weight" slowly inward till the palms almost touch.
▶ During these movements, keep your alignment. Be sure that your shoulders are down and your ribs held high. Feel that the strength is coming from your back and chest muscles.

Repeat four times at first; increase to eight times.

To shape and firm thighs and legs

Stand in correct alignment and spread your legs so that you are standing securely on a broad base. Point your feet outward at about a 30° angle.
▶ Bend the knees and shift the entire weight of the body onto the left foot, leaving the toes of the right foot resting lightly on the floor.
▶ Now shift the weight from the left foot entirely onto the right foot, leaving the toes of the left foot resting lightly on the floor.
▶ During these shifting movements, keep the torso upright and in alignment.

Repeat slowly 10 times; then more quickly, 20 times.

To sit beautifully

Sit on the floor in proper alignment, knees drawn up.
▶ Place the left knee on the floor and extend the lower leg straight back, foot pointed, as you place the right foot against the lower thigh and knee of the left leg.
▶ Shift both legs to the original sitting position, with knees drawn up.
▶ Now reverse the movement.

Repeat four times.

To shape arms and legs

Stand in correct alignment and move one foot straight ahead about six inches.
▶ Slowly rise up on the flat of your toes.
▶ Raise both arms above your head, keeping the shoulders down, elbows flexed, and the hands and fingers pointed straight up, palms facing each other.
▶ Holding this position, walk slowly forward on the flat of the toes.

Take 10 steps; rest and repeat.

To shape and to firm hips and thighs

Lie on your back in correct alignment, with knees bent. Keep shoulders down throughout the exercise.
▶ Raise your arms over your head, elbows slightly flexed, palms up, and back of hands resting on the floor. Press heels against the floor, bending feet up.
▶ With the legs pressed firmly together, turn both knees to the right so the right leg touches the floor. Then extend the feet.
▶ Bring legs and feet back to the first bent-knee position and repeat to the left.

Repeat three times very slowly; gradually increase to six times.

To shape and firm legs

Kneel on the floor and bend forward to rest forearms on the floor, palms down and wrists touching. Place your forehead on your wrists.
▶ Raise and extend the right leg back, keeping the knee slightly flexed and the foot pointed. Be sure that the shoulders are kept down but are not hunched and that the back is straight.
▶ Bring the leg back to the original kneeling position.
▶ Repeat the movement with the left leg.

Slowly repeat both movements four times; gradually increase to eight times.

Energy boosters

*Directions for this exercise
on following page*

See color illustration, page 37

Sit in correct alignment on edge of stool, knees and feet together.

▶ Extend lower legs forward as far as you can, knees slightly flexed, heels raised, toes touching floor.

▶ With toes pointed, swing right leg from pelvis as high as you can, simultaneously swinging right arm back and left arm up.

Alternating legs, repeat 10 times; then faster 20 times, swinging arms back and forth in rhythm.

Stand in correct alignment—feet together and parallel, knees slightly flexed, ribs up, shoulders down, chin drawn in, and head held squarely on top of the spine.

▶ Raise arms overhead, palms turned inward, keeping shoulders down and elbows slightly flexed.

▶ Swing the torso and the arms from side to side.

Swing 10 times slowly and then faster 20 times.

Standing in correct alignment, raise arms overhead, palms in, keeping the shoulders down and the elbows slightly flexed.

▶ In one continuous movement, bend the torso forward as far as you can, swinging the arms down and backward at the same time, and then swing torso and arms up to the first standing position. Take care not to hunch your shoulders during the movement.

Repeat the whole movement five times slowly; then faster 10 times.

Lie on back and throughout the exercise keep the whole back against the floor.
▶ Keeping shoulders down and chin in, raise arms overhead, palms up.
▶ Press knees together and raise them close to the chest, toes pointing down.
▶ Lower left arm overhead to floor, at the same time swinging right leg up.
▶ Repeat with right arm down and left leg up.

Repeat slowly 10 times and then faster 20 times.

Standing on right leg with knee flexed, swing left leg forward as high as you can, right arm forward and left arm back.
▶ Swing the left leg back, bringing right arm back and left arm forward. Keep toes pointed and do not bring the leg too far on the backward swing.

Repeat 10 times, alternating legs and keeping the movement smooth and rhythmic.

Stand in correct alignment and raise arms overhead, palms turned inward.
▶ Raise right knee hip high, toes pointed down, and swing the lower leg up and down, taking care not to stiffen the knee on the upward movement.
▶ Change legs and repeat.

Alternating legs, repeat the whole movement five times slowly and then faster for 10 times.

EXERCISES TO SLIM AND TRIM YOU

DOES spot-reducing work? This question is not yet conclusively answered, but many women find emphasis on exercise for a particular body part does make a difference in inches.

When you diet, the body first takes fat that is most easily available—from the fatty layers under the skin. As a reducing diet goes on, other fat resources in the body are tapped. Fat cannot be "worn away." Spot reducing thus seems to be a muscle-firming effect—the slimming is really a smoothing of body lines.

Exercises for hips and thighs

Heavy hips and thighs are a figure problem for many women—it is natural for a woman's body to be somewhat full here. Your girdle cushions these areas too, encouraging softness and fat accumulation; sitting a great deal—and particularly sitting on the thighs instead of the buttocks — helps produce unwanted "spread." Along with exercising to slim and trim the hips and thighs, work at correct sitting posture: Sit on the buttocks, not on the thighs—and keep the spine straight.

Exercises for the waist and back

The waist is the easiest part of the body to slim—and a slim waist does much to make for a youthful trim look. At the same time you slim your waist, strengthen your back muscles and practice holding yourself tall so the midriff narrows and feels long and slender.

Exercises for legs and ankles

The legs and ankles respond well to exercises to make them more shapely. Exercise that firms and strengthens the legs also makes other exercises easier to do. Often, however, an overweight woman has legs that are slender for the rest of her; exercises that firm leg muscles give slender legs better shape.

Exercising in water does much to make the legs more shapely. Pushing against the weight of the water gives plus value to such exercises as the frog kick *(page 56)*; because the rest of the body is buoyed up by the water, exercising is less of a strain.

Exercises for arms and shoulders

Strengthening the arms and shoulder muscles is good for posture as well as for body contour. Arm-and-shoulder exercises, and other mild exercises as well, can be done while you are lying down—they help relax the body while you rest.

Exercises for neck and chin line

Holding the back of the neck straight is your most youthful action—it improves your chin line and does away with the slumped look that speaks of age even in the not-so-old.

Exercises to improve your morale

Exercise can lift your spirits, relieve tension, and make the day's work easier to do. When critical moments in your diet come, exercise can renew your enthusiasm.

Exercises on pages 42-63 are by Evelyn Loewendahl, physical therapist. Spot reducers *(pages 64-65)* are by Adele Kenyon, specialist in figure beauty.

Exercises for hips and thighs

Gentle stretch to streamline hips

Lie on your back on the floor, arms stretched out, shoulder height, at the sides.
▶ Cross left leg over right knee. Do not cross at a higher point.
▶ Keeping the knee straight, toes pointed upward, give a good long pull on the whole leg. PULL. Back to position.
▶ Now cross right leg over left knee. PULL. Back to position. If you are doing this stretch correctly, you will feel the pull all the way up at the hip.

10 stretches on each leg.

Hip toner and firmer

Lie face down, arms at sides.
▶ Tighten buttock muscles hard and lift legs about 10 inches above the floor.
▶ Do quick scissors kicks, knees straight and buttock muscles tight, to the count of 10.
▶ Relax and repeat.

The count may be increased to 20, 30, or more daily for faster streamlining.

Firm stretch for streamlining

Lie on back, arms stretched out at sides.
▶ Bring left leg across right leg, with the big toe leading toward right wrist.
▶ Keep knee straight, toes up, and fling the leg over loosely, reaching up as far as possible. This gives the hip stretch.

10 flings, each side.

Strong stretch for streamlining

Stand, balancing with one hand on back of chair.
▶ Bring your free leg back and start it swinging forward, letting it go as high as possible. Keep toes pointed upward throughout the swing.
▶ Force your foot as high as you can. Don't stop at your limit. Try for a higher swing.

10 swings, each leg.

Side-hip shaper

Lie on right side, right leg bent for comfort.
▶ Lift left leg as high as possible.
▶ Change to other side and repeat.

Start with 10 lifts daily, increase to 20.

Side-hip stretch

Stand, feet together, left arm overhead, right hand on hip.
▶ Bend trunk to the right, pushing against hip as you bend. PUSH HARD—HARD. For the movement to be most effective, you should feel the pull directly over the hip you are stretching.
▶ Come up straight.
▶ Repeat to the left side.

10 hard pushes to each side.

To reduce hip spread

Kneel, hands on floor, right knee bent, left leg held straight out behind you.
▶ Bring the straight leg up as high as possible in 10 quick kicks.
▶ Change leg positions and repeat.

For faster results, increase kick count to 20.

If your hip width needs attention

Lie on side, head resting on arm.
▶ Raise upper leg straight up and, with the foot, make a complete circle in the air—forward, up, back, and down.
▶ Repeat, making big round circles. If you feel this movement in your hip, you are doing it correctly. You might feel the pull more on one side than the other. These muscles then need your attention.
▶ Change sides; circle other leg.

10 circles daily, each leg.

43

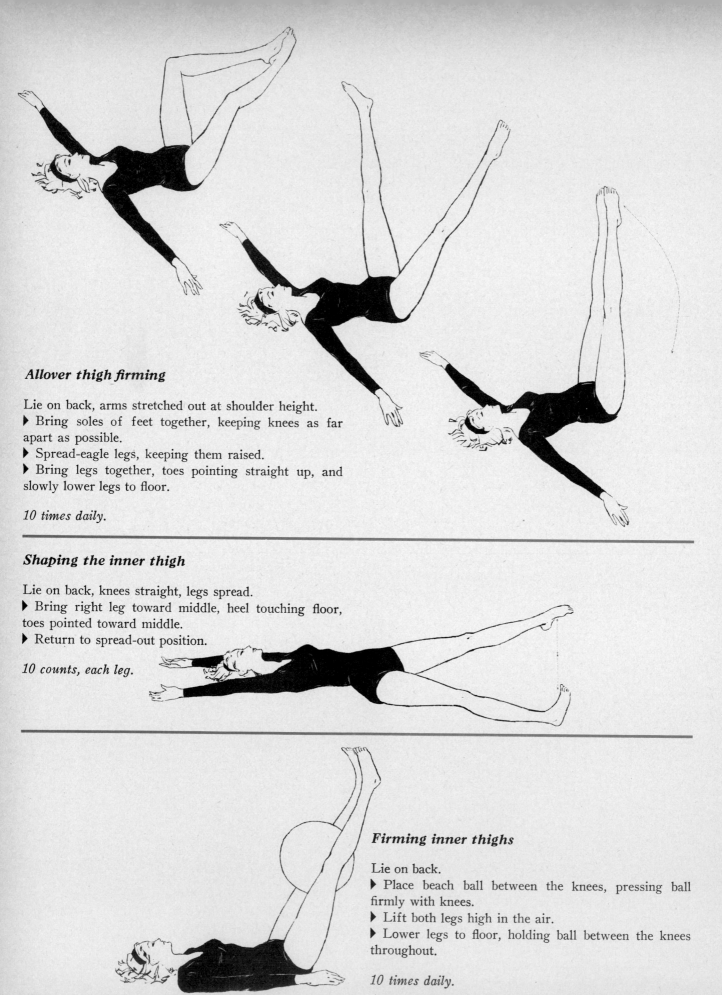

Allover thigh firming

Lie on back, arms stretched out at shoulder height.
▶ Bring soles of feet together, keeping knees as far apart as possible.
▶ Spread-eagle legs, keeping them raised.
▶ Bring legs together, toes pointing straight up, and slowly lower legs to floor.

10 times daily.

Shaping the inner thigh

Lie on back, knees straight, legs spread.
▶ Bring right leg toward middle, heel touching floor, toes pointed toward middle.
▶ Return to spread-out position.

10 counts, each leg.

Firming inner thighs

Lie on back.
▶ Place beach ball between the knees, pressing ball firmly with knees.
▶ Lift both legs high in the air.
▶ Lower legs to floor, holding ball between the knees throughout.

10 times daily.

44

For firm front thighs

Stand straight, arms at sides.
▶ Lift legs alternately in quick rhythm, bringing knees high for a count of 16.
▶ Relax and repeat.

16, each leg.

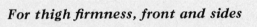

Strengthening inner thigh

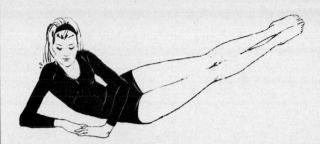

Lie on right side, with left leg resting upon right leg.
▶ Tighten buttock muscles.
▶ Using left leg as a weight, lift, and lower right leg, keeping buttock muscles tight throughout the lifts.

10 lifts, each side.

For thigh firmness, front and sides

Stand, balancing with right hand on back of chair.
▶ Lift knee of outer leg and, with the knee, make a complete circle.
▶ Make five circles and relax.
▶ Repeat with other leg.

Five circles, each leg.

For shapelier thighs

Stand, holding a towel overhead, arms straight. Hold towel tightly. Tuck buttocks under to carry weight of spine on the hips.
▶ Now bend right knee, holding left leg straight.
▶ Shift from one knee to the other five times and then come up straight.

Start with five shifts before coming up straight; work up to 10 shifts.

Exercises
to firm legs
and ankles

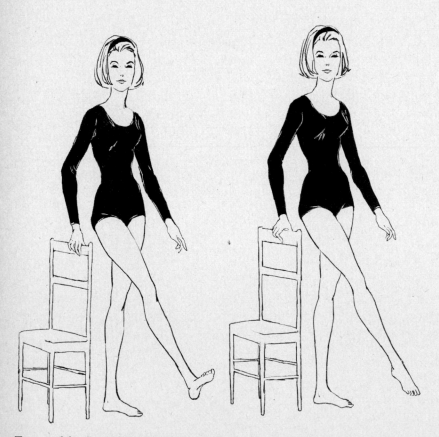

For ankle flexibility and good posture and for streamlining the calves

Stand, supporting yourself with one hand on chair back, and lift one leg forward.

▶ Press hard with heel so that the whole leg is stretched from the back of hip to the heel.

▶ Relax and repeat.

To start, 10 heel pushes with each leg.

Stand in the same position, steadying yourself with one hand on the back of a chair.

▶ Extend one leg and point the toe hard, feeling the stretch on front of leg and thigh.

▶ Relax and repeat.

To start, 10 toe stretches with each leg.

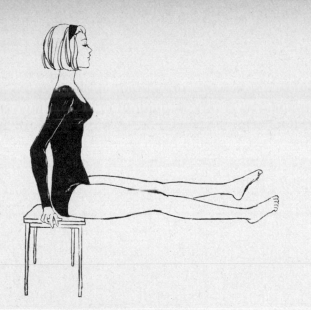

To develop calf muscles, strengthen knees

Stand, supporting yourself if necessary with one hand on the back of a chair.

▶ Rise on toes, stretching hard with knees.
▶ Hold for the count of 10.
▶ Relax and repeat.

To start, five leg stretches.

For foot flexibility and for relief of leg fatigue

Sit on a low stool and extend both legs.

▶ Curl the toes tightly. HOLD.
▶ Stretch the toes as far apart as possible so that all leg muscles feel the stretch. HOLD.
▶ Relax and repeat.

Repeat 10 times to start.

Stand, supporting yourself if necessary with one hand on the back of a chair.

▶ Stand on heels and raise front part of foot as high as possible.
▶ Hold for the count of 10.
▶ Relax and repeat.

To start, five heel stands.

Sit on low stool and extend one leg.

▶ Pushing hard with heel, rotate the ankle first in one direction and then in the other.
▶ Repeat with other leg.

To start, 10 circles in each direction with each ankle.

Slim while you rest

To slim the midriff

Lie on back, legs straight, arms at sides.
▶ Reach right arm far back on the floor, making the arm as long as possible.
▶ At the same time lengthen your right leg, pushing with the heel, the toes pointed up, making the leg as long as possible.
▶ Stretch from fingertips to heel.
▶ Repeat to the other side.

Do 10 times, alternating sides

To flatten upper abdomen

Lie on back, arms at sides, legs straight.
▶ Raise head and shoulders about 10 inches off the floor and hold to the count of three.
▶ Slowly lower the head to the floor.

Repeat 10 times.

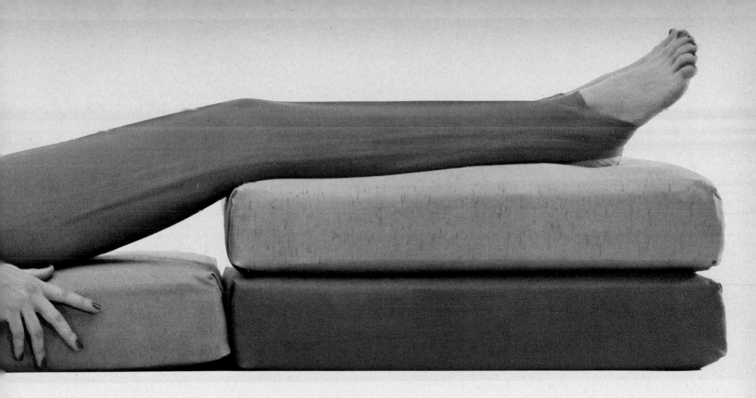

For relaxation, posture improvement, and waist slimming

Whenever you lie down—while you lounge, sun, or half doze—keep your body long, your shoulders flat, your neck straight. For the full treatment in relaxation, posture improvement, and waist slimming, lie on your back with hips higher than the head, legs higher than the hips. In this position the abdomen is flattened, the internal organs assume their proper place.

▶ Breathe regularly while you count slowly to 100.

To firm bosom and to slim midriff

Lie on back, knees bent, feet flat on the floor, arms at sides.

▶ Raise both arms overhead, stretching them high.
▶ Lower arms to the floor behind head.
▶ With arms on floor, return them to the side position.

Repeat 10 times.

To flatten lower abdomen

Lie on back, arms at sides, legs straight.
▶ Raise right leg about 10 inches off the floor and then quickly lower the leg to the floor.
▶ Raise the left leg and quickly lower it.
▶ Lift legs alternately in a quick and rhythmic scissors kick to the count of 10.

Relax and repeat.

▶ Now raise legs together about 10 inches off the floor.
▶ Hold for the count of three.
▶ Lower legs and repeat.

Twice to start; as the abdominal muscles get stronger, increase to five times and then to 10.

To firm hips

Lie, face down, arms at sides, forehead resting on floor.
▶ Raise both legs off the floor and alternate legs in a scissors kick, brisk and rhythmic, to a count of 10.

Relax and repeat.

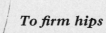

To firm hips

Lie, face down, arms folded, head slightly raised.
▶ Roll legs outward so the heels turn outward, toes touching.
▶ Tighten buttock muscles firmly so the whole leg is rolled inward and heels touch. Feel the pull all the way into the hips.
▶ Release the buttocks so the heels again roll outward.

Repeat 10 times; relax and repeat another 10 times.

To loosen muscles of the neck and shoulders and to strengthen the back for better posture

Lie, face down, hands clasped behind back.
▶ Raise head, shoulders, and midriff off the floor.
▶ Hold for a count of three.
▶ Return to face-down position.

Repeat 10 times.

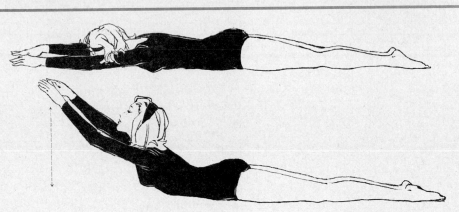

To firm arms and shoulders and to relax rib cage

Lie, face down, arms forward, flat on floor, elbows straight.
▶ Raise arms, head, and shoulders off the floor.
▶ Hold for a count of three.
▶ Return to a flat-on-floor position.

Repeat 10 times.

To strengthen low-back muscles, to reduce hips, and to improve posture

Lie, face down, arms at sides.
▶ Tighten buttock muscles, making the hips as narrow as you can.
▶ Raise both legs; get them as high as possible.
▶ Hold to a count of three and then lower legs to floor.

Five lifts to start; increase to 10.

To strengthen back, to slim hips, and to straighten head and shoulders

Lie, face down, arms straight ahead, elbows straight.
▶ Tighten buttocks, narrowing hips.
▶ Keeping the legs together, raise arms, head, and shoulders, and then both legs off the floor.
▶ Hold for a count of three.
▶ Return to resting position.

Repeat 10 times.

51

Exercises for waist and back, arms and shoulders

To slim waist, strengthen back muscles

Stand, arms above head, hands clasped, with right side toward a wall.
▶ Place the right hip against the wall as if it were pinned there.
▶ Bend upper torso to the left so that the left arm is pulling the right arm as far to the left as possible while the right hip stays firm against the wall.
▶ Straighten slowly.
▶ Change sides and repeat, with left hip pinned to the wall and right arm pulling left arm as far to the right as possible.
▶ Straighten slowly.

Three times to each side, twice daily.

To slim waist, strengthen back and rib cage

▶ Stretch the right arm up and out and the left leg back as far as possible, pointing the toes and the fingers and lifting the head and chin. If you do not feel the ribs lift while you do this stretch, you are not doing it correctly.
▶ Reverse to stretch the left arm up and out and to stretch the right leg backward.

Repeat 10 times, each side.

To strengthen arm muscles

Stand an arm's length away from a wall or other immovable object, with one side toward the wall.
▶ Place palm of near hand flat against the wall, straighten elbow, and push hard.
▶ Hold for a count of five.
▶ Rest and repeat.
▶ Change sides and repeat.

Five pushes with each arm.

To eliminate flabbiness and to straighten shoulders

Stand in good-posture position, feet pointing straight ahead, shoulders down and level, shoulder blades flat and slightly spread.
▶ Place fingertips on shoulders and rotate elbows in a wide circle—forward, up, back, and down.
▶ Make 10 circles.
▶ Reverse direction, now rotating elbows back, up, forward, and down.

To start, 10 elbow circles each direction.

To strengthen back and shoulder muscles

Sit on floor, legs spread, knees straight, toes pointing straight up.
▶ Clasp the right foot with the left hand and bring the forehead down toward the right knee.
▶ Force the head down as close to the knee as possible and bounce twice.
▶ Come up slowly to sitting position.
▶ Repeat to other side.

Repeat 10 times each side.

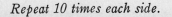

In-water exercises

To firm the thighs

Stand on pool floor, with side to pool wall, holding onto the pool edge with the near hand.
▶ Make a large circle with the outer knee, keeping knee under water throughout. Repeat five times. Keep the circles large and round.
▶ Change sides and make five large complete circles with the other knee.

Start with five circles, each knee, and build gradually to 10 circles, each knee.

Hip slimmer

Face side of pool, holding onto pool edge with hands.
▶ Starting high in the buttocks, knees straight, kick upward with each leg alternately in a rapid scissors action. This is *not* a "flutter kick." Keep the whole leg, including the buttocks, under water. The head may be kept above water if you choose.
▶ Continue for a count of 25. Rest and repeat.

Start with 10 25-count sessions, resting between them. Work up gradually to 50-count sessions.

Frog kick to firm inner thigh

Lie on back, facing away from edge of pool, holding on-to the pool edge with the hands.
▶ Place soles of feet together, knees spread, and then bring the knees up as close to the chest as possible.
▶ Spread legs, stretching them as far apart as possible, knees straight, feet out to the side.
▶ Knees straight, bring legs strongly together and then down.

Repeat 10 times.

Leg streamliner

Turn onto one side, with the shoulder toward the pool wall, supporting yourself with your hands.
▶ Kick upper leg back and lower leg forward, in a strong sideways scissors action to the count of 10. Pushing against the water, muscles work hard to complete this side swing.
▶ Change sides and repeat.

Start with 10 scissors kicks on each side; increase count as leg muscles strengthen.

56

To slim waist and streamline back of legs

With both arms straight, hang from the end of a low diving board, your body dangling loosely. The head need not be under water.

▶ Feet together, knees straight, bring the legs up till the toes reach the level of the hips.

▶ Now, with a deliberate pull, lower the legs, keeping them together, till you are again straight for your full length. Rest and repeat.

Start with five lifts and work up to 10.

Midriff stretch

Hold with hands to the end of a low diving board.

▶ With both arms straight, hang loosely and easily for a count of 10. The head need not be under water. This simple stretch, so effective under water, will do wonders for the waistline if practiced often. The rib cage is elongated, and circulation is stimulated in the midriff area.

Relax arms, rest, and repeat.

To firm slack arm muscles

Stand in good-posture position.

▶ Grasp towel at both ends; bring the arms high over-head.

▶ Now swing arms back, keeping elbows straight.

▶ Rest and repeat. If you feel a decided pull at the front of the shoulders, you need this stretch for shoulder-straightening too.

To start, 10 towel stretches daily.

Thigh firming

Sit on pool edge, supporting your straight back with your arms. Knees are bent and lower legs are in the water.

▶ Straighten each knee alternately, lower legs in the water, so water comes just to knee level of the straight leg.

▶ Repeat.

To start, 10 knee straightenings; increase gradually. You may tire after a count of 10, but as muscles get firm, you can increase your score.

Exercises for neck and chin line

To relax stubbornly tight neck muscles

Sit comfortably and place the chin in the palm of one hand.
▶ With the other hand, force the elbow of the supporting hand outward to turn the chin to the side as far as possible.
▶ When you feel a pull in the neck muscles, give an extra push to the elbow to stretch the neck.
▶ Release the chin slowly and easily.
▶ Repeat to the opposite side.

Do three times daily.

To prevent a double chin

Sit with hips well back in chair seat, arms at sides.
▶ Drop the head as far back as possible, keeping the mouth open.
▶ While head is still far back, close the mouth. If you feel a decided pull in the throat, you are doing this correctly.
▶ Open and close the mouth 10 times.
▶ Bring head up straight and relax.

Do daily to the count of 10.

Exercises
to improve your morale

To chase morning gloom

Stand, feet together.
▶ Bend loosely forward, letting the arms fall freely.
▶ Try to touch the floor with your fingertips.
▶ Bounce . . . bounce . . . bounce . . . and come up straight, feeling refreshed.

Repeat five to 10 times.

To relieve late-afternoon tiredness in arms and shoulders

Stand, feet together, and swing your arms alternately in large circles—forward, up, back, down, and forward.

Do five to 10 circles with each arm—and relax.

For a midmorning pickup

Stand, feet together, arms at sides.
▶ Clapping hands above head, jump so that your legs are spread apart sideways.
▶ Jump again, bringing arms back to sides and feet together.

Repeat quickly several times—and experience new energy.

To relieve stiff hips and legs after sitting

A gentle and simple stretch from the hips to the heels removes fatigue.
▶ While seated comfortably, loop a towel around the ball of one foot.
▶ Keeping the toes pointed up and knees straight, raise the leg to hip level and pull on the towel.

Five pulls, each foot.

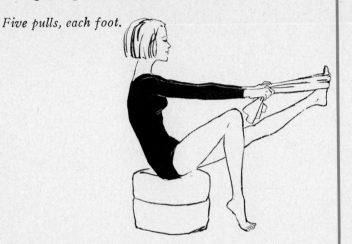

To free tension in hands

Stand, arms at sides, and make two tight fists.
▶ Raise the hands, fists clenched, high overhead and then open the hands till the palms are turned back at right angles to the wrists.
▶ Bring the arms back to your sides with the hands in this palm-back position.

Relax arms completely and then repeat.

To relieve evening tension and fatigue

Lie on back, knees bent, feet flat on floor, arms at sides, and breathe slowly.
▶ As you inhale, raise both arms overhead and back to touch the floor.
▶ As you exhale, bring the arms again overhead forward and down to lie again at your sides.

Repeat five to 10 times.

Lie on back, knees bent, feet flat on floor, arms at sides.
▶ Raise the right arm straight up, clench the fist firmly, and then let the whole arm limply drop.
▶ Repeat with the left arm.

Repeat five to 10 times.

To relieve tightness and stiffness at the back of the neck

To relieve the strain, lie on a bed or sofa so the head can fall loosely and comfortably over the edge.
▶ Raise the head slowly and try to pin the chin to the chest.
▶ Force the head forward to get a good stretch.
▶ Lower the head completely and relax.

Repeat 10 times.

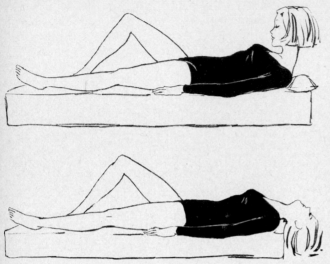

To relieve tightness in the shoulders

Sit cross-legged on the floor or upon a large cushion. Grasp ends of a towel in your hands.
▶ Pull the towel taut and hold it before you at arms' length.
▶ Raise the towel overhead, keeping your elbows straight, and then lower the towel all the way down behind your back.
▶ Bring the towel overhead and forward again.

Repeat 10 times.

Stand and grasp sides of desk or a table top.
▶ Lean in to the desk, lowering your chest to the desk.
▶ Straighten the arms to raise chest.
▶ Lower chest again to the desk top.

Repeat three times.

To relieve tension in leg muscles

Approach a flight of stairs (or front steps) in good alignment. Keep the back very straight and the head high.
▶ Walk up, putting all the weight on the legs and with each step give a strong push upward.

Three to four steps, and repeat.

To relieve tiredness from sitting

While sitting, grasp arms or sides of chair.
▶ Lift yourself completely off the seat.
▶ Sit back and lift yourself again.

Repeat three times.

To relieve tired feet

Sit, with one leg crossed over the other above the knee.
▶ Circle elevated ankle.
▶ Reverse legs and circle other ankle.

Do 10 circles with each ankle.

Spot reducers

To slim waist, to flatten derriere, and to improve posture

Stand in good posture alignment, arms raised.

▶ Bend forward and down from the groin, upper torso and head down and the arms loose.

▶ Relax knees and "scoop up" slowly, squeezing buttocks in to flatten derriere.

▶ Hold till you have straightened to good-posture position.

Repeat eight times.

To trim thighs and buttocks, to strengthen back and leg muscles

Squat on toes, with hands placed for balance on the floor between slightly spread feet. (Or you may hold chair back for balance at start.)

▶ Bounce the derriere up and down eight times.

▶ From squatting position, dart right leg out to side; bring back and dart left leg out to side. Alternate leg darts four times.

▶ Now alternately jet legs forward four times.

Increase by four counts daily till you can do 40 leg jets and darts.

To strengthen shoulder and abdominal muscles

Go into a kneeling position and then sit back on heels, elbows straight, palms pressed hard against floor.
▶ Straighten legs and lock knees, pulling abdomen up and in.
▶ Raise and lower torso, bending and straightening knees.

Repeat eight times.

To smooth hip and derriere bumps

Lie, face down, on floor, elbows bent, and hands palm-down at sides of chest.
▶ Kick toes up to buttocks 16 times.
▶ Then, keeping hands palm-down on floor, push yourself into a double-kneeling position.
▶ Pulling in tight at the groin, push buttocks backward toward heels, straightening elbows.
▶ Then press derriere forward to bump pelvic area hard toward the floor.

Repeat derriere pushes eight times; build to 32 times.

THE PSYCHOLOGY OF STAYING ON A DIET

WHILE you reduce, one of the strongest psychological pressures you will have to deal with is the urging of others to break your diet "just this once." Well-meaning or not, friends and family often press food upon the would-be dieter in social situations. Here are some sound ways of building your resistance:

▶ *Don't think you need to clean your plate.* Take small portions if you serve yourself, eat slowly so that you finish when the heavier eaters do, and if possible, leave some food on your plate. This helps in resisting pressure to have second helpings—you still have food left.

▶ *Eat slowly and carry the conversational ball.* Eating slowly helps you achieve appetite appeasement in the course of the meal—you don't finish hungry. You will notice too, if you eat with a group, that the ones who talk the most eat more slowly than the others. When you eat with nondieters, you do the talking and let them do the eating.

▶ *Learn to say no gracefully.* If you refuse second helpings with a gracious, "No, thank you. Everything was perfectly delicious," your hostess will accept your refusal easily. If you say, "I wish I could, but you know I'm on a diet," others out of sympathy for your deprived state are likely to encourage you to overeat.

There are other advantages to you and to others in keeping any mention of the subject of dieting away from the dinner table:

▶ If you mention dieting, you are likely to make others self-conscious about their own weight and perhaps about their own enjoyment of the meal.

▶ If you talk diet, you leave yourself open to being tempted by friends or family to go ahead and live it up a little—just this once.

▶ If you mention your diet, you may feel deprived because you can't eat more—and you may then go ahead and eat more (just this once?).

Keep your motivation strong

There are other compelling reasons for keeping your diet largely a private affair. True, it is helpful to discuss your diet problems with your doctor or with another interested individual who is supervising your weight-loss program. Out of such discussions can come strengthened motivation and renewed enthusiasm. But what about diet as small talk?

Realize that in its early stages it may interest your friends and family—but after that, diet talk can become a bore. Interest won't revive till you've really slimmed down. Then your overweight friends will want to know how you did it.

Except in well-directed discussions with your diet supervisor, talking about your diet can lower your determination to stick with it by dissipating your emotional impetus.

Snacking and night eating

There are said to be three kinds of overeaters—those who like good food but can be educated to control their weight while enjoying treats within reason; those who eat from nervous tension and who need a considerable amount of moral support in order to stay on a diet; and

Ten tested ways to control your weight

THERE will be critical days in any weight-control program; there will be backsliding, too. But it is possible to stay with your weight-loss program if, in any difficulty, you act promptly and wisely. Here, from Dr. John E. Eichenlaub, M.D., is a 10-step plan that has worked for others—and for himself. He starts by putting one bugaboo to rest:

"The key to weight loss," he points out, "is *not* will power. Overweight persons with just as much will power as anyone can still find themselves driven toward extra eating by emotional pressures beyond conscious remedy.

"Motivation, emotional support, and a deliberately gratifying food program are the basis of this 10-step plan. Even if you have failed a dozen times in reducing efforts, you may well find that this one works."

1 Try hard to enlist the entire sympathy of those persons whose co-operation and support is important to you. Hesitant or halfhearted co-operation with your program—or even simple lack of enthusiasm for it—among family members can wreck or severely hamper your weight-control program. If you cannot achieve the goal of family encouragement, you may need sympathetic support from new attachments— a helpful friend or a good doctor-patient relationship —to meet your emotional needs during weight reduction.

2 Set a goal you believe in. You will have to agree that the new weight will be right, not only according to your build and musculature but according to your personality, attitudes, and interests.

You can't buck this particular force. If weight loss beyond a certain point threatens your feeling of identity, your brain simply won't let you reduce any farther. Not that you can't get your weight down ultimately. After you have your new weight range for a year or two, you may feel comfortable with the idea of weighing a few pounds less, revising your self-image as the years go by.

those who have deep emotional problems that have to be solved before any weight-control program can be effective.

Evening snacking for persons of the first category may often be due to a relaxed and pleasant atmosphere and the presence of good things to eat. Occupying your time—or at least your hands—in activities that take you out of the food environment will do much for your resistance.

Getting up at night and going to the refrigerator can become a habit like anything else. Daily exercise to make you tired enough to sleep through the night will be helpful. A glass of water may suffice in allaying hunger pangs. In other cases night hunger may be emotionally triggered. If you have a continuing problem, discuss it with your doctor.

For those in the educable category, the part that

foresight can play in dealing successfully with snacking and night eating should be considered. First of all, you can make up your daily portion of snacks and eat-alone meals and wrap them in plastic wrap so that they will not lose nutrients. Prepared ahead, they are there when it is time to eat them; unless middle-of-the-night meals are scheduled, you won't have them to nibble on. If they are scheduled, they will be part of your calorie allowance.

A good deal of the success of a diet depends upon your conscious knowledge that you are being fed enough to live on—you *are not* starving. You may, in fact, be nutritionally better fed than you were previously.

What about emotional hunger?

Diet blues and other common threats to your weight-control program have to be dealt with. Above, you will find a program that has been helpful to others and can

But don't immediately attempt reduction beyond the point you currently believe to be a reasonable goal. And don't pull the rug out from under yourself by constantly revising that goal as you get close to it. If you feel inclined to go below your goal (many persons feel so inclined once they find how easy well-planned reduction really is), restrain the impulse for the time being. Enjoy the fruits of your success for six months or so and then set a new objective if you wish.

3 List in writing all the ways in which you expect to benefit from weight control. This will aid your motivation and desire and will give you a handy reminder to use whenever your incentive flags.

Most persons put "improved appearance" at the top of their list. "More energy" comes next, but this actually deserves little emphasis. A few persons gain energy immediately through diet, but most do not notice any big improvement till they have maintained their lower weight for a year or more. "Longer life" usually rates at the bottom of the list, though most doctors would give it first rank.

4 Set a definite daily or weekly schedule for eating, work, and play. Persons disposed toward overweight usually crave food when they feel at loose ends; when they know exactly what they will be doing next, this craving disappears. A reasonably rigid daily or weekly schedule cuts down food desire. Perhaps the keystone is fixed mealtimes. Eat every meal as close to exact schedule as is humanly possible, both while reducing your weight and while trying to maintain it.

Schedule your work and play, settling your use of open periods at least six hours in advance. If you schedule Friday night, for example, for recreation, you need not always limit yourself to the same activity—a movie, bowling, or bridge. You should, however, make up your mind by lunch time exactly what you will do during the evening. If you don't, the old "loose-ends hunger" will catch up with you.

5 Establish your basic food program to supply *all* your nutritional needs, to keep your fuel supply from food well below the amount your body burns each day, and to give you enough pleasure and satisfaction to assuage food cravings. A well-chosen variety of natural foodstuffs (see pages 79-87) can meet your nutritional needs—including vitamins, minerals, proteins, and certain essential fats—without vitamin capsules or nutritional substitutes.

To get satisfaction from your food—which is quite different from getting enough bulk to fill your stomach—include at least one all-you-want food with each meal. This category includes the low-calorie vegetables and fruits and some virtually calorie-free condiments.

Assemble a list of foods that—because of their nature, intrinsic appetite satisfactions, or the like—you normally take in reasonably small or not-too-caloric servings. Work such items into your program as often as possible for increased food gratification without excess fuel intake.

Assemble another list of foods that afford a high level of food gratification in relation to their fuel value—broiled steak or chops or dietetic cottage cheese—and use these foods as appetite appeasers.

6 Enlist a diet monitor and never break away from your fixed program without calling your diet monitor and clearing the change with him or her. The forces that lead an overweight person to eat more fuel than his body burns act mainly when he makes food decisions. If you let someone else make the decisions for you, those forces usually prove much easier to control. You can accomplish this without doctor bills if you can get someone in your family or one of your friends to serve as diet monitor. Discuss your preferences and difficulties with your monitor and let the

help you. It takes into consideration the emotional as well as the physical aspects of hunger.

Do you know when to stop?

Can you stop eating when you've had enough? Do you feel hungry a half hour or so after eating? Knowing the times when hunger may haunt you, you can help yourself overcome these threats to your weight-loss program. For example, it may prove wise to plan activities right at the end of your meals and in the hour or so immediately following them so that temptation at such times will not overwhelm you.

In speaking of the sensations of hunger and satiety Harry N. Hoffman, M.D., chairman of the committee on dietetics of the Mayo Clinic reports:

"A recent study revealed no significant differences in these sensations [hunger and satiety] between obese and nonobese subjects. In fact, a somewhat greater number of obese persons experienced very few or no hunger sensations after prolonged food deprivation, and the urge to eat was similar in both groups. Most interestingly, it was at the end of meals that differences were greatest. Obese subjects reported that they required more will power to stop eating, even though they more frequently reported sensations of physical discomfort such as fullness and nausea at the end of meals. In addition, the obese subjects more frequently became preoccupied by thoughts of food a half hour after meals, a rare phenomenon among the nonobese subjects. Hence, rather than hunger, it seems that abnormalities in satiety may characterize the obese."

The too-highly-set appetite-control center in the brain may thus be victimizing you. Yielding to its demands may only defer the time when you will feel satisfied

Ten
tested ways...

monitor make all the decisions—and you stick by them.

Whenever you feel the urge to break away from your food program, even in the middle of the night, call your monitor. Talk the situation over before you take that first liberty that means the end of real food control.

If an unusual situation puts you under heavy pressure toward transgression, the fact that someone else is concerned about you and your progress usually makes you feel better. If the problem is not unusual but simply that your food program needs adjustment, the monitor should decide what those changes should be.

7 Each week go over your progress and complaints with your diet monitor. Besides being available in case of need, your monitor should go over your progress and complaints with you once a week. He should actually weigh you and compare your weight with previous records. Then he should ask a series of questions and revise your food program according to your replies:

▶ *Have you consistently suffered hunger at any one period of the day?* Hunger an hour to an hour and a half after a meal usually comes from a blood-sugar drop. You can stop mild hunger of this sort by replacing some of the preceding meal's sugars and starches with slower-burning protein foods—an extra serving of meat or cottage cheese, for example, in place of an equivalent amount of bread or potato. More intense blood-sugar-type hunger requires a small snack (reserved from the previous meal) to be taken just before the usual hunger period.

Hunger in the late morning or afternoon simply signifies an empty stomach. An appetite-spoiling snack split off from the next projected meal usually solves this problem.

Late hours or social pressures may require some evening eating; if so, you do better to split off a snack from the preceding evening meal than to try to make up for violations later.

▶ *Have you felt tired at any one time of day?* Some stringent dieters get a letdown feeling, fatigue, or mental fuzziness in the last hour before a meal. Such complaints disappear when snacks are provided on the pattern described for hunger before meals.

▶ *What about constipation?* When one eats less, the size and frequency of stools usually decrease, and this need not cause concern. Difficult passage, abdominal cramps, headache, or nausea does, however, call for constipation-fighting measures.

▶ *Indigestion?* Dieters often eat large amounts of "hay" in the mistaken notion that bulk assuages appetite. Actually, high-fiber foods sometimes overload the intestine, causing gas pains and a feeling of fullness without gratifying food desires.

You can get perfectly good control of hunger without bulk if you are willing to wait 15 minutes after each meal before deciding whether your appetite is satisfied.

▶ *Any other complaints or difficulties?* It helps to discuss with your monitor any difficulties you attribute to your weight-control program or any living situation that you find upsetting. Merely airing your complaints and miseries lets you feel somewhat better. Your monitor's concern helps to replace the emotional uplift that many overweight persons get from indulgence in sweets and from other food gratifications and combats "dieter's depression."

A well-balanced weight-control program does not, incidentally, make you any more likely to catch cold. And though patients sometimes feel that they need extra sleep during a diet, records show no increase in bed-bound hours. Most other similar complaints attributed

with a food intake that you know to be a really adequate one for you.

In this same talk, given before the Grocery Manufacturers of America Food Forum, Dr. Hoffman gave this hope to those who stick with their program:

"Success [in diet and treatment programs] was more directly dependent upon how carefully and consistently the patient adhered to the program, rather than the specific structure of the program itself. . . . Most importantly, [these facts] emphasize the prominence of the complex psychologic factors at work in obesity, the great importance of realistic motivation on the part of the patient, and sincere interest and support by the physician.

"Fortunately, the great majority of obese persons are mildly obese and of reasonably normal emotional stability. Most of these can effectively reduce their weight with modest attention from their physicians and less alteration of their normal habits."

What about a weight-off group?

Some women find their motivation strengthened in the atmosphere of a reducing club. If you need such help (and if it works for you), fine! There is, however, one thing to watch out for. If you find yourself slipping from your club's standards, you may be tempted to drop out simply from guilt. This guilty feeling may hang on and make you feel helpless. You may find it hard to get back on your program again.

You should also understand that weight-control is a long-term—indeed, a lifetime—project. You have to depend on yourself for the long haul. If a club can get you over the first hurdle, that's good; use what you learn in helping yourself keep weight off thereafter.

to diet have no relation to the food program itself; rather they are the result of emotional stresses in the reducing effort.

8 Judge progress fairly. Weight loss tends to occur in spurts instead of in steady progression. Most reducers lose eight to 10 pounds quite easily and then hit a weight plateau. Waist and other measurements may continue to decrease, but the weight remains about the same for a week or more. Then further weight loss occurs abruptly.

This step pattern probably comes from the body's need to convert fat into water or into a different chemical form before mobilizing it. Your weight will ultimately change in complete accordance with the difference between fuel value of your food and the fuel consumed by body activity.

While your weight hangs on an unchanging plateau, you may feel quite discouraged. Persons whose reducing pattern starts with a plateau are especially likely to give up their program after a week or two of strenuous food restriction has apparently caused no real weight loss. Other reducers become overly optimistic when their weight plunges downward in the initial phase and then become discouraged when weight seemingly hits a barrier and remains the same for weeks.

Don't let your weight's temporary ups and downs discourage you unduly. If your program is sound and you follow it carefully, you will undoubtedly reduce.

Don't weigh too often—once a week is plenty. More frequent weighings only raise and then dash false hopes.

9 After you reach your goal, don't expect to stay on a lifelong "weight-maintenance diet." No one with a major weight problem ever stays on a rigid diet for life. Let your body be your calorie bookkeeper. When you reach your weight objective, make up a graph on which to record your future weight. Five pounds above your weight objective draw a red line across the graph and swear a solemn oath not to let your weight curve go above that line. Then weigh yourself on the same scale at the same time each week. Continue weekly weighings for the rest of your life.

10 Go back to your reducing diet the minute your weight hits the five-pound limit. You might as well face the facts right now. The overeating that makes you fat is not just a bad habit. Bad habits cease to trouble you once they have been broken. The tendency to eat for emotional comfort that characterizes persons with a weight problem usually remains a part of their make-up for life.

When you complete a weight-reduction program, your tastes have adjusted considerably. You once took two teaspoonfuls of sugar in your coffee; now you find that half a teaspoon makes the beverage sweet enough. But these changes do not last. In time the old pressures start to reassert themselves, the old patterns recur. Your weekly trip to the scale signals your need for real caution—you are rapidly approaching the diet level. You eat a bit less and more carefully and slow the upward march—but you can't completely stop it. Ultimately you hit the red line on your weight chart.

This is the critical moment. If you put off action, the weight will sneak up 10 pounds, and then you won't be able to face the stern necessity for a long reduction program. You will glide 15 to 20 pounds upward before you start your diet.

But if you get back on your program at once while you have only five pounds to lose, a couple of weeks of effort will put you back on the track. Your tastes will again adjust themselves, this time for nine months to a year.

This is the important factor in lifelong weight control. If you take that one step back to your diet quite soon, the process becomes brief and reasonably easy—not completely easy, for weight control never is, but well within your reach and worth the effort of attainment.

Keep up your appearance

Part of your motivation in controlling your weight is to look better. And keeping up your looks contributes to keeping your program going well.

Make a good-grooming program a part of your daily routine. All grooming matters become simpler as you slim—it's easier to get in and out of the bathtub, to brush your hair, to polish your toenails.

Here are ways to get a lift with good looks:

▶ Freshen up for your meals, even for a snack. Comb your hair, repair your make-up, take off your apron.

▶ Wear a well-fitted foundation garment to improve your figure even more than your exercises and weight loss have done.

▶ Deal now with any beauty problems. If you need a new permanent, a new hair color, a new make-up, get it now while your spirits need a boost. Now is the time to give your complexion a treat.

▶ Consider your wardrobe. Don't wait till you've reached your ideal weight before treating yourself to a few new clothes that do things for your improved figure. For economy, buy compromise clothes that, with a few tucks or a tighter belt, you can wear even after you've slimmed.

▶ Strive for the right kind of compliments: "You're looking wonderful!" (Not: "What's the matter? You've lost weight. Have you been sick?") Face-firming and figure-toning exercise helps here.

▶ Avoid snapshots. Few of us ever look our best in random photographs—and the camera is said to add pounds. Until you reach your ideal weight, avoid the discouragement of seeing your figure immortalized by the camera.

With today's lean, lower-calorie pork, a dieter really strikes it rich.   This thick Glazed Pork Chop (recipe on page 122) bakes juicy tender atop a big onion slice and is served with a perky vegetable kebab and soy-sauce dip.   Rest of the menu includes Green-bean—carrot Saute (recipe on page 135), plump Baked Tomato Moon (recipe on page 133) and Double Green Salad (recipe on page 137)

Total calories per serving: 423

DIET AND WEIGHT LOSS

WHY must we go on a reducing diet if we want to lose weight? The answer is simple: Because consciously or unconsciously (and probably both) we have been on a weight-gaining diet in order to put on our added pounds. We have been systematically overfeeding ourselves with results that now show up on the scale and around hips, waist, and chin line, and probably elsewhere. Now we must reverse the process.

We are going to be underfed—but only in one important respect. We are going to supply the body with each and every nutrient it needs for daily life and to keep up its reserve—except fuel. The diet is going to be calorie-deficient.

This means that for some of the energy it needs for activity, the body will be forced to burn its own fat. If this calorie-deficient diet is continued for long enough, we shall gradually shrink into a form that is more to our liking. Most of the surplus fat that makes us look and feel overweight is stored in the layers beneath the skin. It is this excess fat that, with a consistent calorie-deficient diet, will gradually be used up.

What is a calorie?

A calorie is a unit of measurement of the heat-producing, or energy-producing, value of fuel. It is not itself a nutrient. When we say that a glass of milk has 166 calories, we mean that "when burned in the tissues of the body, the food will produce a certain amount of energy that can then be expended by the muscles or by other body activity." The nutrients and the fuel we need to get from our food are found in proteins, fats, carbohydrates (sugar and starch), vitamins, and certain minerals (see pages 79-87). Proteins, fats, and sugars and starches all can be burned in the body to produce energy; the energy they provide is measurable in calories.

When we count calories, we are counting units of energy—and this is why we can count the energy we expend in activity as well as the food we take in when we are planning a reducing program that will work for us. To lose a pound a week on your diet you will have to take in 500 fewer calories (or use up an extra 500) than you require each day. This 500-calorie deficit will then be made up from stored body fat.

What are your calorie needs?

Energy (measured in calories) is needed to digest and store the food you eat—and energy is also used to keep other body processes going. The beating of the heart, the circulation of the blood, the activity of the brain and other organs—these all consume fuel. The average 120-pound woman uses about 1,300 calories in 24 hours, even in a state of rest. This is, however, an average figure only. A great deal depends upon body size, metabolic rate, and so forth. You can, however, assume that your basic body need for fuel is about 0.45 calories an hour per pound. For example: 0.45 calories x 120 pounds x 24 hours = 1,296 calories per day—or about 1,300.

In addition to the calories needed to keep the body processes going, body fuel is needed to meet the demands of the muscles. Your daily calorie requirement thus depends to a great extent upon how active you are. The table on page 76 shows how many extra calories you are able to use up per hour in various activities. The more active you are, the higher the calorie allotment on your weight-loss diet can be. And this is why it is suggested that you increase your activity along with cutting calories—your calorie cut can be less drastic if you burn up more fuel daily in your work and play.

If you find that the calorie allotment in the table on page 10 is far higher than you are now taking in—if you are gaining weight on a calorie allotment that is considered normal—it may mean that you are below normal in your range of activity.

Age is another factor. Your basic body calorie needs gradually decline as the body processes gradually slow. For each decade of life after age 25 this calorie allotment must be reduced (see table, page 10).

Today a 1,500-calorie diet can be considered a weight-maintenance diet for many 40-plus women. For others—particularly younger women—it will be a reducing diet. How will it work for you?

Planning your diet

The best way to find the diet that will lower your weight by a pound a week is to go to your doctor and let him work it out for you. You should do this anyway if you have any health problem, if you are pregnant or nursing, or if you are 10% or more overweight.

If you have a reasonable number of pounds to take off, you can work out your diet for yourself.

Start by making a list of all the foods you ordinarily eat each day. Be sure the list is complete and includes snacks, the extras such as mayonnaise, sugar, and cream, and fairly accurately estimated portions of any food—meat, vegetables, desserts, and so forth.

With this list in hand, calculate each item for its calorie content (see page 157) and total them—this is your average daily calorie intake.

Are you gaining on this diet? If so, multiply the number of pounds you have gained by 3,500 (calories per pound of body fat) and divide by the number of days it has taken you to gain this amount. This will give you your average daily calorie surplus. Deduct this number from your daily calorie intake, and you have what should be your daily calorie intake for maintaining your present weight. By cutting another 500 calories from this amount, you will have a calorie budget on which you should lose a pound a week.

If you are simply maintaining your overweight on your present diet, you need only drop to a calorie count that is 500 below your present diet, and see how rapid is your weight loss. If 1,500 calories a day would maintain your weight, drop to the 1,000-calorie-a-day diet—or to the 1,200-calorie-a-day diet (page 104) and increase your activity by another 200-calorie expenditure daily—and again you will have a loss of about a pound a week.

The simplest method is to assume that the daily calorie allowance for your desirable weight (see table, page 10) will be a reducing diet for you.

How low must you go?

With any diet there has to be some experimenting—you have to see how you respond. If you gain or maintain your weight on the program you set up for yourself, you will have to decrease the calorie allotment still further or increase your activity still more.

But take care to give your diet a fair chance before you decide it is not working. In the early weeks of a diet, water may replace fat—and your weight loss will not immediately show up on the scale. Or you may at the start lose as you expect to—and then maintain weight on the diet for the several weeks that follow. Again, this may be a result of water-fat balance. Or you may also have to consider weight gain from retention of body fluids in the monthly cycle.

At the end of six weeks you should know whether you are actually losing and whether the weight loss is going on at a reasonable rate.

If there is no change by this time, you may have to reduce your calorie intake by dropping to a still lower calorie count.

Sometimes it is necessary for the reducer to take in no more than 900 or even 800 calories a day to realize an adequate weight loss. Any diet under 1,000 calories should have your doctor's approval and supervision. All food needs other than calories can barely be provided in an 800-calorie diet. Planning of menus at this low-calorie intake must be extremely careful to ensure that you are not losing needed nutrients as you cut calories.

What should your diet do for you?

There are several factors involved in the calorie requirement for an individual—age, body size, sex, physical activity, and the type of food. Whatever your calorie requirement, there are certain important things your diet should do for you:

▶ Your diet should be nutritionally sound (see pages 79-87); this means it gives all the basic nutrients you need to keep going each day and to have a reserve for any emergency.

▶ Your diet should also fit into your regular menu plan so that you need not always be eating apart from family or friends.

▶ Your diet should provide portions of food to be eaten at the times of day when you are most likely to feel actual hunger or emotionally triggered food desire.

▶ The diet must also provide fewer calories than you use during a day—so that the body is forced to use stored fat for fuel.

If you follow such a diet plan, you can continue on a calorie-deficient diet as long as is necessary to reach your desired weight and you can thereafter—making allowances for decreased calorie requirement with age, lessened activity, and smaller body size once desired weight is reached—stay within a desirable range.

74

For the added necessity of reeducating your tastes it is wise to plan your weight loss over a fairly long period of time—at least six to 12 weeks—so that you can adjust to new food habits and can accustom your body to metabolizing body fat for energy.

Put your monitor back in control

Your body itself should control the amount of food you feel like eating; this control is provided by a natural appetite monitor in the midbrain.

Because in certain conditions the body needs to have fuel reserves, we are physically constructed so that we can store reserve fuel as fat. This was useful to our ancestors. Fat can be stored in seasons of plenty as a reserve to be used in seasons of food shortage. In the past human survival probably often depended upon this ability.

The body's food-intake monitor in the midbrain— the area that controls our waking and sleeping, our temperature, and other body functions—can be adjusted to the habit of overeating regardless of the body's need for fuel. It can also be readjusted so that the appetite is satisfied with a smaller portion of food. If your diet is to succeed, this adjustment must take place.

Experience with a new food-intake level over weeks or months is necessary if your appetite monitor is to be reset to a lower demand.

Be aware of body changes

For any dieter some or many of the hungers that threaten a weight-loss plan will be emotional. Food can serve as a substitute satisfaction for many needs other than those of the body for nourishment. The need to give yourself a treat, the need to relieve tension, the need for companionship are a few. Still, some of the seemingly psychological urges to break your diet can arise from the changes that are going on in your body as you lose weight.

For the body to burn its own fat rather than to get instant fuel from food intake means a change in body processes. Your constitution may well express alarm at having to call upon its reserves for its present needs. And you may well react emotionally with a feeling of depression, of deprivation, and of anxiety. Compare the situation with the desperation you might experience if, in an emergency, you had to start making a cake from basic ingredients when always before you've had instant cake mix.

To force your body to burn its own fat, your diet must be calorie deficient. But your diet must also be planned to satisfy many of your physical and emotional needs.

Your diet will go better if each of your daily portions is planned ahead to be most satisfying to both these needs. Realize that the meal plan you use should be the one that works best for you. The generally accepted food allotment pattern is 40% of your calories at breakfast, 20% at lunch, black coffee only at morning and afternoon snacks, 40% at dinner. The milk allotment can be kept, if desired, for between-meal or bedtime snacks.

Some women prefer to eat a smaller portion at breakfast and more at lunch and dinner; some women get along perfectly all right without snacking. Others feel they must have a larger allotment for their between-meal nibbling. So long as you don't go over your daily calorie quota, you will lose weight no matter at what time of day you take your food.

What about skipped meals?

It is usually advisable to set up your menus on a three-meal-a-day plan. This gives you food intake during the day when you are using most fuel for activity. Blood sugar will thus not fall below normal, and you will not be overcome by lassitude or fatigue. With a three-meal-a-day diet—the meals eaten at the same time of day each day—a rhythm of eating and fasting is established that can make it easier to stay on your diet without snacking.

Each of us is, however, an individual—and we have to use the plan that works well for us. Recent medical studies have shown that some women who could not lose on a 1,000-calorie three-meal-a-day diet could lose on an 1,100-calorie daily ration if they consumed their food on a two-meal-a-day basis. Another study has shown that a "nibble" diet—six small meals a day— has been effective for some persons who couldn't lose weight on conventional three-meal menu plans. If you get along perfectly well by skipping lunch or another of your meals and find that everything goes better that way, no one will gainsay your doing what works best for you. It is important to realize, however, that diet-planners who work with large groups of would-be reducers suggest that the three-meal-a-day menu plan be followed.

Make your calories count

Important on the low-calorie diets that most of us must undertake, if we are to have impressive weight loss, is that we should have at least some of the things we like along with the things that are good for us.

But too many of the so-called "empty" calories can bring a weight-loss program down in defeat. These empty calories are the ones that exist in table sugar and alcohol—and "empty" merely means that these two foods provide calories without providing other nutrients the body needs (vitamins, proteins, and so forth). If too many of these empty calories creep into the diet, the nutrient calories may be slighted or the diet will go over the calorie limit to supply them.

Other considerations include overuse of meats such as beef, pork, and lamb to the exclusion of fish, chicken, and other good protein sources. In steaks and chops there are likely to be hidden fats. Meat is an excellent source of protein, but take care in your diet menu planning not to exclude other good sources.

Part of your diet program is the reeducation of your eating habits. Unless you really work at eating the foods

THE ENERGY COST OF ACTIVITIES

Activity	Calories per pound per hour	Activity	Calories per pound per hour
Bedmaking	1.9	Piano playing (Mendelssohn's *Song Without Words*)	0.9
Bicycling (century run)	4.0	Piano playing (Beethoven's *Appassionata*)	1.1
Bicycling (moderate speed)	1.6	Piano playing (Liszt's *Tarantella*)	1.4
Boxing	5.7	Reading aloud	0.7
Carpentry (heavy)	1.5	Rowing	5.0
Cello playing	1.1	Rowing in race	7.8
Cleaning windows	1.7	Running	3.7
Crocheting	0.7	Sawing wood	3.1
Dancing, moderately active	2.2	Sewing, hand	0.7
Dancing rhumba	2.8	Sewing, foot-driven machine	0.8
Dancing, waltz	1.9	Sewing, electric machine	0.7
Dishwashing	0.9	Singing in loud voice	0.9
Dressing and undressing	0.8	Sitting quietly	0.7
Driving car	0.9	Skating	2.1
Eating	0.7	Skiing (moderate speed)	5.2
Exercise		Standing at attention	0.8
very light	0.9	Standing relaxed	0.7
light	1.1	Sweeping with broom, bare floor	1.1
moderate	1.9	Sweeping with carpet sweeper	1.2
severe	3.0	Sweeping with vacuum sweeper	2.2
very severe	4.0	Swimming (2 mi. per hr.)	4.1
Fencing	3.8	Tailoring	0.9
Football	3.6	Tennis	2.8
Gardening, weeding	2.3	Typing, rapidly	1.0
Golf	1.2	Typing, electric typewriter	0.7
Horseback riding, walk	1.1	Violin playing	0.8
Horseback riding, trot	2.5	Walking (3 mi. per hr.)	1.4
Horseback riding, gallop	3.5	Walking rapidly (4 mi. per hr.)	2.0
Ironing (5-lb. iron)	1.0	Walking at high speed (5.3 mi. per hr.)	4.3
Knitting sweater	0.8	Washing floors	1.0
Laboratory work	1.5	Writing	0.7
Laundry, light	0.6		
Lying still, awake	0.5	Walking down stairs, calories per pound per 15 steps	0.011
Office work, standing	0.8	Walking up stairs, calories per pound per 15 steps	0.034
Organ playing (1/3 handwork)	1.2		
Painting furniture	1.2		
Paring potatoes	0.8		
Playing cards	0.7		
Playing table tennis	2.5		

Adapted from "Foundations of Nutrition," 6th edition, by Clara Mae Taylor and Orrea Florence Pye. Copyright © 1966, The Macmillan Company.

that give you a low calorie intake while providing all the nutrients—and adjust your tastes to this kind of eating—you will find yourself on a diet merry-go-round. Your weight will fall while you diet and rise again as soon as you go back to your old eating ways.

This is a particular hazard if your traditional menus have been heavy in rich desserts, fried foods, high-caloric snacks; these are the forbidden foods of the weight-watcher.

Face the fact that your food habits have made you overweight; changing your food habits can help you control your weight for your lifetime.

Your diet and family meals

The menu plans and recipes in this guide are designed for a woman who will be eating with the family—and it should be possible for you to eat at least some of many items your family eats. Sometimes breakfast, lunch, and between-meal snacks can be planned for you to eat alone (if your diet requires this), but dinner for a family woman should be a family affair.

Plan ahead what portions you will have, what foods you can share, and try not to call attention to what the family can eat and you can't touch. Keep mealtime a relaxed and cheerful occasion, and this means: *Don't complain*. Stimulate conversation and eat slowly so that you finish with the family—even if they go on to second helpings.

A good deal of your diet success in the family eating pattern will depend on your planning your food allotment for the whole day and in your knowing clearly what portions you can have.

It is also important that the different calorie needs of family members be considered. Family members also differ in nutritional needs *(see pages 82-83)*. Each of your family members will probably have a higher calorie requirement than your own. Your husband can probably take in more calories because of body size and activity. Children need calories for both growth and activity. The need for added calories persists through teen years.

What about crash diets?

You will often hear from your friends—and perhaps your family—that someone went on a one-food diet and lost 10 pounds in two weeks, and why don't you try it? Or that someone else eats everything she wants and still loses, because the diet she read about in such-and-such a place lets you do just that. Or some clinic or some university or some Government agency has tried a new diet, and this is the great thing. After all, it's scientific, isn't it?

Many of the diets that are being tried in clinics and hospitals throughout the country and that get wide publicity are designed for use in controlled circumstances or for persons with certain specific problems for which conventional reducing programs are not useful. Other reported "medically proved" diets are disowned by the agency or hospital or clinic at which they are supposed to have originated.

In addition, dietetical tests are made in circumstances where doctors are in attendance and can constantly watch over the patients—check the blood pressure and urine and blood count and so forth while the dieting is going on. Although many such diets might not do great harm if used for a brief period without medical supervision, in a certain number of cases the body might not be able to stand the strain. Until such experimental diets become approved for public use, it is best to stay with nutritionally accepted menu planning.

The same cautious attitude should apply to total fasting. Although by total fasting many obese persons have been able to lose weight, this treatment is advisable only in a hospital—again, medical supervision is a necessity. And it is important to note that in at least one study of total fasting as against conventional reducing, the subjects who fasted lost more muscle tissue than did others on conventional diets. The conventional dieters, for their part, lost what they wanted to lose—fat.

One runs still another hazard with experimental diets or one-food diets. These diets usually are designed for rapid short-term weight loss. The eating habits are not really changed, and weight gain is often resumed once the 14-day or three-week diet regimen ends.

Water and weight loss

Will you lose weight if you drink less water? Will it help your weight loss to cut down on fluids? Cutting water and salt intake as well as the use of diuretic drugs (drugs that induce release of body fluids) can help with weight loss—temporarily. But this has little to do with your actually losing fat. One should take in enough water to keep the body well-supplied with fluids—enough to produce about a quart of urine a day. Water is lost not only through the bladder. It is also lost through perspiration and through breathing.

The body can, in fact, get along better without food than it can without water. Those who are dehydrated become fatigued and restless and nervous. And water often proves to be a good appetite appeaser when taken between meals and after exercising.

It is true that water is produced by fat in the process of its being oxidized, and this may make your weight loss slow to show up on the scale. This condition is only temporary, and your body will usually secrete the fluid in good time; as you continue on your diet you will lose weight. Soft fat that is high in water content is usually lost first—and thus weight loss is actually easiest at the start of the diet, slower as the diet progresses. If you know that your reducing diet is nutritionally sound and calorie-correct for weight loss, the knowledge will help you to stay with your weight-loss program long enough to reach your desired weight. Keep these facts in mind:
▶ The older you are or the less you have to lose the slower your weight reduction should be.
▶ The more pounds you have to lose the greater your weekly rate of loss can be.
▶ If you are a young and active adult, you can undertake a more drastic diet than an older less-active person.

A sandwich needn't be taboo for a dieter. Just make it open-face. Here, Ham-and-cheese Bonanza (recipe on page 122) calls for sliced ham and cheese, tomatoes, lettuce, cucumber rounds, and tangy onions—all heaped on rye bread. Another secret: Zippy cheese spread from a jar to go on the bread snips off calories. For a beverage, choose low-calorie cola or ginger ale

Total calories per serving: 414

NUTRITION AND THE REDUCING DIET

CAN better nutrition help you lose weight? Yes, it can. You are less likely to get hungry on a diet if you fortify your body every day with all the nutrients it needs for its complex processes. Well-nourished, you will eventually have more energy—and you perhaps will become more active and thus burn up more calories. Possibly you'll be less nervous—and will feel little impelled to seek food as a tranquilizer. Sooner or later you will experience other health benefits from sound nutrition. These could show up in a fresher complexion, brighter eyes, better sleep.

Good nutrition is one of the advantages a whole family can gain when the woman of the house goes on a sensible weight-watching program. The reducing menus in this book are planned to provide the essentials of your nutritional needs—except for calories. If you eat a variety of foods within your accepted calorie quota, you will be well fed and you *will* lose weight.

What is good nutrition?

Good nutrition is to be well-fed on the basis of meeting the body's needs for its growth, maintenance, energy, and tissue repair rather than to be well-fed simply on the basis of an abundant table and a full stomach. But good nutrition does not mean that your meals cannot be interesting, taste-satisfying, and completely enjoyable—as a glance at the food pictures and recipes in this guide will tell you.

The body has a variety of food needs—some are for very small quantities of certain minerals; often demands, such as that for protein and calcium and vitamin C, are so great that it takes careful menu planning to meet them on a reducer's diet. Some nutrients the body can store. Others must be supplied daily in adequate amounts if you are to stay in good health.

The key is to eat foods daily from each of the four basic food groups. The dairy group—milk, cheese, and ice cream; the meat group—meats, the variety meats, fish, poultry, eggs; the fresh-fruit-and-vegetable group—including good sources of both vitamin C and vitamin A daily; and the cereal group—breads, rice, breakfast cereals, and macaronis. You can include dried peas and beans (high in protein but also in carbohydrates) and nuts (high in protein but also in fats).

Fortunately, the nutrients for all daily needs are readily available in the foods that you find on your market shelves and in its fruit and vegetable and dairy and meat departments. By eating a variety of foods and choosing some each day from each of these four basic food groups, you can (if you are a nonpregnant nonnursing adult and not on a reducing diet) get your complete nutritional quotas (*see table, pages 82-83*).

By varying your food choices within each group and not overemphasizing one group to the neglect of the others, you will be supplying yourself and your family with their basic nutritional needs—proteins, fats, carbohydrates (starches and sugars), and a variety of vitamins and minerals.

What are the energy foods?

The body needs nutrients to maintain itself, for growth, for tissue repair—and for energy. Carbohydrates—sugars and starches (the body converts starches to sugars)—are the natural sources of quick energy. But they also are readily turned into body fat if the energy that they could provide is not used.

We get sugar from many foods—fruits and vegetables and milk, for example—that provide us with other nutrients. Starchy foods—bread, cereals, and some vegetables (potatoes, for example)—also contribute to the carbohydrate intake (and provide other nutrients) and thus supply energy. For the dieter, sweets, such as sugar, candy, syrups, cake frosting, and other high-sugar desserts that have no other food value, should be kept to a minimum. It is better to get the needed sugars and starches from foods that provide for other nutritional needs. This also helps keep total calorie intake down.

Fats are a natural source of slow energy; they must be changed to sugar to be used by the body as fuel. Fats are packed with twice as many calories per unit of weight as sugar and so are very concentrated sources of energy. The dieter's own body fat must supply the great part of the fat requirement and about one half of the daily calorie need if one is to lose weight. Some fat should, however, be included in the reducing diet. For one thing, fat is appetite-appeasing. For another, some fat makes the diet more interesting as well as more satisfying. Fats are available within many meats even after the visible fat is trimmed. Butter, margarine, salad oil, and nuts also are fat sources, and some of these foods can be included in a reducing diet.

What are the body builders?

Some proteins also can be burned as fuel—if there is a need for it. But the body will burn available protein only when there are no sources of fat or carbohydrate. Certain protein foods are appetite-satisfying because they are digested and assimilated slowly.

Proteins are chiefly needed for the body's muscle-building, maintenance and repair of organs and all systems, and are involved in the structure of every body cell. Because protein cannot be stored, the body's requirement must be met each day. Proteins are abundant in meats (including fish and shellfish) and also in milk, eggs, cheese, nuts, and enriched bread.

Because meeting the daily protein requirement (see table, pages 82-83) is a necessity, care in planning this part of the reducing menu is of utmost importance; though meat such as beef is a good source of protein, other good sources should not be overlooked—fish, poultry, skim milk and skim-milk cheese, for example.

We also need fluids

The body is about two thirds fluid, and its water supply is constantly diminished through breathing and perspiration as well as through the kidneys. Thus water is another daily essential that the dieter may have to take some care to supply to the diet. You get water from many solid foods—even soda crackers have some; vegetables and fruits have high water content — and, of course, from the liquid foods you consume: Milk, soup, fruit juices. If you cut your food intake greatly—particularly soft drinks and other such fluids—you should maintain your body fluid by drinking more water. Three to five glasses of water a day are suggested.

Essential minerals

Drinking water, depending on the soils through which it has percolated, also supplies the body with some essential minerals. The minerals the body needs are these:

Calcium	Manganese
Phosphorus	Copper
Potassium	Iodine
Sulphur	Cobalt
Sodium	Fluorine
Chlorine	Silicon
Magnesium	Zinc
Iron	

These minerals are essential, but some of them only in traces, and in most cases you need not be concerned with them nutritionally. Cobalt, fluorine, silicon, and zinc are needed in only minute quantities. These minerals, with phosphorus, potassium, sulphur, magnesium, manganese, and copper are readily available in common foods in adequate amounts; if a variety of foods is eaten, all the body's needs for these elements is readily supplied. Oversupply of some minerals — notably iron, cobalt, copper, and fluorine—can in fact be dangerous.

The need for two other minerals—sodium and chlorine—is supplied (if not oversupplied) by the use of table salt (sodium chloride); unless, of course, you are on a sodium-restricted diet. Because salt in some cases causes the body to retain fluids, it is suggested that the dieter get accustomed to salting food just a little less than has been usual.

Another essential mineral is iodine, and this is often added to table salt for use in areas where iodine is scant in the natural water and food supply. Sea foods also are rich in iodine.

Iodine is necessary to prevent goiter (enlargement of the thyroid gland) and also to enable the thyroid to manufacture hormones that play a vital role in body well-being.

Calcium and iron

Minerals take part in every body process and enter into the make-up of every body cell, and two particularly have to be carefully worked in sufficient supply into the menu—of both the dieter and each of the family members. These minerals are iron and calcium. Phosphorus and potassium are also needed in generous amounts, but if your diet is adequate in calcium and other nutrients, you will usually get enough phosphorus and potassium.

Iron is an essential in the red cells of the blood; infants, children, and growing boys and girls have a high daily iron requirement. This high requirement persists

HOW MUCH YOU NEED Recommended Daily Allowances *(higher levels are recommended during pregnancy and lactation)*	WHY YOU NEED THEM	MAJOR DIETARY SOURCES
VITAMIN A *(Fat-Soluble)* 5000 International Units (applies when ⅔ of Vitamin A activity is supplied as carotene, as occurs in average diet)	Helps to form and maintain healthy eyes, skin, hair, teeth, gums, and the various glands. Vitamin A is also involved in fat metabolism.	Whole milk, butter, fortified margarine, eggs, liver, deep green leafy vegetables,* yellow fruits and vegetables**
VITAMIN D *(Fat-Soluble)* *(including D₂ and D₃)* Requirements for adults is not known but there are indications that a small need does exist.	Needed for strong teeth and bones. Helps the body to use calcium and phosphorus properly.	Under normal circumstances, from sunlight and usual mixed diet. When not exposed to sunlight, sources are Vitamin D fortified milk and other fortified foods.
VITAMIN E *(Fat-Soluble)* *(a-Tocopherol)* 25 to 30 International Units (varies with polyunsaturated fatty acid content of diet)	Needed to help form normal red blood cells, muscles and other tissues. Protects the fat in the body's tissues from abnormal breakdown.	Vegetable oils, margarine, cabbage, other vegetables and fruits, whole-grain cereals
VITAMIN K *(Fat-Soluble)* Allowance has not been determined but a need has been established. Normally, most is manufactured by microorganisms in the intestine.	Needed for normal blood clotting.	Deep green leafy vegetables*
VITAMIN B₁ *(Water-Soluble)* *(Thiamine)* 1.0 to 1.4 mg.	Helps get energy from food by promoting proper use of sugars.	Milk, liver, poultry, pork, fish, whole-grain enriched breads
VITAMIN B₂ *(Water-Soluble)* *(Riboflavin)* 1.5 to 1.7 mg.	Functions in the body's use of carbohydrates, proteins and fats, particularly to release energy to cells.	Milk, eggs, liver, lean meats, deep-green leafy vegetables,* whole-grain enriched breads
VITAMIN B₆ *(Water-Soluble)* *(Pyridoxine)* 2.0 mg.	Important in metabolism, particularly in formation of certain proteins and in use of fats. Aids in forming red blood cells.	Lean meats, deep green leafy vegetables,* green beans, whole-grain cereals
VITAMIN B₁₂ *(Water-Soluble)* *(Cobalamin)* 5.0 to 6.0 mcg.	Helps in building nucleic acids for cells. Aids in forming red blood cells. Aids the functioning of the nervous system.	Milk, liver, lean meats, kidney, oysters, salt-water fish
BIOTIN *(Water-Soluble)* Requirement not established but 150.0 to 300.0 mcg. considered adequate. Normally, most is manufactured by microorganisms in the intestine.	Involved in formation of certain fatty acids and production of energy from the metabolism of glucose. Essential for working of many body chemical systems.	Eggs, liver, kidney, green beans, deep-green leafy vegetables*
FOLIC ACID *(Water-Soluble)* *(Folacin)* 0.4 mg.	Helps in forming certain body proteins and genetic materials for cells. Helps form cells, especially red blood cells.	Liver, deep green leafy vegetables*
NIACIN *(Water-Soluble)* *(Niacinamide)* 13.0 to 18.0 mg. (assuming an equal amount is formed from tryptophan, which we get from dietary protein)	Present in all body tissues and involved in energy-producing reactions in cells.	Eggs, liver, lean meats, whole-grain enriched breads and cereals
PANTOTHENIC ACID *(Water-Soluble)* Requirement not established but 5.0 to 10.0 mg. is probably adequate.	Involved in changing foods into molecular forms needed by body. Needed to form some hormones and nerve regulating substances.	Eggs, liver, kidney, nuts, deep-green leafy vegetables*
VITAMIN C *(Water-Soluble)* *(Ascorbic Acid)* 55.0 to 60.0 mg.	Needed to keep bone, teeth and the blood vessels healthy. Important in formation of collagen, a protein that helps support body structures as skin, bones, tendons.	Citrus fruits, berries, tomatoes, melons, new potatoes, green peppers, cauliflower, cabbage, deep green leafy vegetables*
Measurements One gram (g.) is one twenty-eighth of an ounce One milligram (mg.) is one thousandth of a gram One microgram (mcg.) is one millionth of a gram An International Unit (I.U.) is a standard of biological activity set by an international scientific committee		***Deep Green Leafy Vegetables** include: broccoli, Brussels sprouts, chard, kale, mustard greens, spinach, turnip greens ****Yellow Fruits and Vegetables** include: apricots, cantaloupes, carrots, pumpkin, rutabagas, squash, sweet potatoes

Adapted from VITAMINS AND YOUR BODY, courtesy of Vitamin Information Bureau and RECOMMENDED DIETARY ALLOWANCES, National Academy of Sciences

in women through the child-bearing years because of the iron losses through menstruation. Infections also may be a cause of iron loss. Foods high in iron (see table, page 87) should be brought into the diet in adequate amounts to keep up your reserve.

Iron-deficiency anemia is a common problem in women and in teen-age girls. A simple test in the doctor's office can reveal such deficiency—and the cause can be treated. Iron supplements may be prescribed, but such supplements should not be taken except on a physician's advice. (Iron supplements should be kept out of the reach of children, for accidental iron poisoning from such tablets is a hazard.) For all normal needs, adequate iron can be had from the foods on a reducing diet.

Calcium, apart from its bone-building role that makes the quart of milk a day a must during childhood, is used in many other body functions — including the rhythm of the heartbeat and the response of nerves to stimulation and the clotting of blood in injuries.

Milk and milk products are the important source of calcium for grownups as well as for infants and children. The need for milk as a food never stops—adults should have at least a pint a day, children and teen-agers require at least a quart; pregnant women and nursing mothers have a still higher milk requirement. The dieter should take it as skim milk, which differs from whole milk only in having fewer calories and slightly less vitamin A. Other calcium-rich foods (see table, page 87) should also be included in the family eating pattern because of the great need for this mineral in all age groups.

Calcium supplements, like iron supplements, are sometimes prescribed by physicians, but in ordinary circumstances, including most weight-control diets, the calcium can be obtained along with other nutrients from the foods on the menu.

The vital vitamins

Vitamins, organic compounds found in various foods, spark the vital processes that go on within the body; today there are about 15 that are considered essential to life, and the discovery of others is still going on. Along with these discoveries, more knowledge is being gained about what vitamins do and how they do it. The major vitamins are found chiefly in the green and yellow vegetables, in milk, in fruits, and in cereals and meats. Today many common foods are enriched with vitamins; by eating a variety of foods an adult can satisfy his or her basic vitamin needs without resorting to supplements. Infants and children and teen-agers and nursing mothers and pregnant women usually require supplementary vitamin D, needed for growth and health of bones.

It is important to health that vitamins be supplied by

RECOMMENDED DAILY DIETARY ALLOWANCES
Designed for the maintenance of good nutrition of practically all healthy people in the U.S.A.

	AGE (years) From Up to	WEIGHT (kg)	WEIGHT (lbs)	HEIGHT (cm)	HEIGHT (in)	CALORIES	PROTEIN (gm)	FAT-SOLUBLE VITAMINS VITAMIN A ACTIVITY (IU)	VITAMIN D (IU)	VITAMIN E ACTIVITY (IU)
Infants	0 – 1/6	4	9	55	22	kg × 120	kg × 2.2	1,500	400	5
	1/6 – 1/2	7	15	63	25	kg × 110	kg × 2.0	1,500	400	5
	1/2 – 1	9	20	72	28	kg × 100	kg × 1.8	1,500	400	5
Children	1 – 2	12	26	81	32	1,100	25	2,000	400	10
	2 – 3	14	31	91	36	1,250	25	2,000	400	10
	3 – 4	16	35	100	39	1,400	30	2,500	400	10
	4 – 6	19	42	110	43	1,600	30	2,500	400	10
	6 – 8	23	51	121	48	2,000	35	3,500	400	15
	8 – 10	28	62	131	52	2,200	40	3,500	400	15
Males	10 – 12	35	77	140	55	2,500	45	4,500	400	20
	12 – 14	43	95	151	59	2,700	50	5,000	400	20
	14 – 18	59	130	170	67	3,000	60	5,000	400	25
	18 – 22	67	147	175	69	2,800	60	5,000	400	30
	22 – 35	70	154	175	69	2,800	65	5,000	—	30
	35 – 55	70	154	173	68	2,600	65	5,000	—	30
	55 – 75+	70	154	171	67	2,400	65	5,000	—	30
Females	10 – 12	35	77	142	56	2,250	50	4,500	400	20
	12 – 14	44	97	154	61	2,300	50	5,000	400	20
	14 – 16	52	114	157	62	2,400	55	5,000	400	25
	16 – 18	54	119	160	63	2,300	55	5,000	400	25
	18 – 22	58	128	163	64	2,000	55	5,000	400	25
	22 – 35	58	128	163	64	2,000	55	5,000	—	25
	35 – 55	58	128	160	63	1,850	55	5,000	—	25
	55 – 75+	58	128	157	62	1,700	55	5,000	—	25
Pregnancy						+200	65	6,000	400	30
Lactation						+1,000	75	8,000	400	30

Adapted from RECOMMENDED DIETARY ALLOWANCES, National Academy of Sciences

the diet in adequate amounts every day, for each vitamin has its own work to do and is essential to the life processes *(see table, page 81)*.

Planning your diet and that of your family so that there are adequate amounts of the essential vitamins—and being sure that the vitamin-rich foods that are served are eaten—is a homemaker's responsibility. The vitamins that will most concern you in planning menus are these:

Vitamin A, which protects the skin and mucous membranes and inner organs, is found in liver, kidney, egg yolk, butter and margarine, and other dairy products; and the green and yellow vegetables and tomatoes are sources of a substance the body can convert into vitamin A. An excess of vitamin A can be hazardous, and supplements of this vitamin should be taken only on a physician's recommendation.

The B vitamins (there are now believed to be a dozen or more) are found in the cereal food group—whole-grain cereals, breads, and macaronis—and in meats, milk, and other foods. Each B vitamin has its own function; a deficiency can result in nervousness and can lead to a host of general complaints.

Vitamin B_1 (thiamine) has much to do with keeping heart, nerves, and muscles functioning well. It is available in good amounts in pork, beef, lamb, green peas,

lima beans, in whole wheat, oatmeal, milk, and egg yolk.

Vitamin B_2 (riboflavin) has much to do with tissue health and the state of the skin. It is found in milk, eggs, meat, and in whole-grain cereals and dried fruits.

Niacin aids the nervous system and helps in conversion of food to energy. It is found in lean meats, liver, dried yeast, cereals, enriched bread, eggs, and tuna fish.

Vitamin B_6, important for healthy teeth and gums and the health of the blood vessels, is found in wheat germ, liver, dried yeast, meats, and whole-grain cereals.

Vitamin B_{12} helps prevent certain forms of anemia and contributes to the health of the nervous system. It is found in liver, kidney, milk, salt-water fish and sea food, and lean meat.

Folic acid helps prevent anemia and is involved in protein metabolism. It is present in leafy green vegetables, food yeast, and meats and is synthesized in the healthy digestive system.

The daily need for vitamin C (ascorbic acid) dictates our custom of taking a glass of morning orange juice. Vitamin-C deficiency can lead to many ailments, for this vitamin is essential to build strong body cells and blood vessels. Citrus fruits are a good source as are tomatoes, melons, red berries, and leafy green vegetables. These are foods that often are slighted, particularly by teenagers. Vitamin C must be supplied daily.

The allowance levels are intended to cover individual variations among most normal persons as they live in the United States under usual environmental stresses. The recommended allowances can be attained with a variety of common foods, providing other nutrients for which human requirements have been less well defined.												
WATER-SOLUBLE VITAMINS							MINERALS					
ASCOR-BIC ACID (mg)	FOLA-CIN (mg)	NIA-CIN (mg equiv)	RIBO-FLAVIN (mg)	THIA-MIN (mg)	VITA-MIN B_6 (mc)	VITA-MIN B_{12} (mcg)	CAL-CIUM (g)	PHOS-PHORUS (g)	IODINE (mcg)	IRON (mg)	MAG-NESIUM (mg)
35	0.05	5	0.4	0.2	0.2	1.0	0.4	0.2	25	6	40
35	0.05	7	0.5	0.4	0.3	1.5	0.5	0.4	40	10	60
35	0.1	8	0.6	0.5	0.4	2.0	0.6	0.5	45	15	70
40	0.1	8	0.6	0.6	0.5	2.0	0.7	0.7	55	15	100
40	0.2	8	0.7	0.6	0.6	2.5	0.8	0.8	60	15	150
40	0.2	9	0.8	0.7	0.7	3	0.8	0.8	70	10	200
40	0.2	11	0.9	0.8	0.9	4	0.8	0.8	80	10	200
40	0.2	13	1.1	1.0	1.0	4	0.9	0.9	100	10	250
40	0.3	15	1.2	1.1	1.2	5	1.0	1.0	110	10	250
40	0.4	17	1.3	1.3	1.4	5	1.2	1.2	125	10	300
45	0.4	18	1.4	1.4	1.6	5	1.4	1.4	135	18	350
55	0.4	20	1.5	1.5	1.8	5	1.4	1.4	150	18	400
60	0.4	18	1.6	1.4	2.0	5	0.8	0.8	140	10	400
60	0.4	18	1.7	1.4	2.0	5	0.8	0.8	140	10	350
60	0.4	17	1.7	1.3	2.0	5	0.8	0.8	125	10	350
60	0.4	14	1.7	1.2	2.0	6	0.8	0.8	110	10	350
40	0.4	15	1.3	1.1	1.4	5	1.2	1.2	110	18	300
45	0.4	15	1.4	1.2	1.6	5	1.3	1.3	115	18	350
50	0.4	16	1.4	1.2	1.8	5	1.3	1.3	120	18	350
50	0.4	15	1.5	1.2	2.0	5	1.3	1.3	115	18	350
55	0.4	13	1.5	1.0	2.0	5	0.8	0.8	100	18	350
55	0.4	13	1.5	1.0	2.0	5	0.8	0.8	100	18	300
55	0.4	13	1.5	1.0	2.0	5	0.8	0.8	90	18	300
55	0.4	13	1.5	1.0	2.0	6	0.8	0.8	80	10	300
60	0.8	15	1.8	+0.1	2.5	8	+0.4	+0.4	125	18	450
60	0.5	20	2.0	+0.5	2.5	6	+0.5	+0.5	150	18	450

The 4 basic foods

Milk, cheese, and butter or margarine make up this class. For the two glasses of milk you need every day, you may substitute skim milk for whole-milk goodness with about half the calories. And depend on low-count uncreamed cottage cheese—it's only one fourth as caloric as Cheddar. Allow a tablespoon of butter or margarine every day

This group includes meats, fish, poultry, and eggs, and everyone should have two or more servings each day. With such a wide variety to choose from, monotony need never be a problem. In cooking meat for dieters, trim all fat—and no gravy, please! Less tender cuts that are braised are just as good for you as broil-roast kinds, count fewer calories

Each of the food groups here holds the key to a well-balanced diet, and each is equally important. Learn to think in terms of this basic pattern every day, and soon good meals will just fall into line naturally without any further fuss or bother

Fruits and vegetables—Make oranges, grapefruit, or tomato juice (or melon or strawberries in season) a daily must for vitamin C, and add your choice of two other fresh or canned diet-pack fruits. Daily servings of vegetables should include one green, one yellow, one raw, and one other. (Some of our menu plans even call for a plain small potato)

Breads and cereals or their equivalents—spaghetti, macaroni, noodles, hominy grits, rice, and crackers or other baked goods—should be a part of every day's diet. Check labels and buy enriched white, whole-grain, or high-protein breads. On the other foods, keep to small quantities. The menus on pages 98-107 will show you just how much a calorie-counter rates

Vitamin D has been widely used to fortify foods. For adults (except pregnant women and nursing mothers) no daily requirement has been established. In the young, vitamin D helps calcium and phosphorus in the building of bones and teeth. This vitamin is abundant in fish-liver oil; but the adult body, when exposed to sunlight, can manufacture in the skin the vitamin D it needs. An excess of this vitamin can be as devastating as a deficiency, and the amount of vitamin D that may be added to foods is now being limited.

Should you take a vitamin supplement?

The key to success in a reducing diet is to plan menus that are nutritionally sound—that give you all the nutrients you need from the foods you eat. If you follow such a diet plan, you can watch weight indefinitely without endangering your well-being. A sound diet plan (see pages 91-107) has these requirements:

Milk (a pint each day for an adult; a quart for a child; a quart or more for a teen-ager); fruits and vegetables high in vitamin C—one or more servings of citrus fruit, tomato, cabbage, or salad greens; two servings daily of foods high in vitamin A—leafy green or yellow vegetables; eggs—at least three to five a week; meats, poultry, fish, or cheese—two or more servings daily; cereals and breads; a modified amount of fat; sweets in a small amount.

With the wide availability of nearly all foods, nutritionists today emphasize that vitamin supplements are not always necessary. If you question this in your own case, you should talk to your physician. He may suggest, as some physicians do, that you, as a dieter, need vitamins to avoid a health hazard. But care should be taken not to take a supplement instead of eating your diet quota of vitamin-rich foods, for these foods provide other nutrients as well. And realize that continued success with a weight-control diet depends upon the menu's supplying the basic body needs from the foods themselves.

Weight control in pregnancy

During pregnancy, weight control often becomes a problem. Weight gain is preferably held to 18 to 24 pounds—and if you are overweight already, your weight gain should be less than 24 pounds. Ask your physician's advice on pregnancy weight-watching.

Good nutrition during pregnancy—and during nursing—is vital both for the health of the infant and that of the mother. Particularly important is increasing the protein, calcium, and vitamin-D intake to provide for the growth of the unborn infant and, while nursing, to provide the mother's own body needs and milk supply for her baby.

Your doctor will encourage you to watch your weight during pregnancy—and he will also encourage you to improve your nutrition. Usually a pregnancy diet of about 2,500 calories is the maximum for women of normal weight. Milk intake is increased to bolster calcium and protein supply.

Pregnant women also have increased need for other food essentials (see table, pages 82-83), and the nursing mother's needs, particularly for calories, are also higher.

Feeding the dieter's family

Basic dietetic requirements vary with each family member. Your husband will probably need considerably more calories than you do—to support a larger better-muscled frame and because he is probably more active than you are. He will also need more protein (again a matter of frame size and muscle), but his iron requirement will be lower. Some of his vitamin requirements and yours will be about the same; other vitamins he will need in greater amounts (see table, pages 82-83).

The calorie requirement of men diminishes, as does that of women, with age and lessened activity. While working with your diet and your family's menus, encourage others in the family to eat the basic foods and also, if necessary, to control their calorie intake.

Children need calories for growth as well as for activity; throughout the growth period, and particularly in the teen years, the needs for many of the other basic foods, especially protein, run higher than those of adults. Vitamin D is needed from infancy through the teens and is usually supplied by diet supplement—fish-liver oil; fortified milk and sunshine are other sources.

Vitamin C (ascorbic acid) and iron requirements are high in the young, and fulfillment of the requirement should be watched carefully, particularly in your teen-agers. Teen-agers have hearty appetites—but they tend to eat fun foods (carbohydrates and fats) and neglect other basics, particularly fruits and vegetables.

Why you can overeat and be underfed

Why do those who overeat so often find themselves undernourished? The reason is that the overweight often find themselves eating foods that provide only energy—and these foods (the fats and carbohydrates) are stored as fat when activity is not sufficient to require their being burned.

Undernourishment can also be a result of family eating habits. There are lean families as well as fat families—fruit-and-vegetable families as well as meat-and-potatoes families; hamburger-and-hot-dog families and whipped-cream-and-mayonnaise families; there are pasta families and families in which the only really important part of the meal is the dessert. In many families hot cereals are neglected; in other families fish and variety meats are ignored; in still others vegetables are limited to peas and beans with no exploring of the variety of other vegetables that can provide additional nutrients.

True, a great deal of consideration must be given to family eating habits and family tastes. It is unwise for the dieter to put herself or her family on a totally unfamiliar menu pattern just because she thinks it will be better for them. Instead, within your family eating tradition, make the changes that will correct nutritional deficiencies and that will cut down any daily calorie oversupply for any family member.

FOODS HIGH IN CALCIUM

FOODS HIGH IN IRON

The recommended daily dietary allowance of calcium for normally active healthy adults is 800 mg. It is very important to increase dietary calcium during pregnancy and lactation. (See table on page 82.)

The recommended daily dietary allowance of iron for women of child-bearing age is 18 mg. But as individual requirements vary greatly, increasing the dietary iron through fortification may be desirable.

Food	Measure or Weight	Calcium mg.	Food	Measure or Weight	Iron mg.
Almonds	¼ cup	83	Almonds	¼ cup	1.7
Apricots, dried	¼ cup	25	Apple juice	1 cup	1.5
Beans, cut green	½ cup cooked	32	Applesauce, no sugar	1 cup	1.2
Beans, lima, dried	½ cup cooked	28	Apricots, dried	¼ cup	2.1
Beans, lima, green	½ cup cooked	40	Asparagus, canned	½ cup	2.0
Beans, navy, dried	½ cup cooked	48	Avocado	½ medium	0.8
Beans, red kidney, dried	½ cup cooked	37	Banana	1 medium	0.8
Bran flakes, 40%	1 cup	25	Beans, lima, dried	½ cup cooked	3.0
Bread, white	1 slice	21	Beans, lima, green	½ cup cooked	2.2
Bread, whole wheat	1 slice	24	Beans, navy, dried	½ cup cooked	2.6
Broccoli	½ cup cooked	68	Beans, red kidney, dried	½ cup cooked	2.3
Cabbage, shredded	1 cup	34	Beef, ground, broiled	3 ounces	2.7
Cheese, American	1 ounce	198	Beef, pot roast	3 ounces	2.9
Cheese, Cheddar	1 ounce	213	Beef, steak, broiled	3 ounces	2.5
Cheese, cottage, creamed	½ cup	115	Bran flakes, 40%	1 cup	12.3
Cheese, cottage, dry	½ cup	90	Braunschweiger	2 slices	1.2
Cheese, Parmesan, grated	⅓ cup	383	Bread, whole wheat	1 slice	0.8
Cheese, Swiss	1 ounce	262	Brussels sprouts	½ cup cooked	0.9
Chocolate, semi-sweet	1 cup pieces	51	Chicken, broiled	3 ounces	1.4
Clams, canned	3 ounces	47	Chocolate, semi-sweet	1 cup pieces	4.4
Collards	½ cup cooked	145	Clams, canned	3 ounces	3.5
Cream, dairy sour	¼ cup	48	Dates, pitted	¼ cup	1.3
Cream, heavy	¼ cup	44	Egg	1 large	1.1
Cucumber	1 medium	35	Fruit cocktail, canned	1 cup	1.0
Egg	1 large	27	Ham, boiled	3 ounces	2.4
Endive, curly and escarole	1 cup pieces	46	Lamb, roast	3 ounces	1.4
Fruit cocktail, canned	1 cup	23	Lettuce, Boston	¼ head	1.1
Ice cream	½ cup	97	Liver, beef, fried	3 ounces	7.5
Ice milk	½ cup	102	Macaroni, enriched	1 cup cooked	1.4
Kale	½ cup cooked	74	Molasses, light	2 tablespoons	1.8
Milk, buttermilk	1 cup	296	Oatmeal	1 cup cooked	1.4
Milk, evaporated, undiluted	1 cup	635	Oysters	½ cup	6.6
Milk, skim	1 cup	296	Peanuts	¼ cup	0.8
Milk, whole	1 cup	288	Peas, green, canned	½ cup	2.1
Molasses, light	2 tablespoons	66	Peas, split green	½ cup cooked	2.1
Oysters	½ cup	113	Plums, canned	1 cup	2.2
Peas, green, canned	½ cup	25	Pork, roast	3 ounces	2.7
Pineapple, canned	2 large slices	26	Potato, sweet, baked	1 medium	1.0
Pineapple juice	1 cup	37	Prune juice	½ cup	5.3
Prunes	½ cup cooked	30	Prunes	½ cup cooked	2.3
Potato, sweet, baked	1 medium	44	Raisins	¼ cup	1.5
Raisins	¼ cup	26	Rhubarb	½ cup cooked	0.8
Rhubarb	½ cup cooked	106	Rice, enriched	1 cup cooked	1.8
Sardines, canned	3 ounces	372	Sardines, canned	3 ounces	2.5
Salmon, canned	3 ounces	167	Sauerkraut	1 cup	1.2
Sauerkraut	1 cup	85	Shredded wheat	1 biscuit	0.9
Shrimps, canned	3 ounces	98	Shrimps, canned	3 ounces	2.6
Spinach	½ cup cooked	84	Spinach	½ cup cooked	2.0
Squash, summer	½ cup cooked	26	Strawberries	1 cup	1.5
Squash, winter	½ cup cooked	29	Sugar, brown	2 tablespoons	0.9
Strawberries	1 cup	31	Tomato	1 large	0.9
Sugar, brown	2 tablespoons	24	Tomato juice	1 cup	2.2
Tomato	1 large	24	Tuna, canned	3 ounces	1.6
Turnip, yellow	½ cup cooked	27	Veal, roast	3 ounces	2.9
Yogurt, plain	1 cup	294	Walnuts	¼ cup	1.9

Adapted from NUTRITIVE VALUE OF FOODS, United States Department of Agriculture and RECOMMENDED DIETARY ALLOWANCES, National Academy of Sciences

Diet tricks and treats

As a dieter you will discover for yourself many tricks that make it easier and pleasanter to be a calorie-counter. And you will also find ways to introduce into your daily menu diet treats that don't break the calorie barrier. Here are suggestions you may find useful. Perhaps they will bring to mind other ways to use your calorie allotment creatively.

Breakfast brighteners

The surest way to tire of eggs is to eat them cooked the same way every morning of the week. For a change:

▶ Poach your egg in skim milk to serve on toast with the hot milk sauce spooned over it.

▶ Prefer your egg fried? Then diet-fry it this way: Pour cold water into a small frying pan just to cover the bottom; break an egg into the pan; season with salt and pepper. Cover the pan and steam slowly till the egg is done as you like.

▶ French toast not for dieters? Try it this way: Combine bread, milk, and eggs from your diet allowance into a tasty 310-calorie breakfast. A tablespoon of honey adds only 50 calories. To make the toast dip, beat 1 egg with 2 tablespoons of skim milk (this makes enough dip for 1½ thin slices of bread). Dip the bread into the mix and then saute in 1½ teaspoons butter or margarine.

▶ For another breakfast delight stretcher, use whipped butter or margarine (softened before using for greater spreadability). These spreads give greater coverage at lower calorie cost.

▶ Honey, jam, jelly, molasses, or syrup in tiny amounts —not more than a tablespoonful—can be an occasional 50-calorie breakfast treat for the calorie-counter. Or you can sprinkle cereals with a tablespoonful of brown sugar for a flavor change.

Helps for diet family meals

If your family is away from home at lunchtime and you can pick and choose for yourself, depend on a cup of bouillon, a big vegetable or cottage-cheese salad sparked with lemon or lime juice, and skim milk or buttermilk to start off a good afternoon. If lunch (like dinner) is a family-round-the-table meal, here is your chance to star one main dish with a low-calorie twist for all. (See Calorie-counter's Recipes, pages 109-157.) On tuna-salad day, for example, save your portion to dress with lemon juice or a zippy no-calorie tomato dressing and serve a choice of salad dressings to the others.

▶ Skim every smidgen of fat from homemade soup before tasting it. And speaking of tasting, try not to sample your cooking more than once. Many a good cook has eaten her meal allowance before reaching the table.

▶ Trim all fat from your portion of meat. When cooking your portion with the family meal, use foil to protect your portion from the cooking fat or oil.

▶ Remember—no gravy for the dieter.

▶ To cook meat without fat or oil, simmer or bake it in a sauce made of canned tomatoes and green pepper with spices and herbs for extra zip.

▶ Poach fish—don't fry it.

▶ For variety, cook vegetables in bouillon, adding herbs and spices for flavor.

▶ Small amounts of grated cheese can also be added to vegetables to give flavor variety.

▶ Take out the dieter's serving of vegetables before adding butter or sauces to the family's portion.

▶ Let seasonings take the place of fats and oils in meats, vegetables, and salads. Meat tenderizers enhance meat flavors. Season with lemon, vinegar, wines, onions, garlic, salts, spices, or herbs.

Nibbles

Keep low-calorie vegetable snacks fixed and handy in your refrigerator. If they're not ready and you have to stop to clean them, you'll probably pass them by for a higher-count nibble. All you want of the following items won't add up to more than 25 calories:

Sliced raw cauliflowerets	Green-pepper sticks
Celery	Water cress
Cucumber sticks	Radishes
Carrot curls	Lettuce wedges

By saving from your mealtime allowance of fruit and other foods, you can have a variety of snacks between meals without adding calories to the daily allowance:

▶ Dip fresh sweet strawberries into creamy yogurt. (Perfect, too, as a dinner dessert.)

▶ Grapes taste equally satisfying served this way—and one half cupful is less than 50 calories.

▶ Save breakfast orange or grapefruit (half a small one) for a midmorning treat.

▶ Make a jellied compote of 1 envelope low-calorie lemon-flavor gelatin dissolved in 1 cup boiling water; combine with 1 can (1 pound) diet-pack fruit cocktail. Chill just till set and then divide into 6 servings (each only 46 calories).

▶ Slice half an unpared apple thinly; spread with 2 tablespoons of dry cottage cheese if you can afford a 25-calorie extra.

▶ Combine diced cantaloupe and honeydew melon; then flavor with a squeeze of fresh lime and chopped fresh mint for a refresher.

▶ Keep low-calorie diet-pack fruits—peaches, apricots, pears, fruit cocktail—chilled in the refrigerator. Enjoy them plain, or add a little lemon juice.

▶ Open and drain a can of mushroom caps or slices or slice unpeeled fresh mushrooms. Dip with picks into any of these no-calorie seasonings: Seasoned salt, lightly salted lemon juice, chopped parsley or dill, chopped water cress sprinkled with paprika.

▶ If you are entertaining, arrange mushrooms and dip choices around a table-type hibachi; spear mushrooms with picks and heat before dipping.

▶ Here are other daytime or party munchers—each under 25 calories:

1 saltine	2 dried apricot halves
1 small rye wafer	2 teaspoons raisins
½ cup unbuttered popcorn	1 medium-size dried prune
6 pretzel sticks	1 large dill pickle
	1 large sweet pickle

Drinkables

Between-meal drinks are refreshing and often at no calorie cost to you. Or your milk allowance can be saved from your daily menu to give you an afternoon refresher. Skim milk or buttermilk—both are good pickups.

▶ Enjoy a mug of hot beef or chicken bouillon made with cubes, paste, or the instant kind packed in tiny envelopes. Calories—almost zero.

▶ Rich canned condensed beef broth, diluted with an equal part of water, or poured right from the can over ice, adds up to 17 calories for ⅔ cup.

▶ Make tomato juice your midmorning pickup. Add one envelope of unflavored gelatin for extra protein and goodness. To fix, sprinkle gelatin into juice and then stir. Sip cold—or heat just till the gelatin dissolves.

▶ Plain tea or coffee—with no sugar or cream—has zero calorie count. Hot, these beverages stimulate; iced, they refresh as well. Add fresh lemon or lime juice or a no-calorie sweetener with a clear conscience.

▶ Check the many no-calorie carbonated beverages in your supermarket. Their count is zero.

▶ Combine milk and eggs from your daily allowance into an eggnog and flavor it with vanilla or almond extract and no-calorie sweetener. This may also be baked as a custard or frozen to make ice cream.

Fool-the-eye diet tricks

Enjoyment—satisfying the taste buds and the eye—is an important factor in being sure a diet works. Make your diet meals as pretty as a picture (see the many illustrations in this book). And try these simple fool-the-eye tricks:

▶ So your portion won't look small on the plate, serve yourself on small or medium-size dishes.

▶ Slice all foods very thin so they will look like more.

▶ Sprinkles of parsley on potatoes, mushrooms on meat, herbs, spices, and other gourmet touches make diet food more tempting and thus more satisfying.

▶ Fool the taste buds too—eat slowly so you really savor and enjoy everything you eat.

Diet tips for dining out

If eating in a restaurant, order roasts or other plain meats or broiled fish rather than dishes with sauce. For dessert, choose plain fruit or cheese. Other tips:

▶ Choose a low-calorie white wine rather than a high-calorie cocktail as an appetizer.

▶ Don't ask your hostess to provide special diet foods for you. Instead, eat small portions of what you are served. If your diet is drastic, you can decline an invitation for a meal by saying: "Sorry, I am on a strict diet. I shall, however, be delighted to join you and your other guests for after-dinner coffee."

▶ If you use less than the total of your calorie budget in any day, do *not* make up for it the next day. If you plan to dine out, save part of your calorie allowance from other meals to add to your dinner allowance.

▶ If you use more than your calorie allowance in one day, cut down the next day at lunch or dinner.

Depend on popular sea food to be a winner for any meal, yet keep the calorie count down. And even the men will go for this hearty Bouquet Crab Bowl (recipe on page 128) dressed up invitingly with sunny hard-cooked egg. To eat with the salad, serve your favorite bran muffins baked in tiny pans. (Allow three for a dieter.) Beverage go-with: Iced or hot tea sparked with lemon

Total calories per serving: 251

DIET PLANS AND MENUS

THERE'S nothing like the lift you get or the zip you feel when unwanted pounds vanish. And eating right while trimming down can be a pleasant game. Most important to remember: Don't shortchange any meal—just short-cut the calories.

Once you learn proportions and portions, the rest is easy—whether your goal is to take off pounds or simply hold the line. Keep in mind that any be-svelte training program should include lean meats, fruits and vegetables, milk and dairy products, and whole-grain breads and cereals, for these are the foods that keep you fit. Does this mean the same old thing every day? No, indeed, for these foods, with a little imagination, can be turned into all kinds of inviting dishes. For example: Lean ground beef, combined with tomato as the vegetable and herbs for seasoning, becomes a topper for spaghetti (it takes the place of bread). With little extra effort, your milk and egg allowances, plus flavoring and no-calorie sweetener, is custard; fruit, eggs, and milk may go souffle-fancy. Raw or cooked vegetables in low-calorie gelatin make a sparkly molded salad.

Diet arithmetic made easy

As a guide for meal planning, you'll find exchange lists on pages 94-95. Here foods with the same nutritional value are grouped together, and while you may make substitutions within each group, it's important not to switch back and forth between groups or you'll cheat yourself of the valuable proteins, minerals, and vitamins you need for pep and good health.

Turn the pages for sample menus of 1,000, 1,100, 1,200, and 1,500 calories a day showing how interesting breakfast, lunch, and dinnertime can be. (Starred recipes start on page 110.) If you're a beginner dieter, you'll find it easiest to follow these plans until you get into the swing of things. Then branch out on your own and juggle the calorie combinations as you wish. But remember to stick to the basic diet pattern—and keep the day's total the same.

Let's measure up!

At first, measuring amounts of foods may seem unnecessary and fussy work, but because "servings" vary from person to person, they are not an accurate guide. Cups, tablespoons, and teaspoons as used in cooking are standard, so make them your calorie-counting tools. After a while, you'll be able to judge the size of a helping by eye—whether eating at home or away.

Sample menus do not allow for snacks or between-meal refreshers, but you may have them. Just save something from your regular mealtime allowance to nibble or sip later, or choose the no-calorie kind. (Your supermarket has morale-boosters aplenty.)

Ready to go? Then start with the idea that dieting can be a rewarding experience, for nothing ventured—nothing lost!

Your shopping guide to diet foods

A treasure hunt—that's what shopping for these wonder foods is, for meat and produce counters, dairy and freezer cabinets, and grocery shelves up and down the aisles hold the makings of inviting meals to help you and your family be fit and stay fit. It pays to know and use all the varieties your store offers, for they make meal-planning easier, more fun and exciting. Notes here tell you the inside facts on these diet-right helpers.

Why are they different?

Manufacturers have worked out carefully researched substitutions for low-calorie or special diet foods. For example: If a label reads "sugar-free," you can be sure that the sweetening is either the natural flavor of the food or one of the popular no-calorie sweeteners. In some cases, syrups and oils are replaced with water, or for gluten bread, a special formula uses no-fat, high-protein flour to replace regular flour.

Where do you find them?

Some supermarkets stock low-calorie foods in one convenient section, but new products appear fast and may show up anywhere in the store. Look around, for you may find the low-calorie salad dressings with the regular ones, low-sugar spreads in the jam and jelly section, or low-calorie crackers and gluten bread in the cracker and bread departments. Now and then, it pays to allow a few extra shopping minutes just to browse for new ideas.

How can you recognize diet foods?

Check the label, for they are some of the most clearly marked products in your supermarket. Each specifically states whether it is sugar-free, or artificially sweetened, salt-free or no salt added, low-calorie, or 90% fat-free. Each label also lists the ingredients, as well as the percentage of carbohydrate, fat, and protein. And what's best, there's no guesswork about calories, for packers have worked them out for you, right down to the specific number in a cup, tablespoon, or teaspoon.

Are these foods good buys?

Indeed they are! Many of the canned fruits, vegetables, jellies, and salad dressings cost no more than the regular products. A few are even cheaper. Nonfat dry milk and fluid skim milk are thriftier than homogenized milk. Whipped toppings are more economical than the regular products. In the main-dish line, complete meals may seem to cost more, but when you're cooking for a family in addition to a calorie-counter, these specialties save time.

Do they taste good?

Food manufacturers can take a sweeping bow, for low-calorie items not only look like their higher-calorie twins, but match them in flavor. (No wonder many non-dieters prefer them!) The great popularity of low-calorie beverages and ice milk is proof of good taste.

What is available?

As with regular foods, supermarkets stock the diet-slanted varieties most popular with their customers, so knowing what your store carries will speed your shopping. The list below describes the leaders, many of which are called for in the meal plans and recipes in this book.

WEIGHT-WATCHING CHOICES

Juices

You'll find canned unsweetened grapefruit and pineapple juices and bottled low-calorie cranberry juice cocktail. Unsweetened citrus and other fruit juice concentrates come frozen in handy six- and twelve-ounce cans.

Meats, main dishes, fish, and cheese

Obvious is the wide selection of fresh meats—always on the side of the calorie-counter. Buy the leanest cuts and trim off visible fat. To enhance the ever popular broiled chicken, use new low-calorie, low-fat seasoned coating. For easy flavor variety, try the ready-to-heat low-calorie dinners-in-a-can—Chili beans and beef, Rice and chicken, Spaghetti and meat sauce, and three others. And don't miss the assortment of low-calorie dinners in the frozen food case. To pep up your menus, remember fish and cheese—frozen fish (mostly filleted and ready to cook), tuna packed in water, dry cottage cheese, low-calorie cheese spreads, and low-calorie soft Neufchâtel that looks and tastes like cream cheese.

Vegetables

These are canned without salt and are usually available in 8- and about-16-ounce sizes. Choices include corn, peas, tomatoes, green beans, beets, carrots, asparagus.

Fruits

What would we dieters do without these morale boosters? Besides fresh fruits, there are canned diet-pack apricots, cherries, figs, fruit cocktail and fruits for salad, sliced peaches and peach halves, pears, purple plums, and mandarin oranges. Also pineapple in natural juice, unsweetened applesauce, and grapefruit sections. Most fruits come in 8-ounce and about-1-pound sizes.

Spreads

Here's another morale-boosting family that includes low-sugar fruit jellies and preserves in popular flavors: apple, blackberry, apricot-pineapple, grape, raspberry, strawberry. And look for low-calorie pancake syrup.

Breads and cereals

Dietetic and gluten breads, melba toast, seasoned or plain rye wafers, and unsalted crackers, along with some high-protein dry cereals make up this group.

Salad dressings

Salad lovers take note, for you have almost endless choices. Flavors include French, Italian, Roquefort; Cole slaw, Thousand Island, and a mayonnaise type that is almost fat-free. And if you would prefer to whip up your own with water, buttermilk, or tomato juice, there are perky seasoned dry mixes in an envelope.

Desserts

Have your cake and stick to your diet, too, for just look at this selection: Six flavors of low-calorie gelatin, three flavors of puddings, rennet powder, and ice-cream mixes. Even several canned pie fillings are "calorie-reduced." Dietetic ice cream and ice milk are prepared in popular flavors, plus such other tempters as coffee, lemon, and peppermint. Topping powders to whip up at home or toppings from a pressurized can are excellent limited-calorie alternates for whipped cream. And do look above the ice-cream cabinet for low-calorie syrup toppings.

Beverages

The market is rich with low-calorie carbonated drinks, powders, and tablets; noncarbonated fruit drinks; iced-tea mixes—with and without lemon—in family-size jars and the packages of convenient envelopes. And remember that skim milk, a must for all dieters, is available in the dairy case both plain or with extra proteins, minerals, and vitamins, and on the shelves, as instant-dissolving nonfat dry milk.

Sweeteners

Most dieters are familiar with these no-calorie sweeteners sold as tablets, crystals, liquid,—and some are used just like sugar. Be sure to follow label directions carefully for their sugar equivalents.

Diet supplements

These very popular foods—in liquid or powder form—or as cookies—are nutritionally complete meals to use for periodic weight control. All forms come in a variety of popular flavors—chocolate, vanilla, strawberry, eggnog, and coffee among others. The liquid may be chilled or frozen, the powder mixed with whole or skim milk. The cookies (nine to an envelope) could also be used as a high-nutrition snack. All labels list calorie count as well as complete nutrition information.

Your food choices

Good nutrition is a must if you are dieting or not. A good diet allows for your daily needs, subtracting calories without sacrificing the minerals, vitamins, and other food requirements. A good reducing diet can be as varied as you are imaginative. Once you know how to combine foods you can pick and choose from all those listed here. But it is important that you select foods from each of the groups in the portions suggested.

Group I
MILK

On any diet, a pint of skim milk a day is a must, and counts 180 calories. Drink it as a beverage with your meals or as a between-meal snack. Use it in cooking, too. Substitute a pint of buttermilk made from skim milk or two cups of reconstituted instant nonfat dry milk if you prefer.

Group II
MEATS

This includes not only beef, veal, lamb, pork, and poultry, but also fish, cheese, and eggs. You need five units of cooked lean meat (trimmed of fat and bone) or their equivalent every day. Count each unit of cooked meat as 75 calories. For a three-unit serving choose:

1 slice prime-rib roast, 5"x3½"x¼"
1 slice sirloin or eye-round roast, 5"x4"x¼"
1 slice roast lamb, 4"x4"x¼"
1 slice baked ham, 5½"x3½"x¼"
2 slices roast pork, 3"x1½"x½"
1 slice roast veal, 3"x2"x¼"
1 slice broiled sirloin steak, 3"x2"x1"
1 broiled loin lamb chop (6 ounces raw)
1 broiled pork chop (5½ ounces raw)
1 broiled veal chop (6 ounces raw)
1 broiled ground-round beef patty (4 ounces raw)
2 slices roast turkey breast meat, 3"x3"x¼"
3 slices roast chicken, 3½"x3"
1 fried chicken breast
½ cup boned, canned chicken
1 piece broiled halibut, 4"x3"x½"
1 piece fresh broiled or baked salmon, 4"x3"x½"
1 cup cream-style cottage cheese

For a two-unit serving choose:

1 piece liver, 3½"x2½"x¼"
3 medium-size chicken livers, broiled
¼ of an about-2-pound chicken, broiled
2½ slices canned corned beef, 3"x2¼"x¼"
3 slices boiled tongue, 5"x3"x⅛"
2 slices bologna

1 thin frankfurter
3 slices crisp bacon
2 square slices packaged boiled ham
6 medium-size shrimps (20 to the pound)
2 large California-type, tomato-packed sardines, 4"x1½"
4 small Atlantic-type sardines, 3"x1¼", drained
1 piece poached cod, 4½"x4"x¾"
1 piece broiled mackerel, 4"x2"x1½"
1 piece broiled haddock, 4½" x 4" x ½"
½ cup canned salmon
½ cup canned tuna
1 codfish cake, 2½" diameter
2 poached, hard-, or soft-cooked eggs
¾ cup uncreamed cottage cheese
1 cube Cheddar cheese, 1½"x1½"x1½"

For a one-unit serving choose:

6 medium-size oysters
6 cherrystone clams
½ cup crab meat

Group III
VEGETABLES (DARK GREEN AND YELLOW)

Your best friends in any diet are the low-calorie vegetables which are high in essential minerals—iron, calcium, and phosphorus—and in vitamins A and C (ascorbic acid). Winter (acorn or Hubbard) squash, carrots, and pumpkin contain about 35 calories per half cup. The others vary but average less than 20 calories per half cup. A 1-cup serving of the starred (★) vegetables will supply all the vitamin A you need daily. Use two or more of the others to supply your daily needs.

Asparagus, 6 spears	Lettuce
Broccoli	★Mustard greens
★Carrots	★Pumpkin
★Collards	★Spinach
★Dandelion greens	Tomatoes
★Escarole	Turnip greens
Green beans	★Winter squash
★Kale	

Group IV
VEGETABLES (OTHER)

The following vegetables, too, contribute varied amounts of the nutrients you need, so include them in your diet plans. Beets, onions, peas, parsnips, and turnips count about 50 calories per half cup. The others average about 15 calories for the same amount. Use one or more servings every day but do not substitute these for the vegetables listed in Group III.

Bean sprouts	Mushrooms
Beets	Okra
Brussels sprouts	Onions
Cabbage	Parsnips
Cauliflower	Peas
Celery	Radishes
Chard	Sauerkraut
Cucumbers	Summer squash
Endive	Turnips
(Belgian)	(white or yellow)
Kohlrabi	

Group V
FRUITS (HIGH VITAMIN C)

One serving of any of these will meet your daily need for vitamin C. Count 70 calories for all except strawberries which contain 50 calories.

- 1 cup grapefruit sections (fresh or canned, unsweetened)
- 6-ounce glass of grapefruit juice
- 1 medium-size orange
- 6-ounce glass of orange juice
- 1 cup papaya cubes
- 1 cup fresh strawberries

Group VI
FRUITS (MEDIUM-HIGH VITAMIN C)

Use two servings of these, or one plus one of the starred vegetables in Group III. Count 40 calories for each.

- ¼ cantaloupe
- ½ grapefruit
- ½ cup red raspberries
- 1 tangerine
- 1 cup tomato juice

Group VII
FRUITS (OTHER)

When serving diet-pack fruits, check the calorie listing on the label. Other choices in 40-calorie servings are:

- 1 small apple
- ½ cup unsweetened applesauce
- 2 fresh apricots
- 4 halves dried apricots (uncooked)
- ½ small banana
- ½ cup fresh blackberries
- ½ cup fresh blueberries
- 10 dark sweet cherries
- 2 dates
- 2 fresh or dried figs
- ¼ cup grape juice
- ½ cup Malaga, Tokay, or Thompson Seedless grapes
- 1 wedge honeydew melon, 7"x2"
- 1 cup cubed watermelon
- ½ mango

- ⅓ medium-size papaya
- 1 medium-size peach
- 1 small pear
- ½ cup cubed fresh pineapple
- ⅓ cup unsweetened pineapple juice
- 2 medium-size fresh plums
- 2 tablespoons seedless raisins

Group VIII
BREADS, CEREALS, AND OTHER HIGH-STARCH FOODS

It may surprise you to see what's included here but this list covers bread, cereals, rice, beans, the macaroni and noodle family, potatoes, and any other vegetables that are about as rich in starch and protein as bread. Each amount as listed counts about 70 calories.

- 1 slice bread (any variety)
- 1 two-inch dinner roll
- 2 medium graham crackers
- 20 oyster crackers
- 5 square saltines
- 3 square soda crackers
- 3 rectangular plain or seasoned rye wafers
- ½ cup oatmeal
- ⅔ cup cooked farina
- ½ cup cooked granulated whole-wheat cereal
- ¾ cup dry cereal flakes or puffs
- ⅓ cup cooked rice
- ½ cup cooked hominy grits
- 1 small baked or boiled white potato
- ½ cup mashed white potatoes (with milk only)
- ½ medium-size baked sweet potato
- ½ cup cooked spaghetti
- ⅓ cup cooked noodles or macaroni
- ⅓ cup cooked navy or kidney beans
- ⅓ cup fresh or frozen cooked lima beans
- ¼ cup baked beans without pork
- ½ cup canned whole-kernel corn
- ⅓ cup canned cream-style corn
- 1 cup popcorn

Group IX
BUTTER OR MARGARINE, FATS, OILS

To make your diet meals more inviting, a smidgen of these foods—or their equivalents—has been included. For about 45 calories, you may choose any of these:

- 1 pat butter or margarine (1/16 of a stick)
- 1 teaspoon vegetable or olive oil
- 2 tablespoons light or table cream
- 1 tablespoon cream for whipping
- 2 tablespoons dairy sour cream
- 1 teaspoon mayonnaise or salad dressing
- 1 tablespoon cream cheese
- 1 tablespoon French dressing
- 9 small olives
- 6 small nuts

Spaghetti fans: Here's a way to enjoy your favorite and stick to your diet, too. And this Meat-ball Spaghetti Bowl (recipe on page 116) boasts the same zesty flavor as its Italian twin. A diet serving allows a plump, low-fat veal ball, ½ cup sauce, 1 cup spaghetti, and a sprinkle of cheese for a bonus. Just to be different, why not start your dinner with Bouquet Salad (recipe on page 137). It tastes amazingly satisfying

Total calories per serving: 483

What a matchless choice for calorie-counters and nondieters alike. Each person rates a Pepper Beef Loafette (recipe on page 112) striped with crunchy water chestnuts and green pepper. Cauliflower Supreme (recipe on page 135) goes glamorous with a "hollandaise-sauce" topper, and a colorful Relish Ruffle (recipe on page 141) dresses the plate most invitingly. For a starter, serve a bowlful of Jellied Appetizer Cubes (recipe on page 111)

Total calories per serving: 403

1,000-calorie-a-day meal plans

The first menu gives the basic diet pattern, using foods described in the food lists on pages 94-95. Others show how to combine these same foods into interesting and varied meals, including some of the recipes on pages 110-157. All calorie counts are approximate, since a few calories more or less make no difference.

BASIC DIET PATTERN

BREAKFAST
1 serving high vitamin-C fruit
1 serving from bread-cereal group plus 1 egg,
or 2 servings from bread-cereal group
(use part of skim milk with cereal)
1 pat butter or margarine
1 cup skim milk

LUNCH
2-unit serving from meat group
1 serving dark green or yellow vegetable
1 serving other 15-calorie vegetable
1 serving any 40-calorie fruit
1 cup skim milk

DINNER
3-unit serving from meat group
1 serving dark green or yellow vegetable
1 serving other 15-calorie vegetable
1 serving any 40-calorie fruit
Black coffee or tea with lemon

1

Breakfast
1 cup grapefruit sections
1 poached egg on
1 slice white toast
1 pat butter or margarine
1 cup skim milk

Lunch
3 broiled chicken livers
½ cup stewed tomatoes
½ cup steamed cabbage
Wedge of honeydew melon
1 cup skim milk

Dinner
1 broiled loin lamb chop
6 spears steamed asparagus
½ cup broiled mushrooms
★Lotus Blossom Salad
Black coffee or tea with lemon

2

Breakfast
6-ounce glass orange juice
½ cup oatmeal
1 slice raisin toast
1 pat butter or margarine
1 cup skim milk

Lunch
Salad Plate
(★Cucumber-cool Relish-salad
with 6 medium shrimps,
½ cup cooked chilled broccoli,
and lemon wedges)
½ cup Thompson Seedless grapes
1 cup skim milk

Dinner
1 slice baked ham
★Green-bean Mingle
★Creamy Coleslaw
★Jewel Parfait
Black coffee or tea with lemon

3

Breakfast
1 cup fresh strawberries
★Baked Egg Ramekin
1 slice whole-wheat bread
1 pat butter or margarine
1 cup skim milk

Lunch
Open-face Grilled Cheese Sandwich
(1 slice bread, mustard,
1 slice process Cheddar cheese)
¾ cup salad greens with
1 tablespoon bottled low-calorie
blue-cheese dressing
1 cup cubed fresh pineapple
1 cup skim milk

Dinner
★Celery-clam Broth
★Lamb Kebabs
½ cup kale
½ cup stewed celery
★Lemon-lime Royale
Black coffee or tea with lemon

4

Breakfast
6-ounce glass grapefruit juice
½ cup cooked granulated
whole-wheat cereal
1 slice rye toast
1 pat butter or margarine
1 cup skim milk

Lunch
¼ broiled chicken
½ cup steamed spinach
★Skillet Squash
★Tomatoes Vinaigrette
1 cup skim milk

Dinner
★Mushroom Chip Salad Bowl
★Lamb Ragout
½ cup fresh blueberries
Black coffee or tea with lemon

5

Breakfast
1 medium-size orange
1 soft-cooked egg
1 slice whole-wheat toast
1 pat butter or margarine
1 cup skim milk

Lunch
★Poached Shrimps
½ cup steamed summer squash
★Lemon Broccoli
Wedge of honeydew melon
1 cup skim milk

Dinner
1 slice prime-rib roast
½ cup steamed green beans
½ cup steamed cauliflower
⅓ cup diet-pack apricots
Black coffee or tea with lemon

6

Breakfast
1 cup tomato juice
¾ cup dry cereal flakes
with ¼ banana, sliced
1 slice white toast
1 pat butter or margarine
1 cup skim milk

Lunch
Salad Plate
(2½ slices canned corned beef with
★Tomato-bean Cup)
¼ cantaloupe
1 cup skim milk

Dinner
★Veal-vegetable Loaf
6 spears steamed asparagus
½ cup boiled turnip greens
★Choco-chip Pear Velvet
Black coffee or tea with lemon

7

Breakfast
½ grapefruit
1 poached egg on
1 slice whole-wheat toast
1 pat butter or margarine
1 cup skim milk

Lunch
★Tomato Consommé
Fruit Plate
(½ cup uncreamed cottage cheese,
1 slice diet-pack pineapple,
1 tablespoon dairy sour cream,
2 lettuce leaves)
2 slices melba toast
1 cup skim milk

Dinner
★Cucumber Frappé
★Golden Chicken
★Parslied Carrots
★Spring Broccoli
★Iced Fruits
Black coffee or tea with lemon

8

Breakfast
1 medium-size orange, sliced
½ cup uncreamed cottage cheese
½ toasted English muffin
1 cup skim milk

Lunch
★Bouquet Crab Bowl
1 tomato, sliced
1 rye wafer
1 medium-size peach, sliced
1 cup skim milk

Dinner
★Oriental Pork and Vegetables
½ cup sauteed mushrooms
★Strawberry Crown
Black coffee or tea with lemon

9

Breakfast
¼ cantaloupe
1 codfish cake
½ slice white toast
1 pat butter or margarine
1 cup skim milk

Lunch
Deviled-egg Salad
(3 egg halves with 1 tablespoon
low-calorie whipped dressing on
1 cup chopped greens with
1 tablespoon bottled low-calorie
French dressing)
★Raspberry Sparkle
1 cup skim milk

Dinner
★Bouillon Imperial
★Liver and Onion Saute
½ cup green beans
★Baked Tomato Moon
★Angel Lime Pie
Black coffee or tea with lemon

Starred (★) recipes start on page 110

1,100-calorie-a-day meal plans

The first menu gives the basic diet pattern, using foods described in the food lists on pages 94-95. Others show how to combine these same foods into interesting and varied meals, including some of the recipes on pages 110-157. All calorie counts are approximate, since a few calories more or less make no difference.

BREAKFAST
1 serving high vitamin-C fruit
1 serving from bread-cereal group plus 1 egg,
or 2 servings from bread-cereal group
(use part of skim milk with cereal)
1 pat butter or margarine
1 cup skim milk

LUNCH
2-unit serving from meat group
1 serving from bread-cereal group
1 pat butter or margarine
1 serving dark green or yellow vegetable
1 serving other 15-calorie vegetable
1 serving any 40-calorie fruit
1 cup skim milk

DINNER
3-unit serving from meat group
½ serving from bread-cereal group
1 serving dark green or yellow vegetable
1 serving other 15-calorie vegetable
1 serving any 40-calorie fruit
Black coffee or tea with lemon

1

Breakfast
½ grapefruit
⅔ cup cooked farina
1 slice raisin toast
1 pat butter or margarine
1 cup skim milk

Lunch
Salad Plate
(1 hard-cooked egg, quartered;
1 tomato, sliced; ¼ cup uncreamed
cottage cheese; dill pickle, sliced;
on 1 cup salad greens with 1 tablespoon
bottled low-calorie Italian dressing)
5 square saltines
¼ cantaloupe
1 cup skim milk

Dinner
★Lamb Kebabs
½ cup steamed kale with
1 tablespoon vinegar
½ cup stewed celery
2 rye wafers
★Orange-pear Rosette
Black coffee or tea with lemon

2

Breakfast
1 cup fresh strawberries
1 poached egg on
1 slice whole-wheat toast
1 pat butter or margarine
1 cup skim milk

Lunch
1 piece poached cod with lemon wedges
½ cup steamed okra
½ slice whole-wheat bread
1 pat butter or margarine
1 tomato, sliced, on 2 lettuce leaves
with 1 tablespoon low-calorie
Italian dressing
⅓ cup diet-pack apricots
1 cup skim milk

Dinner
1 slice roast beef
½ baked potato
½ cup steamed broccoli
½ cup broiled mushrooms
★Cardamom Cup Souffle
Black coffee or tea with lemon

3

Breakfast
6-ounce glass orange juice
¾ cup dry cereal flakes
1 slice white toast
¼ cup uncreamed cottage cheese
1 cup skim milk

Lunch
Salad Plate
(2½ slices corned beef with
★Oriental Cabbage Toss
on bed of lettuce leaves)
1 slice pumpernickel
1 pat butter or margarine
1 cup skim milk

Dinner
1 broiled pork chop
★Green-bean Mingle
½ cup steamed cauliflower
★Coconut Cup Custard
Black coffee or tea with lemon

4

Breakfast
1 tangerine
1 soft-cooked egg
5 square saltines
1 pat butter or margarine
1 cup skim milk

Lunch
1 piece broiled liver
1 baked potato
½ cup steamed green beans
½ cup broiled mushrooms
1 pat butter or margarine
1 peach, sliced
1 cup skim milk

Dinner
1 slice roast veal
6 spears steamed asparagus
Braised Endive
¼ cup canned whole-kernel corn
★Lemon-lime Royale
Black coffee or tea with lemon

5

Breakfast
¼ cantaloupe
¾ cup dry cereal puffs
1 slice raisin toast
1 pat butter or margarine
1 cup skim milk

Lunch
★Strawberry Omelet
½ cup steamed broccoli
½ cup steamed summer squash
½ slice white bread
1 pat butter or margarine
½ grapefruit
1 cup skim milk

Dinner
★Cucumber Frappé
1 piece fresh baked salmon
½ cup steamed spinach with
1 tablespoon vinegar
½ cup steamed cauliflower
★Butterfly Eclairs
Black coffee or tea with lemon

6

Breakfast
6-ounce glass grapefruit juice
★Baked Egg Ramekin
1 slice gluten-bread toast
1 pat butter or margarine
1 cup skim milk

Lunch
3 slices boiled tongue
1 baked potato
1 pat butter or margarine
½ cup steamed kale
★Green Salad Piquant
1 cup skim milk

Dinner
3 slices roast chicken
½ cup steamed broccoli
½ cup baked acorn squash
★Ruffled Tomato Cup
½ cup cubed fresh pineapple
Black coffee or tea with lemon

7

Breakfast
1 medium-size orange, sliced
¾ cup bran flakes
1 slice raisin toast
1 pat butter or margarine
1 cup skim milk

Lunch
★Bouquet Crab Bowl
1 slice white bread
1 pat butter or margarine
★Minted Fruit Cup
1 cup skim milk

Dinner
★Relish Ruffle
1 slice broiled sirloin steak
½ cup broiled mushrooms
½ cup steamed Brussels sprouts
★Tomatoes Vinaigrette
½ cup fresh blueberries
Black coffee or tea with lemon

8

Breakfast
¼ cantaloupe
2 scrambled eggs
1 rye wafer
1 pat butter or margarine
1 cup skim milk

Lunch
3 broiled chicken livers
½ baked potato
1 pat butter or margarine
★Salad-vegetable Saute
★Apricot-raspberry Snow
1 cup skim milk

Dinner
★Bouillon Imperial
1 broiled veal chop
½ cup stewed tomatoes
½ cup steamed cabbage
★Apricot Sponge Torte
Black coffee or tea with lemon

9

Breakfast
1 cup grapefruit sections
1 poached egg
½ cup cooked hominy grits
1 pat butter or margarine
1 cup skim milk

Lunch
★Poached Shrimps
⅓ cup cooked rice
★Double Green Salad
⅓ cup diet-pack pineapple tidbits
1 cup skim milk

Dinner
★Weight-watcher's Lasagna
½ cup steamed kale
½ cup braised endive
★Mushroom Aspic Mold
★Iced Fruits
Black coffee or tea with lemon

Starred (★) recipes start on page 110

Here's a popular twosome—*chicken livers with bacon*—but look how it's gone fancy as *Chicken-liver Kebabs* (recipe on page 124) *atop Saucepan Risotto* (recipe on page 133). *Each diet plate also includes Spinach Mimosa* (recipe on page 137) *and an Orange-pear Rosette* (recipe on page 141) *with double fruits and a creamy dressing*

Total calories per serving: 499

102

Take heart, meat-and-potato fans! Here you may have both and stay with your diet, too. Fruit-crowned Ham Steak (recipe on page 122) *with a Snowcap Carrot Nest* (recipe on page 134) *stretches a long way in eating satisfaction. Zucchini Sticks* (recipe on page 132) *and Garden Relish Plate* (recipe on page 140) *finish the meal*

Total calories per serving: 394

1,200-calorie-a-day meal plans

The first menu gives the basic diet pattern, using foods described in the food lists on pages 94-95. Others show how to combine these same foods into interesting and varied meals, including some of the recipes on pages 110-157. All calorie counts are approximate, since a few calories more or less make no difference.

BASIC DIET PATTERN

BREAKFAST
1 serving high vitamin-C fruit
1 serving from bread-cereal group plus 1 egg,
or 2 servings from bread-cereal group
(use part of skim milk with cereal)
1 pat butter or margarine
1 cup skim milk

LUNCH
2-unit serving from meat group
1 serving from bread-cereal group
1 pat butter or margarine
1 serving dark green or yellow vegetable
1 serving other 15-calorie vegetable
1 serving any 40-calorie fruit
1 cup skim milk

DINNER
3-unit serving from meat group
1 serving from bread-cereal group
1 pat butter or margarine
1 serving dark green or yellow vegetable
1 serving other 15-calorie vegetable
1 serving any 40-calorie fruit
Black coffee or tea with lemon

1

Breakfast
1 cup papaya cubes
★Baked Egg Ramekin
1 slice white toast
1 pat butter or margarine
1 cup skim milk

Lunch
Salad Plate
(½ cup drained tuna and 1 tomato,
cut into wedges, on 1 cup salad greens
with 1 tablespoon bottled low-calorie
Italian dressing)
1 rye wafer
★Raspberry Sparkle
1 cup skim milk

Dinner
★Beef Sukiyaki Tray
★Orange Cartwheel Salad
★Coconut Cup Custard
Black coffee or tea with lemon

2

Breakfast
6-ounce glass orange juice
½ cup oatmeal
1 slice raisin toast
1 pat butter or margarine
1 cup skim milk

Lunch
★Tomato-cheese Puff
6 spears steamed asparagus
★Double Green Salad
3 square saltines
½ cup cubed fresh pineapple
1 cup skim milk

Dinner
★Shrimp Spaghetti
★Bouquet Salad
★Baked Apricot Souffle
Black coffee or tea with lemon

3

Breakfast
1 cup grapefruit sections
1 poached egg on
1 slice whole-wheat toast
1 pat butter or margarine
1 cup skim milk

Lunch
1 piece broiled liver
1 baked potato
1 pat butter or margarine
½ cup steamed broccoli
½ cup broiled mushrooms
1 small pear
1 cup skim milk

Dinner
1 broiled veal chop
½ cup mashed white potato
½ cup steamed kale
★Ruffled Tomato Cup
★Fruits Scandia
Black coffee or tea with lemon

4

Breakfast
1 medium-size orange, sliced
½ cup cooked hominy grits
2 slices crisp bacon
1 cup skim milk

Lunch
Salad Plate
(2 California-type sardines, 2 slices
Bermuda onion, ¼ cup uncreamed
cottage cheese, 1 sliced tomato, and
2 lettuce leaves with
1 tablespoon bottled low-calorie
French dressing)
1 rye wafer
¼ cantaloupe
1 cup skim milk

Dinner
★Gourmet Lamb Chop
★Potato-spinach Nest
½ cup stewed onions
★Strawberry Wonder Torte
Black coffee or tea with lemon

5

Breakfast
1 cup tomato juice
★Bacon-and-egg Bun
1 cup skim milk

Lunch
★Veal-vegetable Loaf
½ cup steamed green beans
½ cup steamed summer squash
½ slice whole-wheat bread
½ pat butter or margarine
½ grapefruit
1 cup skim milk

Dinner
1 piece broiled haddock
with lemon wedges
1 baked potato
1 pat butter or margarine
★Tomato-bean Cup
★Double Green Salad
★Lemon Cheesecake Tower
Black coffee or tea with lemon

6

Breakfast
1 cup fresh strawberries
¾ cup dry cereal flakes
1 slice raisin toast
1 pat butter or margarine
1 cup skim milk

Lunch
2½ slices canned corned beef
★Creamed New Potatoes and Peas
⅓ cup diet-pack apricots
1 cup skim milk

Dinner
★Chicken-liver Kebabs
Golden Rice
½ cup steamed collards
½ cup broiled mushrooms
★Carioca Fluff
Black coffee or tea with lemon

7

Breakfast
6-ounce glass grapefruit juice
⅔ cup cooked farina
1 slice white toast
1 pat butter or margarine
1 teaspoon low-sugar jam
1 cup skim milk

Lunch
★Bouquet Crab Bowl
★Tomatoes Vinaigrette
3 square saltines
2 fresh figs
1 cup skim milk

Dinner
★Egg-drop Soup
★Fruit-crowned Ham Steak
½ baked sweet potato
½ cup steamed spinach
½ cup boiled cabbage
★Strawberry Crown
Black coffee or tea with lemon

8

Breakfast
½ cantaloupe
2 soft-cooked eggs
½ slice white toast
½ pat butter or margarine
1 cup skim milk

Lunch
1 piece poached cod with lemon wedges
★Sesame Asparagus
★Skillet Squash
½ slice whole-wheat bread
½ pat butter or margarine
½ cup diet-pack mandarin oranges
1 cup skim milk

Dinner
1 fried chicken breast
½ cup mashed white potato
½ cup steamed broccoli
½ cup stewed celery
★Blossom Salad
★Cardamom Cup Souffle
Black coffee or tea with lemon

9

Breakfast
½ grapefruit
1 codfish cake
½ slice whole-wheat toast
½ pat butter or margarine
1 cup skim milk

Lunch
Open-face Grilled Cheese Sandwich
(1 slice bread, mustard,
1 slice process Cheddar cheese)
★Lettuce Wedge with Danish Dressing
★Cinnamon Pears
1 cup skim milk

Dinner
1 slice prime-rib roast
1 baked potato
1 pat butter or margarine
6 spears steamed asparagus
½ cup steamed turnips
★Chocolate-orange Torte
Black coffee or tea with lemon

Starred (★) recipes start on page 110

1,500-calorie-a-day meal plans

The first menu gives the basic diet pattern, using foods described in the food lists on pages 94-95. Others show how to combine these same foods into interesting and varied meals, including some of the recipes on pages 110-157. All calorie counts are approximate, since a few calories more or less make no difference.

BASIC DIET PATTERN

BREAKFAST
1 serving high vitamin-C fruit
1 serving from bread-cereal group plus 1 egg,
or 2-unit serving from meat group
(use part of skim milk with cereal)
1 serving from bread-cereal group
1 pat butter or margarine
1 cup skim milk

LUNCH
3-unit serving from meat group
1 serving from bread-cereal group
1 pat butter or margarine
1 serving dark green or yellow vegetable
1 serving other 15-calorie vegetable
1 serving other 50-calorie vegetable
1 serving any 40-calorie fruit
1 cup skim milk

DINNER
3-unit serving from meat group
2 servings from bread-cereal group
1 pat butter or margarine
1 serving dark green or yellow vegetable
1 serving other 15-calorie vegetable
1 serving other 50-calorie vegetable
1 serving any 40-calorie fruit
Black coffee or tea with lemon

1

Breakfast
½ cantaloupe
1 poached egg
½ cup hominy grits
1 slice white toast
1 pat butter or margarine
1 cup skim milk

Lunch
★Chicken-liver Kebabs
1 baked potato
1 pat butter or margarine
½ cup steamed broccoli
½ cup broiled mushrooms
★Salad-vegetable Saute
½ cup diet-pack applesauce
1 cup skim milk

Dinner
★Boiled-beef Dinner
★Lettuce Wedge with Danish Dressing
★Iced Fruits
Black coffee or tea with lemon

2

Breakfast
6-ounce glass grapefruit juice
¾ cup dry cereal puffs
Open-face Toasted Cheese Sandwich
(1-ounce slice process Cheddar on
1 slice buttered white bread)
1 cup skim milk

Lunch
★Golden Clam Puff
6 spears steamed asparagus
★Blossom Salad
1 slice white bread
1 pat butter or margarine
1 small pear
1 cup skim milk

Dinner
★Cucumber Frappé
★Oriental Pork and Vegetables
★Orange-pear Rosette
★Daffodil Ring
Black coffee or tea with lemon

3

Breakfast
1 cup orange and grapefruit sections
2-egg omelet
2 slices crisp bacon
1 slice whole-wheat toast
1 pat butter or margarine
1 teaspoon low-sugar preserves

Lunch
1 broiled ground-round beef patty
1 hamburger bun
1 tomato, sliced, on ½ cup broken
lettuce with 1 tablespoon bottled
low-calorie chef's dressing
Wedge of honeydew melon
1 cup skim milk

Dinner
★Chicken Hawaiian
1 baked potato
1 pat butter or margarine
½ cup steamed kale
½ cup stewed celery
★Baked Apricot Souffle
Black coffee or tea with lemon

4

Breakfast
1 cup fresh strawberries
¾ cup dry cereal flakes
2 slices raisin toast
2 pats butter or margarine
1 cup skim milk

Lunch
★Bouillabaisse Salad
1 slice white bread
1 pat butter or margarine
2 fresh apricots
1 cup skim milk

Dinner
★Gourmet Steak
1 baked potato
1 pat butter or margarine
½ cup steamed spinach
★Double Green Salad
★Lemon-lime Royale
Black coffee or tea with lemon

5

Breakfast
1 cup tomato juice
3 broiled chicken livers
★Baked Egg Ramekin
1 slice white toast
1 pat butter or margarine
1 cup skim milk

Lunch
¾ cup cream of tomato soup
5 square saltines
Fruit Plate
(½ cup cream-style cottage cheese,
1 slice diet-pack pineapple,
sections from ½ orange,
2 tablespoons dairy sour cream)
1 cup skim milk

Dinner
★Bouillon Imperial
★Fillet of Sole Roulade with Vegetables
½ cup steamed green beans
★Orange Cartwheel Salad
★Diet-light Spongecake
Black coffee or tea with lemon

6

Breakfast
6-ounce glass orange juice
½ cup oatmeal
★Bacon-and-egg Bun
1 cup skim milk

Lunch
Club Sandwich
(2 slices chicken, 2 slices crisp
bacon, 3 slices tomato, 2 slices
white toast, lettuce leaf, 1 teaspoon
mayonnaise or salad dressing)
★Spring Fruit Coupe
1 cup skim milk

Dinner
★Water-cress Soup
★Veal Ragout
★Vitamin Relish
★Cardamom Cup Souffle
Black coffee or tea with lemon

7

Breakfast
½ grapefruit
2-egg omelet
2 slices crisp bacon
1 slice rye toast
1 pat butter or margarine
1 cup skim milk

Lunch
1 slice broiled liver
1 slice crisp bacon
½ cup steamed Brussels sprouts
★Relish Tomatoes
1 slice white bread
1 pat butter or margarine
¼ cantaloupe
1 cup skim milk

Dinner
1 slice roast lamb
★Potato-spinach Nest
½ cup steamed cauliflower
½ cup steamed carrots
★Cheery Cherry Roll
Black coffee or tea with lemon

8

Breakfast
1 medium-size orange, sliced
¾ cup dry cereal puffs
1 slice French toast
1 tablespoon maple syrup
1 cup skim milk

Lunch
★Summer Chicken Salad Plate
3 rye wafers
1 cup skim milk

Dinner
6 cherrystone clams with
lemon wedges or cocktail sauce
1 broiled ground-round beef patty
1 baked potato
1 pat butter or margarine
6 steamed asparagus spears
½ cup steamed onions
★Double Green Salad
★Lemon Tapioca
Black coffee or tea with lemon

9

Breakfast
1 peach, sliced
2 soft-cooked eggs
2 slices raisin toast
1 pat butter or margarine
1 cup skim milk

Lunch
★Double-boiler Cheese Souffle with
★Green-pea Sauce
½ cup steamed broccoli
½ slice white bread
1 pat butter or margarine
½ cup diet-pack mandarin oranges
1 cup skim milk

Dinner
★Garden Relish Plate
★Veal Chop and Parisian Noodles
½ cup steamed green beans
½ cup stewed celery
★Iced Fruits
Black coffee or tea with lemon

Starred (★) recipes start on page 110

Bavarian Steak Platter (described on opposite page) *with its hidden cabbage surprise is truly a gold-star way to pamper a dieter*

Total calories per serving: 346

108

CALORIE-COUNTER'S RECIPES

WOULD you believe it? This Bavarian Steak Platter (*recipe on page 116*) with its perky Top-hat Tomato Cups (*recipe on page 133*) adds up to only 346 calories for a diet serving—and it's just a teaser to all the other tempting main dishes, appetizers, salads, vegetables—even desserts—that follow. To make calorie-counting easy, each recipe tells what and how much a dieter may have (only nondieters rate seconds), and includes another bonus as well: Each dish is nutritiously good and one the whole family should eat, so there's no double cooking.

If some of these choices surprise you as diet foods, remember it's the cooking that counts, and there are so many ways to snip off calories with no one but the cook the wiser. Here are a few general tips to help you keep flavor high and calories low, and make mealtime more enjoyable for everyone:

▶ Be a creative cook. Fix old favorites new ways, using little or no fat, nonfat dry milk or skim milk, no-calorie sweeteners. To add interest and variety, take advantage of the wide array of special low-calorie foods your supermarket offers (see pages 92-93.)

▶ Broil or roast meats instead of pan-frying or cooking them in rich sauces.

▶ Cook fresh or frozen vegetables in bouillon-seasoned water and heat canned ones in their own liquids. And do savor the goodness of plain vegetables such as a mealy boiled or baked potato.

▶ Experiment with seasonings, depending on those that perk up flavor and play down calories. A few ideas: Mint on carrots, basil on tomatoes, parsley or chives on boiled potatoes, Italian seasoning on green beans. And juicy lemon wedges, herb vinegar, pickle relish, soy and Worcestershire sauces, and seasoned salt all add zip while adding few, if any, calories.

▶ Skip the rich gravy with stews, pot roasts, or chicken, serving the broth unthickened as a substitute. It tastes so good spooned over mashed potatoes or vegetables— and there won't be any muttering about the gravy that's missing.

▶ Go all out on perky garnishes, for they brighten any plate, taste good, and cost little in calories.

▶ Turn about and serve your salad first. It's amazingly satisfying.

▶ Double up and serve a combination salad and dessert or dessert and beverage. For example: If fruit is your dessert choice, make the portion invitingly big and let it count as the salad too. Skim milk twirled in a blender with ice milk and flavoring tastes rich, and seems like a milk-shake splurge to anyone on a diet.

▶ Avoid mealtime monotony. Plan menus for a week at a time to ensure variety.

▶ Take time — above all — to set a pretty table with flowers, candles, a company cloth, and your fanciest china, for doesn't the plainest food taste even better in a colorful setting?

Appetizers and soups

CURRY-CELERY SOUP

Makes 4 servings, 90 calories each

½ cup finely diced celery
2 tablespoons butter or margarine
2 tablespoons flour
1 teaspoon curry powder
1 teaspoon salt
¼ teaspoon pepper
1 cup skim milk
3 cups water

1. Saute celery lightly in butter or margarine in a medium-size saucepan; remove from heat. Blend in flour, curry powder, salt, and pepper; slowly stir in milk and water.
2. Cook, stirring constantly, until mixture thickens slightly and starts to boil; cover. Simmer 10 minutes to blend flavors.
3. Ladle into heated soup bowls or cups.

Calorie-counter's serving: 1 cup.

WATER-CRESS SOUP

Makes 6 servings, 50 calories each

1 bunch water cress
1 tablespoon flour
3 cups skim milk
1 teaspoon instant minced onion
1 teaspoon salt

1. Wash water cress and dry; set aside 6 sprigs for garnish, then chop remaining stems and leaves. (There should be about 1¾ cups.)
2. Smooth flour and 1 to 2 tablespoons of the skim milk to a paste in a medium-size saucepan; stir in remaining milk, onion, and salt. Cook, stirring constantly, until mixture thickens and boils 1 minute; remove from heat. Stir in water cress.
3. Ladle into heated soup bowls or cups; garnish with saved water cress. (If mixture must stand before serving, keep hot over very low heat, but *do not let it boil*.)

Calorie-counter's serving: ½ cup.

ANTIPASTO PLATES

Makes 6 servings, 72 calories each

1 package (10 ounces) frozen asparagus spears
1 tablespoon cider vinegar
1 tablespoon capers and liquid
1 teaspoon olive oil
Lettuce
1 can (7 ounces) pimientos, drained
1 can (4 ounces) mushroom caps, drained
6 small slices bologna, cut in thin strips (from a 6- or 8-ounce package)
6 green onions, trimmed
6 radishes, trimmed
3 stalks celery, cut in 4-inch lengths

1. Cook asparagus in boiling salted water, following label directions; drain; place in a pie plate. Sprinkle with vinegar, capers and liquid, and olive oil; cover; chill.
2. Just before serving, line 6 salad plates with lettuce; arrange asparagus, pimientos, mushrooms, and bologna, dividing evenly, in separate piles on each plate. Garnish each with a green onion, radish, and celery stalk.
3. Serve with wine vinegar to drizzle over, if you wish.

Calorie-counter's serving: 1 plateful.

APPETIZER VEGETABLES

Makes 4 servings, 43 calories each

4 ten-inch-long stalks of celery
4 large cauliflowerets
1 stalk Belgian endive
Cottage-cheese Dip (recipe follows)

1. Split celery stalks into ½-inch-wide sticks; cut each into 2-inch lengths. Slice cauliflowerets thin; quarter endive.
2. Arrange vegetables in separate mounds on a serving plate; set bowl of COTTAGE-CHEESE DIP in center.
COTTAGE-CHEESE DIP—Press ½ cup cream-style cottage cheese through a sieve into a small bowl; stir in 2 teaspoons finely cut chives, 2 tablespoons chopped parsley, ½ teaspoon Worcestershire sauce, ¼ teaspoon salt, and a few drops red-pepper seasoning. Makes about ½ cup.
Calorie-counter's serving: 10 pieces of celery, 4 slices of cauliflower, ¼ of endive, and 2 tablespoons dip.

CRANBERRY FIZZ

Makes 6 servings, 47 calories each

1 bottle (16 ounces) cranberry-juice cocktail
1 bottle (7 ounces) carbonated water

Mix cranberry-juice cocktail and carbonated water in a pitcher or 4-cup measure. Pour over ice in small glasses.
Calorie-counter's serving: ½ cup.

CUCUMBER FRAPPE

Makes 6 servings, 33 calories each

2 cups cubed pared cucumber
2 tablespoons chopped parsley
1 green onion, trimmed and sliced
½ cup instant nonfat dry milk
1 cup cold water
1 teaspoon lemon juice
1 teaspoon salt
⅛ teaspoon bottled red-pepper seasoning

1. Combine all ingredients in an electric-blender container; cover. Beat until foamy and creamy-smooth.
2. Pour into small juice glasses; garnish with a sprig of parsley, if you wish.
Calorie-counter's serving: ¾ cup.

MINTED FRUIT CUP

Makes 6 servings, 53 calories each

1 can (1 pound) diet-pack pear halves
1 medium-size orange
Fresh mint

1. Drain syrup from pear halves into a medium-size bowl; dice pears and return to syrup.
2. Pare orange and section; cut into bite-size pieces; add to pears. Crush several mint leaves and stir into fruit; chill to blend flavors.
3. Spoon into serving dishes. Garnish with a sprig of mint, if you wish.
Calorie-counter's serving: ½ cup.

BOUILLON IMPERIAL

Makes 6 servings, 26 calories each

2 cans condensed beef broth
1 cup water
½ cup thinly sliced pared carrot
½ cup thinly sliced celery

1. Combine all ingredients in a medium-size saucepan; heat to boiling; cover. Simmer 10 minutes, or just until vegetables are crisply tender.
2. Ladle into soup bowls or cups.
Calorie-counter's serving: ⅔ cup.

CELERY—CLAM BROTH

Makes 4 servings, 20 calories each

2 bottles (8 ounces each) clam juice
1 cup water
½ cup finely cut celery
2 teaspoons finely cut chives
Few drops red-pepper seasoning

1. Combine clam juice, water, celery, 1 teaspoon of the chives, and red-pepper seasoning in a small sauce-pan; heat to boiling; cover. Simmer 15 minutes, or until celery is tender.
2. Ladle into heated soup bowls or cups; sprinkle with remaining 1 teaspoon chives.
Calorie-counter's serving: ¾ cup.

JELLIED APPETIZER CUBES

Makes 6 servings, 33 calories each

2 envelopes unflavored gelatin
1 cup water
1 can (about 13 ounces) consommé madrilene
2 teaspoons lime juice
1 can condensed chicken broth
⅛ teaspoon salt
⅛ teaspoon curry powder

1. Soften gelatin in water in a small saucepan; heat, stirring constantly, over low heat just until gelatin dissolves; remove from heat. Pour half into each of two pans, 9x9x2.
2. Stir madrilene and lime juice into one pan and the chicken broth, salt, and curry powder into the other. Chill both mixtures several hours, or until firm.
3. When ready to serve, cut gelatin in each pan into about-½-inch cubes with a sharp knife. Spoon madrilene cubes into 6 small bowls: top each with the chicken broth cubes. Garnish with lime slices, if you wish.
Calorie-counter's serving: ⅓ cup each jellied madrilene and chicken cubes.

EGG-DROP SOUP

Makes 6 servings, 39 calories each

2 cans (14 ounces each) chicken broth
1 egg, slightly beaten
2 tablespoons chopped parsley

1. Heat chicken broth just to boiling in a medium-size saucepan. Pour in beaten egg very slowly, stirring constantly, just until egg cooks and separates into shreds.
2. Ladle into heated cups; sprinkle with parsley.
Calorie-counter's serving: ⅔ cup.

TOMATO CONSOMME

Makes 8 servings, 25 calories each

2 cups water
4 envelopes instant beef broth
   OR: 4 beef-flavor bouillon cubes
   Handful of celery leaves
1 medium-size onion, peeled and sliced
¼ cup chopped parsley
1 teaspoon salt
½ teaspoon basil
2 bay leaves
1 can (46 ounces) tomato juice

1. Combine water, instant beef broth or bouillon cubes, celery leaves, onion, parsley, salt, basil, and bay leaves in a large saucepan; heat to boiling, then simmer 15 minutes.
2. Stir in tomato juice; heat 5 minutes longer, or until bubbly hot. Strain into heated soup bowls or cups.
Calorie-counter's serving: ¾ cup.

TOMATO SPARKLE

Makes 4 servings, 105 calories each

1 package (3 ounces) lemon-flavor gelatin
1¼ cups hot water
1½ cups tomato juice
2 tablespoons lemon juice
¼ cup thinly sliced celery
2 teaspoons dairy sour cream

1. Dissolve gelatin in hot water in a medium-size bowl; stir in tomato and lemon juices and celery. Chill several hours, or until softly set.
2. Spoon into 4 cups or small bowls; top each with ½ teaspoon sour cream and a sprig of water cress, if you wish.
Calorie-counter's serving: ¾ cup.

APPETEASER SALADS

Makes 4 servings, 51 calories each

2 heads Bibb lettuce, washed and dried
½ small cantaloupe, pared and seeded
4 slices prosciutto ham
1 lemon, cut in 4 wedges

1. Separate lettuce leaves; divide among 4 salad plates.
2. Slice cantaloupe; divide and pile on top of lettuce. Roll ham slices; place one each at edge of plates. Garnish with a lemon wedge.
Calorie-counter's serving: 1 salad.

Main dishes

Beef

BOILED-BEEF DINNER

Makes 6 servings, 385 calories each

3 to 4 pounds lean boneless beef chuck roast
1 tablespoon salt
2 peppercorns
1 bay leaf
6 cups water
6 small potatoes, scrubbed
6 small onions, peeled
6 medium-size carrots, pared and quartered
1 medium-size cabbage (about 2 pounds)

1. Place meat in a kettle or Dutch oven; add salt, peppercorns, bay leaf, and water; cover. Heat to boiling; simmer 1½ hours.
2. Remove meat; let any fat rise to top of broth, then skim off; return meat to kettle.
3. Cut off a band of skin around middle of each potato; place potatoes, onions, and carrots around meat in kettle. Simmer 1 hour longer, or until meat is tender.
4. Cut cabbage into 6 wedges; arrange on top of meat and vegetables; cover. Cook 15 minutes, or until cabbage is tender.
5. Remove cabbage with a slotted spoon and place at one side of a heated large serving platter; place meat in center and carrots at other side. Spoon onions and potatoes into a serving bowl.
6. Skim any last traces of fat from broth; remove bay leaf; spoon broth over vegetables. Carve meat into ¼-inch-thick slices.
Calorie-counter's serving: 1 potato, 1 carrot, 1 onion, 1 wedge of cabbage, 2 slices of meat, and ¼ cup broth.

111

LIVER AND ONION SAUTE

Makes 6 servings, 183 calories each

3 large onions, peeled, sliced, and
　　separated in rings
2 cups water (for onions)
1½ pounds beef or lamb liver
1 teaspoon butter or margarine
2 tablespoons bottled low-calorie
　　French dressing
6 tablespoons water (for sauce)
½ teaspoon salt
¼ teaspoon pepper

1. Cook onions in the 2 cups water in a large frying pan 10 minutes, or just until liquid evaporates. Lower heat and continue cooking, stirring constantly, 3 to 5 minutes, or until onions brown lightly. Remove from pan.
2. While onions cook, snip out veiny parts and skin from liver. (Scissors do a quick job.) Cut meat into 12 even slices. Brown in butter or margarine 1 minute on each side in same frying pan.
3. Return onions to pan. Mix French dressing with the 6 tablespoons water, salt, and pepper in a cup; pour into frying pan; cover.
4. Heat to boiling, then simmer 3 minutes, or just until liver loses its pink color. (Overcooking toughens this delicate meat, so watch it carefully.)

Calorie-counter's serving: 2 slices liver, ⅓ cup onions, and 2 tablespoons sauce.

BEEF-VEGETABLE RAGOUT

Makes 6 servings, 334 calories each

1 small onion, chopped (¼ cup)
1½ cups water
1½ pounds lean beef round or chuck,
　　cut into 1-inch cubes
1 bay leaf
½ teaspoon seasoned salt
¼ teaspoon seasoned pepper
1 can condensed beef bouillon
6 small potatoes, pared
3 cups sliced celery
1 small eggplant, diced (3 cups)
　　Granulated, liquid, or tablet
　　no-calorie sweetener
½ small head escarole, chopped
　　(3 cups)
3 medium-size tomatoes, cut in wedges
3 small dill pickles, cut in thin
　　strips

1. Cook onion in ½ cup of the water in a kettle or Dutch oven 10 minutes, or just until liquid evaporates.

Lower heat and continue cooking, stirring constantly, 3 to 5 minutes, or until onion browns lightly; remove and set aside.
2. Brown beef cubes, a few at a time, in same kettle. (No need to add fat.) Return all beef and onion to kettle; stir in bay leaf, seasoned salt and pepper, beef bouillon, and the remaining 1 cup water; cover. Heat to boiling; simmer 1½ to 2 hours, or until beef is tender.
3. Arrange potatoes on top; cover. Simmer 30 minutes. Add celery and eggplant; simmer 10 minutes longer, or until potatoes are tender.
4. Stir in your favorite no-calorie sweetener, using the equivalent of 1 teaspoon sugar. Lay escarole and tomatoes on top; cover again; simmer 5 minutes, or just until greens wilt. Remove bay leaf.
5. Spoon a potato into each of 6 heated serving dishes; surround with ragout. Garnish with dill-pickle strips.

Calorie-counter's serving: 1⅔ cups ragout, 1 potato, and ½ dill pickle.

PEPPER BEEF LOAFETTES

Bake at 350° for 30 minutes.
Makes 6 servings, 280 calories each

1½ pounds lean ground beef
½ cup fine dry bread crumbs
6 tablespoons instant nonfat dry milk
1 tablespoon chopped onion
1 egg, slightly beaten
¼ cup water
1½ teaspoons salt
⅛ teaspoon pepper
1 small green pepper, halved
　　lengthwise and seeded
8 water chestnuts (from a 5-ounce
　　can)

1. Combine ground beef, bread crumbs, nonfat dry milk, onion, egg, water, salt, and pepper in a medium-size bowl.
2. Set half of the green pepper and 3 water chestnuts aside for Step 4; chop remaining and add to meat mixture; mix lightly.
3. Shape into 6 even-size loaves; place in a shallow baking dish.
4. Cut remaining green-pepper half into 24 one-inch-long strips; cut each water chestnut into 4 slices, then halve each slice. Press 4 pepper strips and 4 water-chestnut slices, alternately, into top of each loaf.
5. Bake in moderate oven (350°) 30 minutes, or until loaves are richly browned.

Calorie-counter's serving: 1 loaf.

WEIGHT-WATCHING LASAGNA

Bake at 350° for 30 minutes.
Makes 6 servings, 271 calories each

1 clove garlic, minced
1 medium-size onion, chopped (½ cup)
½ cup diced celery
½ cup water
½ pound ground lean round steak
3 cups Italian tomatoes (from an about-
　　2-pound can)
¼ cup catsup
¼ cup chopped parsley
1 teaspoon salt
½ teaspoon basil
　　Granulated, liquid, or tablet
　　no-calorie sweetener
1½ cups pot cheese or dry cottage cheese
1 egg
6 lasagna noodles (from a 1-pound
　　package)
½ package (8 ounces) mozzarella
　　cheese, cut into 6 slices
1 tablespoon grated Parmesan cheese
　　Paprika

1. Combine garlic, onion, celery, and water in a medium-size frying pan. Cook 10 minutes, or until water evaporates and vegetables are tender; push to one side.
2. Shape ground steak into a thick patty in same pan; brown 5 minutes on each side; break up into chunks. Stir in onion mixture, tomatoes, catsup, parsley, salt, basil, and your favorite no-calorie sweetener, using the equivalent of 1 teaspoon sugar. Simmer, stirring several times, 20 minutes, or until thick.
3. Mix pot cheese or cottage cheese and egg in a small bowl.
4. Cook noodles in boiling salted water, following label directions; drain well.
5. Place 2 noodles in bottom of a very lightly greased shallow baking dish, 10x6x2; spoon one third of the cheese mixture, then one third of the meat sauce on top. Repeat with remaining noodles, cheese and sauce mixtures to make two more layers of each. Place mozzarella cheese slices on top; sprinkle with Parmesan cheese and paprika.
6. Bake in moderate oven (350°) 30 minutes, or until bubbly hot. Let stand about 10 minutes to set, then cut into 6 even-size blocks.

Calorie-counter's serving: 1 block.

SKILLET STEAK RAGOUT

Makes 6 servings, 219 calories each

1 slice lean boneless round beef steak,
    weighing about 1½ pounds
2 teaspoons salt
1 can (1 pound) tomatoes
2 teaspoons Italian seasoning
½ cup water
12 small white onions, peeled
6 large stalks celery, trimmed and
    cut in 1-inch-long pieces
6 small zucchini, trimmed and cut in
    1-inch-long pieces

1. Trim all fat from steak. Sprinkle salt over bottom of a heated large heavy frying pan; brown steak on both sides. (Salt helps to keep meat from sticking.)
2. Stir in tomatoes, Italian seasoning, and water; cover. Simmer 1 hour.
3. Lay onions around meat; cover again; cook 30 minutes. Place celery and zucchini in pan; cook 30 minutes longer, or until meat and all vegetables are tender.
4. Place meat on a heated large serving platter; arrange vegetables around edge. Carve meat into ¼-inch-thick slices; serve sauce separately to spoon over.

Calorie-counter's serving: 2 slices meat, 2 onions, 6 pieces each celery and zucchini, and 2 tablespoons sauce.

STUFFED BEEF BUNDLES

Makes 6 servings, 218 calories each

1 flank steak (about 1½ pounds)
    OR: 1 piece lean boneless round beef
    steak, weighing about 1½ pounds
1 can (3 or 4 ounces) chopped mushrooms
1 medium-size onion, finely chopped
    (½ cup)
2 tablespoons catsup
1 teaspoon salt
2 medium-size carrots, pared and cut
    in 4-inch-long sticks
2 envelopes instant beef broth
    OR: 2 beef-flavor bouillon cubes
1 cup water
Brown Gravy (recipe follows)

1. Pound steak very thin with a mallet or rolling pin; cut into 6 even-size pieces. (If using round steak, trim off all fat first.)
2. Drain mushrooms, saving liquid in a cup for Step 3. Mix mushrooms with onion, catsup, and salt in a small bowl; spread evenly over steak pieces. Place carrot sticks, dividing evenly, crosswise at end of each; roll up, jelly-roll fashion; fasten with one or two wooden picks.
3. Brown rolls in a medium-size frying pan; add mushroom liquid, instant beef broth or bouillon cubes, and water, crushing bouillon cubes, if using, with a spoon; cover. Simmer 1 hour and 15 minutes, or until meat is tender.
4. Remove to a heated serving platter; take out wooden picks; keep rolls hot while making gravy.

BROWN GRAVY—Pour juices from pan into a 1-cup measure; skim off any fat, then measure 1 tablespoonful and return to pan. Add water, if needed, to juices to make 1 cup. Stir 1 tablespoon flour into fat in pan; add meat-juice mixture. Cook, stirring constantly, until gravy thickens and boils 1 minute. Season to taste with salt and pepper.

BEEF SUKIYAKI TRAY

Makes 4 servings, 349 calories each

1 pound round beef steak, cut
    ½ inch thick
¼ cup soy sauce
1 tablespoon peanut oil
    or vegetable oil
½ pound green beans, tipped and cut
    in 1-inch lengths
2 medium-size yellow squashes,
    trimmed and sliced
1 envelope instant chicken broth
    OR: 1 chicken-bouillon cube
¼ cup water
1 package (10 ounces) fresh spinach,
    washed and stemmed
2 cups hot cooked rice

1. Cut steak diagonally into thin strips; place in a pie plate. Pour soy sauce over; let stand 15 minutes.
2. Lift beef strips from marinade and dry on paper toweling; saute quickly in peanut oil or vegetable oil in a large frying pan; remove and keep hot. Save soy sauce.
3. Place green beans and squashes in separate piles in frying pan; saute, stirring gently, 2 to 3 minutes, or just until shiny-moist.
4. Combine chicken broth or bouillon cube, water, and saved soy sauce in a cup, crushing cube, if using, with a spoon. Pour over vegetables; cover; steam 5 minutes.
5. Lay spinach over vegetables; cover again; steam 5 minutes longer, or just until vegetables are crisply tender.
6. Spoon vegetables, rice, and beef strips in rows on a serving platter; serve broth from pan separately.

*Calorie-counter's serving: 1 wedge.
the steak and three vegetables, ½ cup rice, and 2 tablespoons broth.*

IOWA BEEF PLATTER

Makes 6 servings, 320 calories each

1 lean boneless round beef roast,
    weighing about 2 pounds
2 teaspoons salt
1 teaspoon basil
½ teaspoon rosemary
3 cups water
6 small new potatoes, pared
6 small carrots, pared and cut in
    1-inch-long pieces
3 medium-size yellow squashes, trimmed,
    quartered, and cut in 2-inch sticks

1. Trim all fat from roast. Sprinkle salt over bottom of a heated large heavy frying pan; brown roast on all sides. (Salt helps to keep meat from sticking.)
2. Stir in basil, rosemary, and water; cover. Simmer 2 hours.
3. Lay potatoes and carrots around meat; cover again. Cook 30 minutes. Place squashes in pan; cook 25 minutes longer, or until meat and all vegetables are tender.
4. Place meat and vegetables on a heated large serving platter; carve meat into ¼-inch-thick slices. Serve broth separately to spoon over top.

Calorie-counter's serving: ¼ each of meat, 1 potato, 4 pieces each carrots and squash, and ½ cup broth.

PATTY-CAKE MEAT LOAF

Bake at 375° for 35 minutes.
Makes 6 servings, 260 calories each

1½ pounds lean ground beef
1 jar (about 5 ounces) baby-pack
    strained carrots
½ cup tomato juice
¼ cup chopped parsley
1 small onion, chopped (¼ cup)
1½ teaspoons salt
½ teaspoon Italian seasoning

1. Mix all ingredients just until blended in a large bowl. Form into a thick round patty about 8 inches in diameter; place on rack in broiler pan or set on a wire rack in a shallow baking pan.
2. Bake in moderate oven (375°) 35 minutes, or until brown. Slice patty into 6 wedges.

Calorie-counter's serving: 2 slices

Stew seems like a splurge to a dieter and this measured plateful of Beef-vegetable Ragout (recipe on page 112) allows chunks of lean beef, a potato, and four vegetables. To hold the calories down, meat and onions slow-cook in bouillon. For those who still have room, end the meal with midget-size Butterfly Eclairs (recipe on page 154)

Total calories per serving: 462

With a thick broiled Veal Chop and Parisian Noodles (recipe on page 117), *almost any waistline-watcher will take dieting in stride. Other menu go-withs are Piquant Green Beans* (recipe on page 135) *with a special seasoning trick, and Apple-cheese Whirl* (recipe on page 140) *to eat as a salad or appetizer. Or it can even double as the dessert top-off*

Total calories per serving: 484

GOURMET STEAK

Makes 6 servings, 389 calories each

1 small onion, chopped (¼ cup)
1 small clove garlic, minced
½ cup water
2 teaspoons flour
1 can (3 or 4 ounces) sliced mushrooms
1 envelope instant beef broth
  OR: 1 beef-flavor bouillon cube
1 tablespoon chili sauce
  Granulated, liquid, or tablet
  no-calorie sweetener
1 flank steak (about 2 pounds)
  Instant unseasoned meat tenderizer

1. Heat onion, garlic, and water to boiling in a small saucepan; cook 10 minutes, or just until liquid evaporates. Lower heat and continue cooking, stirring constantly, 3 to 5 minutes, or until onion browns lightly.
2. Sprinkle flour over and stir in; remove from heat.
3. Drain liquid from mushrooms into a 1-cup measure; add water to make 1 cup. Stir into onion mixture with beef broth or bouillon cube and chili sauce. Cook, stirring constantly and crushing bouillon cube, if using, with a spoon, until mixture thickens and boils 1 minute.
4. Stir in mushrooms and your favorite no-calorie sweetener, using the equivalent of ½ teaspoon sugar. Simmer 10 to 15 minutes to blend flavors.
5. Moisten steak and sprinkle with the meat tenderizer, following label directions.
6. Broil, following range manufacturer's directions, 3 to 4 minutes on each side for rare or 5 to 6 minutes for medium.
7. Remove steak to a cutting board; carve diagonally into thin slices. Spoon hot sauce over top.

Calorie-counter's serving: 3 slices steak and 3 tablespoons sauce.

BAVARIAN STEAK PLATTER

Makes 6 servings, 235 calories each

½ head of cabbage (about 1½ pounds)
1½ teaspoons salt
¾ teaspoon caraway seeds
1 flank steak (about 2 pounds)
  Instant unseasoned meat tenderizer
4 tablespoons bottled low-calorie
  Italian salad dressing
  Parsley

1. Place cabbage in a medium-size saucepan with salt, caraway seeds, and enough water almost to cover; cover. Cook 15 minutes, or just until tender.
2. Lift out carefully; drain well, then cut out core. Place cabbage, rounded side up, on a heated serving platter; cut into 6 wedges but leave in shape. Keep warm while cooking steak.
3. Moisten steak with water and sprinkle with meat tenderizer, following label directions. Brush one side with 2 tablespoons of the salad dressing.
4. Broil, following range manufacturer's directions, 3 to 4 minutes; turn; brush other side with remaining salad dressing. Broil 3 to 4 minutes longer for rare or 5 to 6 minutes for medium, or until steak is done as you like it.
5. Remove to a cutting board; carve diagonally into thin slices. Place, overlapping, over cabbage to cover completely. Garnish top with 4 more slices rolled up, jelly-roll fashion, and held in place with wooden picks; tuck a sprig of parsley into each roll.

Calorie-counter's serving: 3 slices steak and 1 wedge of cabbage.

Veal

VEAL-VEGETABLE LOAF

Bake at 350° for 50 minutes.
Makes 6 servings, 178 calories each

1 pound ground lean veal
1 cup (8 ounces) cream-style cottage cheese
3 medium-size carrots, pared and shredded (about 1 cup)
1 small onion, chopped (¼ cup)
1 egg
1 teaspoon salt
½ teaspoon basil
¼ teaspoon pepper

1. Mix all ingredients lightly in a large bowl. Shape into a loaf in a shallow baking pan.
2. Bake in moderate oven (350°) 50 minutes, or until firm and lightly browned on top. Cut into 12 slices.

Calorie-counter's serving: 2 slices.

MEAT-BALL SPAGHETTI BOWL

Makes 6 servings, 443 calories each

Meat Balls

1 pound ground lean veal
1 small onion, chopped (¼ cup)
2 tablespoons chopped parsley
1 cup soft whole-wheat bread crumbs (2 slices)
1 teaspoon salt
⅛ teaspoon pepper
1 tablespoon olive oil

Sauce and Spaghetti

1 medium-size onion, chopped (½ cup)
1 small clove garlic, minced
1 can (about 1 pound) stewed tomatoes
1 can (6 ounces) tomato paste
¾ cup water
1 teaspoon oregano
1 teaspoon basil
1½ teaspoons salt
¼ teaspoon pepper
  Granulated, liquid, or tablet
  no-calorie sweetener
1 package (1 pound) spiral or plain spaghetti
  Grated Parmesan cheese

1. Make meat balls: Mix veal, onion, parsley, bread crumbs, salt, and pepper until well-blended in a medium-size bowl. Shape lightly into 6 even-size balls.
2. Brown in olive oil in a large frying pan; remove with a slotted spoon and set aside for Step 4.
3. Make sauce: Sauté onion and garlic until soft in drippings in frying pan. Stir in tomatoes, tomato paste, water, herbs, salt, pepper, and your favorite no-calorie sweetener, using the equivalent of 1½ teaspoons sugar.
4. Place meat balls in sauce; cover; simmer 1 hour.
5. While sauce simmers, cook spaghetti, following label directions; drain.
6. Spoon spaghetti onto heated serving plates; top each with sauce and a meat ball. Garnish with 3 canned mushroom caps and a green-pepper strip threaded on a wooden pick, if you wish. Pass cheese separately to sprinkle over.

Calorie-counter's serving: 1 cup spaghetti, ½ cup sauce, 1 meat ball, 1 mushroom—green-pepper kebab, and 1 tablespoon grated Parmesan cheese.

VEAL CHOPS SUPREME

Makes 4 servings, 347 calories each

1 can (3 or 4 ounces) chopped mushrooms
1 cup chicken broth (from a 14-ounce can)
2 tablespoons instant-type flour
1 teaspoon lemon juice
4 loin or rib veal chops, cut ¾ inch thick
1 small sweet red pepper, seeded and cut into 12 rings
2 tablespoons chopped parsley
2 cups hot cooked rice (½ cup uncooked)

1. Drain liquid from mushrooms into a small saucepan. (Set mushrooms aside for Step 4.) Stir chicken broth and flour into liquid; cook, stirring constantly, until sauce thickens and boils 1 minute. Stir in lemon juice.
2. Trim all fat from chops; place chops on rack in broiler pan. Brush with part of the sauce.
3. Broil, 4 to 6 inches from heat, 8 minutes; turn; brush again with more sauce. Broil 6 minutes; place pepper rings on rack beside meat. Continue broiling 2 minutes, or until meat is tender and pepper rings are heated through.
4. Stir mushrooms and parsley into remaining sauce; heat until bubbly.
5. When ready to serve, place chops and rice, dividing evenly, on heated serving plates; top rice with pepper rings. Serve sauce separately to spoon over meat and rice.

Calorie-counter's serving: 1 chop, ½ cup rice, 3 pepper rings, and 2 tablespoons sauce.

VEAL CHOPS AND PARISIAN NOODLES

Makes 4 servings, 390 calories each

3 cups uncooked regular noodles (about half an 8-ounce package)
1 can (3 or 4 ounces) sliced mushrooms
½ cup skim milk
2 tablespoons flour
2 envelopes instant chicken broth OR: 2 chicken-bouillon cubes
1 teaspoon lemon juice
2 tablespoons chopped parsley
4 loin or rib veal chops, cut ¾ inch thick
Seasoned salt
½ pimiento, cut in thin strips

1. Cook noodles in boiling unsalted water in a kettle, following label directions; drain. Return to kettle.
2. While noodles cook, drain liquid from mushrooms into a 2-cup measure; stir in milk and enough water to make 1¼ cups. (Set mushroom slices aside for kebab garnish for meat.)
3. Stir liquid into flour until smooth

in a small saucepan, then stir in chicken broth or bouillon cubes. Cook, stirring constantly and crushing cubes, if using, with a spoon, until sauce thickens and boils 1 minute; stir in lemon juice.
4. Pour over noodles; sprinkle with parsley; toss to mix well; keep hot.
5. Sprinkle chops lightly with seasoned salt; place on rack in broiler pan.
6. Broil, 4 to 6 inches from heat, 8 minutes on each side, or until meat is tender.
7. While meat cooks, thread 4 mushroom slices and a strip of pimiento onto each of 4 kebab sticks. Place chops and noodles on serving plates; stick kebabs into chops.

Calorie-counter's serving: 1 chop, ½ cup noodles, and 1 mushroom kebab.

VEAL RAGOUT

Makes 4 servings, 387 calories each

1 pound lean veal shoulder
1 large onion, peeled and sliced thin
2 cups shredded lettuce
1 teaspoon salt
Dash of pepper
½ teaspoon rosemary
1 envelope instant chicken broth OR: 1 chicken-bouillon cube
1 cup water (for meat)
8 small new potatoes
2 medium-size yellow squashes
½ pound green beans
2 tablespoons cornstarch
2 tablespoons water (for gravy)

1. Trim all fat from veal, then cut veal into ½-inch cubes.
2. Combine with onion, lettuce, salt, pepper, rosemary, chicken broth or bouillon cube, and the 1 cup water in a kettle or Dutch oven. Heat to boiling, crushing bouillon cube, if using, with a spoon; cover. Simmer 2 hours, or until veal is tender.
3. About 45 minutes before meat is done, scrub potatoes well; cut off a band of skin around middle of each. Trim squashes and slice thin. Tip beans and cut diagonally into ½-inch-long pieces.
4. Place potatoes on top of meat mixture; cook 30 minutes, or until tender. Cook squashes and green beans in slightly salted boiling water in separate medium-size saucepans 15 minutes, or until crisply tender; drain; keep hot.
5. Smooth cornstarch and the 2 tablespoons water to a paste in a cup; stir into hot meat mixture. Cook,

stirring constantly, until broth thickens and boils 3 minutes.
6. Spoon meat mixture, dividing evenly, and potatoes into each of 4 heated serving dishes; spoon squash and green beans in separate piles at edges.

Calorie-counter's serving: ¼ of the meat mixture, 2 potatoes, and ¼ each of the squash and beans.

Lamb

POLYNESIAN LAMB PLATTER

Makes 6 servings, 455 calories each

6 lamb shanks (about 3 pounds)
1 medium-size onion, chopped (½ cup)
¾ cup water
1 teaspoon salt
1 teaspoon ground allspice
½ teaspoon garlic salt
½ teaspoon ground ginger
¼ cup lemon juice
1 tablespoon bottled steak sauce
1 jar (about 8 ounces) junior prunes
1 jar (about 8 ounces) junior applesauce-and-apricots
Steamed Rice (recipe follows)

1. Trim all fat from lamb shanks; brown shanks very slowly in a kettle or Dutch oven; remove and set aside.
2. Stir onion and 1 tablespoon of the water into kettle; cook, stirring constantly, until onion browns; stir in salt, allspice, garlic salt, ginger, remaining water, lemon juice, and steak sauce.
3. Heat to boiling; stir in junior fruits, then return browned meat; cover. Simmer, stirring several times, 2 to 2½ hours, or until meat is tender.
4. Arrange shanks on a heated serving platter; spoon STEAMED RICE around edge. Spoon part of the sauce over meat, then pass remaining in a separate bowl. Garnish platter with lemon slices and parsley, if you wish.

STEAMED RICE — Combine 1¼ cups water, 1 envelope instant vegetable broth or 1 vegetable-bouillon cube, and 1 teaspoon butter or margarine in the top of a double boiler; heat to boiling over direct heat, crushing bouillon cube, if using, with a spoon. Stir in ½ cup uncooked rice; cover. Cook, stirring once, over simmering water, 45 minutes, or until rice is tender and liquid is absorbed. Fluff up with a fork before serving.

Calorie-counter's serving: 1 lamb shank, ⅓ cup rice, and ½ cup sauce.

A thick juicy chop on a dinner plate will spur about any dieter on! And here, a Gourmet Lamb Chop (recipe on page 119) is served with a pickled red pepper, broiled kidney, and jumbo mushroom. Plate mates include a Potato-spinach Nest (recipe on page 134), Skillet Squash (recipe on page 132), and a Ruffled Tomato Cup (recipe on page 141)

Total calories
per serving: 370

BROWN LAMB STEW

Makes 6 servings, 355 calories each

- 1 shank-end leg of lamb, weighing about 3 pounds
- 18 small white onions, peeled
- 1 clove garlic, minced
- 2 teaspoons salt
- 1 bay leaf
- 2 cups water
- 1 cup sliced pared carrots
  Nutmeg Dumplings (recipe follows)
- 1 package (10 ounces) frozen peas
- 4 cups shredded romaine

1. Cut lamb from bone; trim off all fat, then cut meat into 1-inch cubes. Brown, a few cubes at a time, in a kettle or Dutch oven. (No need to add any fat.)
2. Return all meat to kettle. Add onions, garlic, salt, bay leaf, and water; cover; heat to boiling. Simmer 45 minutes; add carrots; simmer 15 minutes longer, or until lamb is tender.
3. While carrots cook, make NUTMEG DUMPLINGS. Add peas to kettle; heat to boiling again. Drop dumpling batter in 6 mounds on top of hot stew; cover tightly. Steam 20 minutes, or until dumplings are puffy-light.
4. Remove dumplings to a heated serving platter; remove bay leaf. Stir romaine into stew to wilt slightly, then spoon into heated serving bowls. Place dumplings on top.

NUTMEG DUMPLINGS—Combine 1 cup sifted regular flour, 1¼ teaspoons baking powder, ½ teaspoon salt, and ½ teaspoon nutmeg in a small bowl. Add ½ cup skim milk all at once; stir just until flour mixture is evenly moist.

Calorie-counter's serving: 1⅓ cups stew and 1 dumpling.

LAMB KEBABS

Makes 4 servings, 220 calories each

1½ pounds lean shoulder or leg of lamb
2 tablespoons bottled low-calorie
     Italian salad dressing
2 tablespoons water
1 medium-size acorn squash
2 medium-size tomatoes

1. Trim all fat from lamb, then cut
   lamb into 1-inch cubes; place in a
   shallow pan. Mix salad dressing and
   water in a cup; pour over lamb.
   Chill, turning meat often, 1 hour.
2. Cook squash whole in boiling water
   to cover in a medium-size saucepan
   15 minutes, or just until tender;
   drain. Halve; remove seeds; quarter
   each half; brush with marinade
   from lamb.
3. Thread 4 pieces of lamb, alternately,
   with 2 pieces of squash onto each of
   four skewers; lay skewers, not
   touching, on rack in broiler pan.
4. Broil, 4 to 6 inches from heat, turning often and brushing with marinade, 12 to 15 minutes, or until lamb
   is done as you like it.
5. While kebabs cook, cut each tomato
   into 8 wedges; brush with marinade.
   Place on broiler rack 5 minutes before meat is done; broil just until
   heated through.

*Calorie-counter's serving: 1 kebab
plus 4 tomato wedges.*

LAMB RAGOUT

Makes 6 servings, 270 calories each

2 pounds lamb for stewing
1 clove garlic, minced
1 can (about 1 pound) cut green
     beans
1 envelope instant chicken broth
     OR: 1 chicken-bouillon cube
½ teaspoon salt
½ teaspoon marjoram
½ cup water
12 small white onions, peeled
1 can (1 pound) tomatoes

1. Cut all fat from lamb, then cut lamb
   into 2-inch pieces. Brown with garlic in a Dutch oven; pour off fat.
2. Drain liquid from beans and stir
   into meat mixture with chicken
   broth or bouillon cube, salt, marjoram, and water. Heat to boiling,
   crushing bouillon cube, if using,
   with a spoon; cover.
3. Simmer 45 minutes, or until meat is
   almost tender. Add onions; simmer
   45 minutes.
4. Stir in green beans and tomatoes;
   simmer 30 minutes longer, or until
   meat is tender.

Calorie-counter's serving: 1 cup.

GOURMET LAMB CHOPS

Makes 6 servings, 203 calories each

6 loin lamb chops, cut about 1 inch thick
3 lamb kidneys
   Salt and pepper
6 large fresh mushrooms
6 pickled sweet red peppers

1. Trim all fat from chops. Split each
   kidney; snip out tubes and white
   membrane with scissors.
2. Place chops on rack in broiler pan.
   Broil, 4 to 6 inches from heat, 8 to
   10 minutes for medium; turn. Place
   kidneys on rack with chops; broil
   both, turning kidneys once, 8 to
   10 minutes. Sprinkle all lightly with
   salt and pepper.
3. While meat broils, wash mushrooms; cut off stems to within ¼
   inch of cap; flute this way: With a
   sharp thin-blade knife, mark center
   of each cap. Starting here, make a
   curved cut about ⅛ inch deep to
   edge. Repeat around cap to make
   12 evenly spaced cuts. Now make
   a second curved cut just behind
   each line, slanting knife in so you
   can lift out a narrow strip. Heat
   caps in hot water in a small frying
   pan, 2 to 3 minutes, or just until
   the cuts open up slightly.
4. Thread 1 pickled pepper, half a
   broiled kidney, and 1 mushroom cap,
   kebab style, onto skewers; stick
   into each chop on a heated serving
   plate.

*Calorie-counter's serving: 1 chop plus
½ kidney, 1 mushroom, and 1 pepper.*

Pork and ham

SPANISH PORK

Makes 6 servings, 324 calories each

1½ pounds lean boneless pork shoulder
1 large onion, chopped (1 cup)
1½ teaspoons chili powder
1 can (1 pound) tomatoes
¾ cup water
½ cup chopped celery
¼ cup chopped green pepper
1 teaspoon salt
⅛ teaspoon pepper
   Granulated or liquid no-calorie
     sweetener
3 cups cooked hot rice

1. Trim all fat from pork, then cut
   pork into ½-inch cubes. Brown in
   a large frying pan; push to one side.
2. Stir in onion and chili powder;
   saute until onion is soft, then stir

into meat with tomatoes, water, celery, green pepper, salt, and pepper;
cover. Simmer 50 minutes, or until
meat is tender.
3. Just before serving, stir in your
   favorite no-calorie sweetener, using
   the equivalent of 2 teaspoons sugar.
   Serve over rice.

*Calorie-counter's serving: ⅔ cup
meat mixture and ½ cup cooked rice.*

ORIENTAL PORK AND VEGETABLES

Makes 6 servings, 274 calories each

1½ pounds lean boneless pork shoulder
4 tablespoons soy sauce
1 can (6 ounces) unsweetened pineapple
     juice
1½ teaspoons salt
1 cup water
½ pound green beans, tipped and cut
     in 1-inch pieces
2 large yellow squashes, trimmed,
     quartered lengthwise, and cut in
     2-inch-long sticks
2 tablespoons cornstarch
2 tablespoons cold water
   Steamed Celery Cabbage (recipe
     on page 134)
6 cherry tomatoes

1. Trim all fat from pork, then cut
   pork into thin strips; place in a
   shallow dish. Drizzle with soy
   sauce; let stand about 15 minutes
   to season, then drain.
2. Saute strips, stirring several times,
   in a large frying pan 5 minutes;
   stir in pineapple juice, salt, and
   water; cover. Simmer 1 hour.
3. Place green beans and squash sticks
   around meat; cook 15 minutes
   longer, or until meat and vegetables
   are tender.
4. Smooth cornstarch and cold water
   to a paste in a cup; stir into meat
   mixture. Cook, stirring constantly,
   until mixture thickens and boils 3
   minutes. Spoon onto heated serving
   plates; spoon STEAMED CELERY CAB-
   BAGE around edges. Garnish with
   cherry tomatoes.

*Calorie-counter's serving: 1 cup pork-
vegetable mixture, 1 cup cooked cabbage, and 1 cherry tomato.*

Far Eastern foods inspired this diet-fancy of Oriental Pork and Vegetables (recipe on page 119). *And how easy it is to fix! Strips of soy-seasoned pork simmer with squash and green beans in a sweet-sour sauce to serve with Steamed Celery Cabbage* (recipe on page 134). *Lotus Blossom Salad* (recipe on page 140) *blends fruits in a creamy dressing*

Total calories per serving: 341

A lot for little is what a dieter rates with this bright main course. *Chicken Hawaiian* (recipe on page 123) *bakes to a crispy brown in a soy-onion sauce, and is served with a parsley-rimmed pineapple ring and hot Salad-vegetable Saute* (recipe on page 133). *Golden Rice* (recipe on page 135) *cooks beside the chicken in oven with no watching*

Total calories per serving: 475

FRUIT-CROWNED HAM STEAK

Bake at 350° for 1 hour.
Makes 4 servings, 296 calories each

1 slice ready-to-eat ham (about 1 pound)
1 can (1 pound) diet-pack cling peach halves
1 can (about 16 ounces) diet-pack sliced pineapple, drained
1 tablespoon prepared mustard

1. Trim fat from ham; score edge so slice will lay flat during cooking; place in a large shallow baking dish.
2. Drain syrup from peaches into a cup; stud peach halves with two or three whole cloves each for spicy flavor, if you wish. Arrange peach halves and pineapple slices around ham.
3. Stir mustard into peach syrup; pour over ham and fruits.
4. Bake in moderate oven (350°), basting several times with syrup in dish, 1 hour, or until ham and fruits are lightly glazed.
5. Cut ham into 4 even-size pieces; place on serving plates; top each with a peach half and pineapple slice. Garnish with water cress, if you wish.

Calorie-counter's serving: ¼ of the ham, ½ peach, and 1 slice pineapple.

APPLE-GLAZED PORK ROAST

Roast at 375° for 2 hours.
Makes 6 servings, 306 calories each

1 two-pound loin of pork (6 chops)
½ teaspoon salt
⅛ teaspoon pepper
½ cup apple juice
1 small apple, pared, quartered, cored, and sliced
1 tablespoon bottled steak sauce

1. Trim all fat from roast; rub roast with salt and pepper; place on a rack in a roasting pan. If using a meat thermometer, insert bulb into center of roast without touching bone.
2. Pour apple juice over roast; cover pan tightly.
3. Roast in moderate oven (375°) 1½ hours; uncover. Lay apple slices on top of roast; brush with part of the steak sauce.
4. Continue roasting, brushing again with remaining sauce, 30 minutes, or until richly glazed and thermometer registers 185°. Remove to a heated serving platter; carve into chops.

Calorie-counter's serving: 1 chop.

GLAZED PORK CHOPS

Bake at 350° for 45 minutes.
Makes 6 servings, 330 calories each

6 lean pork chops, cut 1 inch thick
1 large onion, peeled and cut in 6 slices
½ teaspoon salt
Dash of pepper
1 envelope instant chicken broth OR: 1 chicken-bouillon cube
2 teaspoons prepared mustard
¼ cup water

1. Trim all fat from chops; brown chops in a large frying pan.
2. Place onion slices in a single layer in a large shallow baking pan; top each with a browned chop; sprinkle with salt and pepper.
3. Combine chicken broth or bouillon cube, mustard, and water in a cup, crushing cube, if using, with a spoon; drizzle over chops; cover.
4. Bake in moderate oven (350°) 45 minutes, or until chops are tender.
5. Place each on its onion slice on a heated serving plate. Garnish with a vegetable kebab, radish rose, and a spear of Belgian endive, if you wish.

Note—To make vegetable kebabs, thread 4 thin rounds of green pepper, 2 slices of water chestnut, and 4 tiny pickled onions each onto wooden picks or skewers.

Calorie-counter's serving: 1 chop, 1 slice of onion, and 1 vegetable garnish.

HAM-AND-CHEESE BONANZA

Makes 1 serving, 409 calories

1 large slice rye bread
1 tablespoon pimiento-cheese spread (from a 5-ounce jar)
2 large leaves iceberg lettuce
½ medium-size tomato, sliced
1 long slice Swiss cheese (from an 8-ounce package)
2 slices boiled ham (from an about-5-ounce package)
¼ medium-size cucumber, scored and cut into 3 thick slices
Parsley sprigs
Tiny pickled onions

1. Spread bread with pimiento cheese; top with lettuce and tomato slices.
2. Roll cheese and ham slices; arrange on top of tomatoes. (Cheese rolls best if warmed to room temperature first.)
3. Thread cucumber slices, parsley, and pickled onions onto wooden picks; stick into ham and cheese rolls, kebab style.

Calorie-counter's serving: 1 sandwich.

HARVEST PORK PLATTER

Makes 6 servings, 299 calories each

6 lean pork chops, cut 1 inch thick
2 medium-size sweet potatoes, pared and sliced thin
2 envelopes instant chicken broth OR: 2 chicken-bouillon cubes
½ cup hot water
1 tablespoon prepared mustard
2 medium-size seedless oranges, pared and sectioned

1. Trim all fat from chops. Brown chops, without adding any fat, in a large frying pan; place potato slices on top.
2. Dissolve chicken broth or bouillon cubes in hot water in a cup; pour over chops; cover. Simmer, basting several times with liquid in pan, 45 minutes, or until chops are tender.
3. Remove chops and potatoes to a heated serving platter; keep warm.
4. Pour liquid in pan into a cup; let stand a minute until fat rises to top, then skim off; return liquid to pan. Stir in mustard and orange sections; heat to boiling. Spoon over chops and potatoes.

Calorie-counter's serving: 1 chop, 6 slices sweet potato, and 3 tablespoons sauce.

PORK CURRY

Makes 6 servings, 364 calories each

1½ pounds lean boneless pork shoulder
1½ cups water
1 small apple, halved, cored, and chopped
1 clove garlic, minced
2 teaspoons curry powder
1½ teaspoons salt
⅛ teaspoon pepper
18 small white onions, peeled
3 cups hot cooked rice

1. Trim all fat from pork, then cut pork into 1-inch cubes. Brown in a large frying pan.
2. Stir in water, apple, garlic, curry powder, salt, pepper, and onions; cover.
3. Simmer, stirring several times, 50 minutes, or until pork is tender.
4. Spoon rice onto serving plates; top with curry mixture.

Calorie-counter's serving: ⅔ cup meat mixture and ½ cup rice.

Chicken

TWIN CHICKEN ROAST

Roast at 375° for 1½ hours.
Makes 4 servings, 421 calories each

    2 whole broiler-fryers (about 1½
       pounds each)
1½ teaspoons salt
    1 large onion, chopped (1 cup)
¼ cup water
¼ teaspoon ground coriander
¼ teaspoon curry powder
    3 medium-size apples, pared, quartered,
       cored, and chopped
       Granulated or liquid no-calorie
       sweetener
    1 teaspoon paprika
½ cup chicken broth (from a 14-ounce
       can)

1. Rinse chickens inside and out with cold water; drain, then pat dry. Sprinkle insides with ½ teaspoon of the salt.
2. Simmer onion in water until soft in a medium-size frying pan; stir in another ½ teaspoon of the salt, coriander, curry powder, apples, and your favorite no-calorie sweetener, using the equivalent of 1 teaspoon sugar.
3. Cook, stirring often, over medium heat 10 minutes, or until apples are slightly soft. Remove from heat.
4. Stuff neck and body cavities of chickens lightly with apple mixture. Smooth neck skin over stuffing and skewer to back; tie legs to tail with string. Place chickens, side by side, in a roasting pan.
5. Mix remaining ½ teaspoon salt and paprika in cup; sprinkle over chickens.
6. Roast in moderate oven (375°), basting several times with chicken broth, 1½ hours, or until drumsticks move easily and meaty part of a thigh feels soft.
7. Remove chickens to a heated serving platter; cut away strings and remove skewers. Garnish platter with parsley and a few thin apple slices, if you wish. Cut each chicken in half, dividing stuffing evenly.
Calorie-counter's serving: ½ chicken plus half of stuffing from one chicken.

SUMMER CHICKEN-SALAD PLATE

Makes 6 servings, 355 calories each

    3 whole chicken breasts (about 12
       ounces each)
    2 cups water
    1 slice onion
       Few celery tops
    1 teaspoon salt
    1 head iceberg lettuce, washed, dried,
       and separated into leaves
    3 oranges, pared and sectioned
½ small honeydew melon, pared and
       cubed
       Water cress
       Tangy Chef's Dressing *(recipe follows)*

1. Combine chicken breasts with water, onion, celery tops, and salt in a large saucepan; cover. Simmer 30 minutes, or just until tender.
2. Remove from broth; cool until easy to handle, then pull off skin and take meat from bones. Chill meat, then cut into thin slices. (Strain broth and chill for soup or gravy.)
3. When ready to serve, place lettuce leaves on 6 serving plates to form cups; arrange chicken slices and orange sections, alternately, in a fan shape inside each. Mound honeydew cubes in front; garnish each with a few sprigs of water cress. Serve with TANGY CHEF'S DRESSING and raisin-bread triangles.
TANGY CHEF'S DRESSING — Blend ½ cup buttermilk and ¼ cup bottled low-calorie chef's-style salad dressing in a cup. Makes ¾ cup.
Calorie-counter's serving: 1 salad plate with 2 tablespoons dressing and 2 raisin-bread triangles (1 slice unfrosted bread and 1 teaspoon butter or margarine).

CHICKEN FRICASSEE

Makes 6 servings, 272 calories each

    3 chicken breasts (about 12 ounces
       each), halved
    1 small onion, chopped (¼ cup)
½ cup finely chopped celery
    2 teaspoons salt
⅛ teaspoon pepper
    1 cup water
    2 tablespoons instant-type flour
½ cup skim milk
       Biscuit Crisps *(recipe follows)*

1. Simmer chicken, covered, with onion, celery, salt, pepper, and water in a medium-size frying pan 30 minutes, or until tender. Remove to a heated serving platter; keep hot while making gravy.
2. Mix flour and skim milk in a cup; stir into hot broth in pan. Cook, stirring constantly, until gravy thickens and boils 1 minute. Serve in a separate bowl to spoon over chicken and split hot BISCUIT CRISPS.
Calorie-counter's serving: ½ chicken breast, 1 biscuit, and ¼ cup gravy.

BISCUIT CRISPS

Bake at 425° for 12 minutes.
Makes 6 biscuits

    1 cup sifted regular flour
1½ teaspoons baking powder
¼ teaspoon salt
    2 tablespoons butter or margarine
⅓ cup skim milk

1. Sift flour, baking powder, and salt into a medium-size bowl; cut in butter or margarine with a pastry blender until mixture is crumbly. Add milk all at once; stir lightly with a fork just until evenly moist.
2. Turn out onto a lightly floured pastry cloth or board; knead gently, flouring hands lightly, 5 or 6 times, then pat into a rectangle about ½ inch thick; cut into 6 squares. Place on a lightly greased cooky sheet; brush tops with more skim milk.
3. Bake in hot oven (425°) 12 minutes, or until lightly browned. Break apart with two forks for serving. (If serving biscuits separately, count 105 calories for each.)

CHICKEN HAWAIIAN

Bake at 350° for 1½ hours.
Makes 6 servings, 287 calories each

    3 broiler-fryers, split (about 1½
       pounds each)
    1 small onion, chopped (¼ cup)
¼ cup soy sauce
1½ cups water
    6 slices diet-pack pineapple (from a
       1-pound, 4-ounce can)
    2 tablespoons chopped parsley

1. Arrange split chickens, skin side down, in a large shallow baking pan. Mix onion, soy sauce, and water in a small bowl; pour over chicken.
2. Bake in moderate oven (350°) 45 minutes; turn. Continue baking, basting several times with soy mixture in pan, 45 minutes longer, or until richly browned and tender.
3. Drain pineapple slices well on paper toweling; roll edge of each in chopped parsley. Serve with chicken.
Calorie-counter's serving: ½ chicken and 1 pineapple slice.

CHICKEN-LIVER KEBABS

Makes 4 servings, 202 calories each

12 chicken livers (about 1 pound)
4 slices bacon, halved
16 cherry tomatoes
2 tablespoons Worcestershire sauce

1. Halve chicken livers; snip out any veiny parts or skin with scissors.
2. Saute bacon slices until partly cooked in a medium-size frying pan; remove and drain well on paper toweling. Wrap slices around 8 of the liver halves; hold in place with wooden picks, if needed.
3. Thread each of 8 long thin skewers this way: Cherry tomato, plain chicken liver half, bacon-wrapped liver, plain liver half, and cherry tomato, allowing about ¼ inch between each. Place on rack in broiler pan; brush with part of the Worcestershire sauce.
4. Broil, 6 inches from heat, 7 minutes; turn. Brush with remaining Worcestershire sauce, then continue broiling 7 minutes, or until bacon is crisp. Remove wooden picks before serving.

Calorie-counter's serving: 2 kebabs.

WEIGHT-WATCHING PAELLA

Bake at 350° for 1 hour.
Makes 6 servings, 406 calories each

1 broiler-fryer (about 2 pounds), cut in serving-size pieces
1 large onion, chopped (1 cup)
1 clove garlic, minced
1 cup uncooked rice
6 small slices salami (about 2 ounces), diced
2 teaspoons salt
1 teaspoon sugar
¼ teaspoon pepper
⅛ teaspoon crushed saffron
1 can (1 pound) tomatoes
1½ cups water
1 envelope instant chicken broth OR: 1 chicken-bouillon cube
1 pound fresh shrimps, shelled and deveined
OR: 1 package (12 ounces) frozen deveined shelled raw shrimps
1 can (4 ounces) pimientos, drained and cut in large pieces

1. Pull skin from chicken pieces, if you wish. Place chicken, meaty side down, in a single layer on rack in broiler pan.
2. Broil, 4 inches from heat, 10 minutes; turn. Broil 10 minutes longer, or until lightly browned; set aside.
3. Pour any drippings from broiler pan

into a medium-size frying pan. Stir in onion and garlic; saute until soft; spoon into a 12-cup baking dish with rice, salami, salt, sugar, pepper, and saffron.
4. Combine tomatoes with water and instant chicken broth or bouillon cube in same frying pan; heat to boiling, crushing bouillon cube, if using, with a spoon. Stir into rice mixture with shrimps. Arrange chicken and pimientos on top; cover.
5. Bake in moderate oven (350°) 1 hour, or until liquid is absorbed and chicken and rice are tender. Garnish with parsley and serve with chopped green onions to sprinkle on top, if you wish.

Calorie-counter's serving: ½ chicken breast, 5 shrimps, and 1 cup of the rice mixture.

GOLDEN CHICKEN

Bake at 400° for 1 hour and 5 minutes.
Makes 6 servings, 210 calories each

3 chicken breasts (about 12 ounces each), halved
3 chicken drumsticks
3 chicken thighs
1 can (1 pound) diet-pack cling peach halves
2 tablespoons lemon juice
1 teaspoon soy sauce

1. Arrange chicken pieces in a single layer in a shallow baking dish, 13x9x2.
2. Drain syrup from peaches into a cup; stir in lemon juice and soy sauce; brush about half over chicken.
3. Bake in hot oven (400°), brushing every 15 minutes with remaining peach-syrup mixture and pan juices, 1 hour, or until chicken is tender and richly browned. Place peach halves around chicken; brush with pan juices. Bake 5 minutes longer, or until peaches are heated through.

Calorie-counter's serving: ½ chicken breast, 1 drumstick or 1 thigh, and ½ peach.

FRIED CHICKEN AND ONIONS

Makes 4 servings, 221 calories each

1 broiler-fryer (about 2 pounds), cut in serving-size pieces
1 teaspoon salt
⅛ teaspoon pepper
2 large onions, peeled and sliced
½ cup water

1. Place chicken, skin side down, in a single layer in a large frying pan.
2. Sprinkle with salt and pepper; place

onion slices on top; cover tightly. (No need to add any fat.)
3. Cook over low heat 30 minutes. Tilt lid slightly so liquid will evaporate; continue cooking 20 minutes longer, or until chicken is tender and golden.
4. Place chicken on a heated serving platter, pushing onions back into pan. Stir in water, mixing with browned bits from bottom of pan; cook until liquid evaporates. Spoon over chicken.

Calorie-counter's serving: ¼ of the chicken and ¼ cup onions.

CHICKEN ORIENTALE

Makes 6 servings, 398 calories each

3 chicken breasts (about 12 ounces each), halved
3 tablespoons soy sauce
1 teaspoon vegetable oil or peanut oil
1 can (1 pint, 2 ounces) unsweetened pineapple juice
4 tablespoons cornstarch
1 can (about 9 ounces) diet-pack pineapple tidbits
2 cans (3 or 4 ounces each) sliced mushrooms
½ teaspoon salt
1 package (10 ounces) frozen peas, thawed
6 cups shredded Chinese cabbage
3 cups hot cooked rice

1. Pull skin from chicken breasts, then cut meat from bones in one piece; slice meat into long thin strips.
2. Place soy sauce in a pie plate; dip chicken strips into sauce; brown quickly in vegetable oil or peanut oil in a large frying pan.
3. Stir just enough pineapple juice into cornstarch in a cup to make a smooth paste; set aside for Step 5.
4. Stir remaining pineapple juice, pineapple tidbits, and mushrooms and liquid into chicken in frying pan; heat to boiling.
5. Stir in cornstarch mixture and salt; cook, stirring constantly, until sauce thickens and boils 3 minutes; cover. Simmer 15 minutes.
6. Stir in peas; place cabbage on top; cover. Cook 8 minutes, or until peas and cabbage are tender. Serve over rice.

Calorie-counter's serving: 1 cup chicken mixture and ½ cup rice.

Fish and sea food

SHRIMP SPAGHETTI

Makes 6 servings, 330 calories each

1 large onion, chopped (1 cup)
½ clove garlic, minced
2 tablespoons butter or margarine
1 bag (1½ pounds) frozen deveined shelled raw shrimps
1 can (1 pound) tomatoes
1 can (6 ounces) tomato paste
1 can (6 ounces) sliced mushrooms
1½ teaspoons oregano
1 teaspoon salt
1 bay leaf
   Granulated, liquid, or tablet no-calorie sweetener
1 package (8 ounces) spaghetti

1. Saute onion and garlic in 1 tablespoon of the butter or margarine until soft in a large frying pan; add frozen shrimps. Heat, stirring often, 10 minutes, or until shrimps thaw.
2. Stir in tomatoes, tomato paste, mushrooms and liquid, seasonings, and your favorite no-calorie sweetener, using the equivalent of 3 teaspoons sugar. Simmer 20 minutes, or until shrimps are tender; remove bay leaf.
3. While sauce cooks, cook spaghetti, following label directions; drain. Toss with remaining 1 tablespoon butter or margarine; keep hot.
4. Spoon spaghetti onto serving plates; top with shrimp sauce, lifting 1 shrimp to top for garnish. Garnish plate with water cress, if you wish.
Calorie-counter's serving: ⅔ cup spaghetti and 1 cup shrimp sauce.

POACHED SHRIMPS

Makes 4 servings, 155 calories each

2 pounds large fresh shrimps
1 tablespoon shrimp spice
   OR: 1 tablespoon mixed pickling spices
2 limes, cut into thin wedges

1. Wash shrimps in cold water; peel off shells, but leave tails on. Make a shallow cut down back of each shrimp with a sharp-point knife; lift out the black line or sand vein.
2. Half-fill a medium-size frying pan with water; season with shrimp or pickling spices; heat to simmering. Add shrimps; simmer 5 minutes, or just until tender; drain well.
3. Arrange, alternately, with lime wedges on serving plates.
Calorie-counter's serving: 8 shrimps and ½ lime.

BAKED STUFFED LOBSTER

Bake at 450° for 10 minutes.
Makes 4 servings, 286 calories each

4 small live lobsters (about 1¼ pounds each)
2 teaspoons grated onion
1 tablespoon butter or margarine
¼ cup flour
1 envelope instant chicken broth
   OR: 1 chicken-bouillon cube
1 can (3 or 4 ounces) sliced mushrooms
2 cups skim milk
4 teaspoons lemon juice
⅓ cup unsalted cracker crumbs
¼ cup grated Parmesan cheese

1. Drop live lobsters into a very large kettle of rapidly boiling salted water; cover; cook over high heat 8 to 10 minutes. Lobsters will turn a bright red. Remove at once with tongs; drain until cool enough to handle.
2. Remove meat from each lobster, saving shell for restuffing, this way: Place lobster on its back; twist off the 2 large claws, then crack and remove meat; set aside.
3. Cut lobster down middle from head to tail, then cut through hard shell of back and the thin membrane on either side of the tail with scissors. Lift out the meat and pink coral (roe), if any. Discard the stomach sac or "lady" from back of the head, black vein running from head to tail, and spongy gray tissue. Dice all meat. Set shells on a large cooky sheet.
4. Saute lobster meat and onion in butter or margarine in a medium-size frying pan 2 minutes; stir in flour, chicken broth or bouillon cube, mushrooms and liquid, and milk. Cook, stirring constantly, and crushing bouillon cube, if using, with a spoon, until mixture thickens and boils 1 minute; remove from heat. Stir in lemon juice; spoon into lobster shells.
5. Mix cracker crumbs and cheese; sprinkle over lobster mixture; dust lightly with paprika, if you wish.
6. Bake in very hot oven (450°) 10 minutes, or until bubbly hot and crumbs are toasted.
Calorie-counter's serving: 1 lobster.

SEA-FOOD CHEF'S SALAD

Makes 4 servings, 211 calories each

1 head Boston or leaf lettuce
1 can (about 7 ounces) crab meat
2 hard-cooked eggs, shelled
10 radishes
   Carrot Curls (recipe follows)
   Marinated Scallops (recipe follows)
1 cup cottage cheese
   Paprika
   Tomato Dressing (recipe follows)

1. Line a large salad bowl with lettuce leaves; break remaining into bite-size pieces into bowl.
2. Drain crab meat; break meat into large chunks and remove bony tissue, if any. Quarter eggs lengthwise. Wash radishes, trim, and slice.
3. Arrange crab, eggs, and radishes in mounds with CARROT CURLS and MARINATED SCALLOPS in a ring on lettuce. Fill center with cottage cheese; dust with paprika. Serve with TOMATO DRESSING.
Calorie-counter's serving: ¼ of the salad with 4 tablespoons dressing.
CARROT CURLS — Pare 2 medium-size carrots and halve lengthwise. Shave into long paper-thin strips with a vegetable parer. Roll each strip around finger; slide off onto a bowl of ice and water; let stand to curl.
TOMATO DRESSING — Combine 1 envelope French-dressing mix, ¾ cup tomato juice, ¼ cup cider vinegar, and 2 tablespoons water in a jar with a tight-fitting lid; shake well to mix; chill. Makes about 1¼ cups. (If serving this dressing on another salad, count 2 calories for each tablespoon.)

MARINATED SCALLOPS

Makes 4 servings

½ pound (about 20) fresh sea scallops
   OR: 1 package (7 ounces) frozen sea scallops
1 slice onion
1 slice lemon
2 peppercorns
3 tablespoons Tomato Dressing (recipe above)

1. Drop fresh scallops into an about-1-inch depth of water seasoned with onion, lemon, and peppercorns in a medium-size frying pan; heat to boiling; cover. Remove from heat; let stand 5 minutes; drain. (If using frozen scallops, cook, following label directions; drain.)
2. Place scallops in a pie plate; drizzle with TOMATO DRESSING; chill at least an hour to season. (If serving scallops as a separate dish, count 45 calories for 5 scallops.)

Dinner needn't say "diet" and look here for three perfect examples.   Bouillabaisse Salad (recipe on page 130) calls for shrimps, scallops, tuna, and three vegetables seasoned with a secret dressing.   Calorie count is amazingly low so you can even add a slice of French bread, if you wish.   In the individual server, Veal Ragout (recipe on page 117) includes potatoes, snippets of green beans, and rings of yellow squash with the meat and gravy.   And what dieter could feel put upon with sparkly-golden Twin Chicken Roast (recipe on page 123)?   Each serving allows a whopping half bird plus mellow apple stuffing

Total calories per serving: Bouillabaisse Salad—228; Veal Ragout—387; Twin Chicken Roast—421

Veal Ragout   Bouillabaisse Salad

Twin Chicken Roast

SOUP-BOWL SHRIMPS

Makes 6 servings, 302 calories each

1 cup sliced celery
1 medium-size onion, chopped (½ cup)
1 clove garlic, minced
1 tablespoon vegetable oil
2 cans (about 1 pound each) stewed tomatoes
1 bay leaf
1 teaspoon salt
1 teaspoon sugar
¼ teaspoon thyme
⅛ teaspoon pepper
1 bag (1½ pounds) frozen deveined shelled raw shrimps
2 slices lemon
  Few celery tops
4 cups hot cooked rice

1. Saute celery, onion, and garlic in vegetable oil until soft in a medium-size saucepan; stir in tomatoes, bay leaf, ½ teaspoon of the salt, sugar, thyme, and pepper; heat to boiling. Simmer 30 minutes; remove bay leaf.
2. While sauce simmers, cook frozen shrimps until tender, following package directions, using an about-1-inch depth of water seasoned with lemon, celery tops, and remaining ½ teaspoon salt in a medium-size frying pan; drain well. Stir shrimps into sauce.
3. Ladle into serving bowls; top each with a mound of hot rice.

Calorie-counter's serving: 1 cup of shrimp mixture and ⅔ cup rice.

FILLET OF SOLE ROULADE WITH VEGETABLES

Makes 6 servings, 246 calories each

1 can (about 7 ounces) crab meat
6 fresh fillets of sole (about 2 pounds) OR: 2 packages (1 pound each) frozen fillets of sole, partly thawed
3 bay leaves
1½ teaspoons salt
1 cup water
2 tablespoons lemon juice
6 medium-size carrots, pared and cut into sticks
2 cups frozen peas (from a 2-pound bag)
3 tablespoons instant-type flour
1 egg
1 lemon, cut into 6 slices

1. Drain liquid from crab meat into a 2-cup measure and set aside for making sauce in Step 6. Break crab meat into large chunks, removing bony tissue, if any.
2. Cut fresh or frozen fillets in half lengthwise. Set aside a few pieces of crab meat for garnish, if you wish, then place remaining, dividing evenly, on thick end of each fillet; roll up, jelly-roll fashion; fasten with wooden picks. Stand rolls in a medium-size frying pan.
3. Add bay leaves, salt, water, and 1 tablespoon of the lemon juice; cover. (Remaining lemon juice is for sauce in Step 7.) Heat to boiling; simmer 15 minutes, or until fish flakes easily.
4. While fish cooks, cook carrot sticks, covered, in boiling lightly salted water in a medium-size saucepan 20 minutes, or until tender; drain; keep hot. Cook peas, following label directions; drain; keep hot.
5. Lift fish rolls from liquid with a slotted spoon; keep hot while making sauce.
6. Remove bay leaves from liquid in pan; combine liquid with crab liquid, adding water, if needed, to make 1½ cups; stir into flour in a small saucepan. Cook, stirring constantly, until sauce thickens and boils 1 minute.
7. Beat egg with remaining 1 tablespoon lemon juice in a small bowl; slowly stir in about 1 cup of the hot sauce, then stir back into remaining sauce in pan. Heat, stirring constantly, 1 minute; remove from heat.
8. When ready to serve, place fish rolls on serving plates; remove picks. Spoon carrots and peas around fish. Spoon hot sauce over all. Garnish each with saved pieces of crab, a lemon slice, and parsley, if you wish.

Calorie-counter's serving: 2 fish-crab rolls, 12 carrot sticks, ⅓ cup peas, 4 tablespoons sauce, and 1 slice lemon.

BOUQUET CRAB BOWLS

Makes 6 servings, 149 calories each

2 cans (about 7 ounces each) crab meat
1 cup chopped celery
½ cup chopped sweet pickles
4 tablespoons bottled low-calorie French dressing
2 heads Boston lettuce, washed and separated into leaves
3 hard-cooked eggs, shelled

1. Drain crab meat; flake and remove bony tissue, if any. Combine crab with celery and pickles in a medium-size bowl; drizzle with French dressing; toss lightly to mix; chill.
2. When ready to serve, arrange lettuce leaves to form cups in individual salad bowls. Mound salad, dividing evenly, in centers.
3. Cut eggs in half lengthwise; scoop out yolks. Cut each white into thin strips and arrange, petal fashion, over salads; press yolks through a sieve on top. Garnish each with celery slices threaded onto a kebab stick, if you wish.

Calorie-counter's serving: ⅔ cup salad, ½ egg, and ⅓ head lettuce.

GOLDEN CLAM PUFF

Bake at 350° for 50 minutes.
Makes 4 servings, 251 calories each

1 can (about 8 ounces) minced clams
  Skim milk
¼ cup instant-type flour
1 teaspoon salt
¼ teaspoon bottled red-pepper seasoning
4 eggs, separated
  Leek Sauce (recipe follows)

1. Grease a 4-cup souffle or straight-side baking dish well.
2. Drain liquid from clams into a 1-cup measure; add skim milk to make 1 cup. Set clams aside for Step 4. Combine liquid with flour, salt, and red-pepper seasoning in a small saucepan; cook, stirring constantly, until mixture thickens and boils 1 minute; remove from heat. Let cool while beating eggs.
3. Beat egg whites just until they form soft peaks in a medium-size bowl.
4. Beat egg yolks until creamy-thick in a large bowl; beat in cooled sauce very slowly; stir in minced clams, then fold in beaten egg whites until no streaks of white remain. Pour into prepared dish.
5. Set dish in a baking pan; place on oven shelf; pour boiling water into pan to a depth of about an inch.
6. Bake in moderate oven (350°) 50 minutes, or until puffy-firm and golden on top. Remove from pan of water. Serve at once with LEEK SAUCE.

LEEK SAUCE—Trim root and tip from 1 medium-size leek, then slice leek thin. (It should measure about 1 cup.) If leeks are not available in your area, use 1 medium-size onion, peeled and coarsely chopped. Parboil leek or onion in water to cover in a small saucepan 5 minutes; drain well. Combine 1 cup skim milk, 2 tablespoons butter or margarine, 2 tablespoons instant-type flour, and ¼ teaspoon salt in a small saucepan. Cook, stirring constantly, until sauce thickens and boils 1 minute. Stir in drained leek or onion. Makes about 1½ cups.

Calorie-counter's serving: ¼ of the puff with about ⅓ cup sauce.

BAKED ORANGE FILLET OF SOLE

Bake at 350° for 15 minutes for fresh
fish, 30 minutes for frozen.
Makes 4 servings, 86 calories each

4 small fresh fillets of sole (about
  1 pound)
  OR: 1 package (1 pound) frozen fillets
    of sole
1 teaspoon grated orange rind
½ teaspoon salt
⅓ cup orange juice

1. Place fresh fillets in a single layer
   or block of frozen fish in a shallow
   baking dish. Sprinkle with orange
   rind and salt; pour orange juice
   into dish.
2. Bake in moderate oven (350°),
   basting once or twice with juices in
   dish, 15 minutes for fresh fish and
   30 minutes for frozen, or until fish
   flakes easily.
3. Place on a heated serving platter;
   garnish with an orange slice and
   parsley, if you wish.

*Calorie-counter's serving: 1 fillet or
¼ of the fish block.*

CURRIED COD BAKE

Bake at 350° for 1 hour and 15 minutes.
Makes 6 servings, 235 calories each

2 packages (1 pound each) frozen cod,
  partly thawed
2 large onions, chopped (2 cups)
1 clove garlic, minced
2 tablespoons butter or margarine
3 medium-size apples, pared, quartered,
  cored, and sliced
1 can (6 ounces) tomato paste
¾ cup water
2 teaspoons salt
1 teaspoon curry powder
⅛ teaspoon pepper

1. Cut cod into 6 serving-size pieces;
   place in a 6-cup shallow baking dish.
2. Saute onions and garlic in butter or
   margarine until soft in a medium-
   size frying pan; stir in remaining
   ingredients. Heat, stirring constantly, to boiling; spoon over fish;
   cover.
3. Bake in moderate oven (350°) 1
   hour and 15 minutes, or until fish
   flakes easily.

*Calorie-counter's serving: 1 piece of
fish plus ½ cup sauce.*

*Behind this bountiful meal
there's many a cooking
trick to hold the calories
down. See what a dieter
may have: Poached Shrimps
(recipe on page 125) with
fresh lime to squeeze over;
Hominy Timbale (recipe on
page 137), Tomato Garni
(recipe on page 134), a cup
of steamed broccoli, and
Orange Cartwheel Salad
(recipe on page 141)*

*Total calories per
serving: 390*

SPAGHETTI WITH SCALLOP SAUCE

Makes 6 servings, 360 calories each

1 large onion, chopped (1 cup)
½ clove garlic, minced
1 tablespoon olive oil
1 can (1 pound) tomatoes
1 can (6 ounces) tomato paste
½ cup water
¼ cup chopped parsley
1 tablespoon Italian seasoning
1½ teaspoons salt
¼ teaspoon pepper
   Granuated, liquid, or tablet
    no-calorie sweetener
1 pound fresh sea scallops, washed and
   chopped
   OR: 1 package (1 pound) frozen sea
   scallops, thawed and chopped
1 package (1 pound) thin spaghetti,
   cooked and drained
   Grated Parmesan cheese

1. Saute onion and garlic in olive oil just until soft in a large saucepan. Stir in tomatoes, tomato paste, water, parsley, Italian seasoning, salt, pepper, and your favorite no-calorie sweetener, using the equivalent of 1½ teaspoons sugar; cover. Simmer 1 hour.
2. Stir in scallops; cook 15 minutes longer to blend flavors.
3. Spoon over spaghetti on serving plates or toss with spaghetti in a bowl just before serving; pass cheese separately to sprinkle on top.

Calorie-counter's serving: 1¼ cups spaghetti, ¾ cup sauce, and 1 tablespoon Parmesan cheese.

•

CAPETOWN LOBSTER

Makes 4 servings, 111 calories each

12 frozen South African lobster tails
   (3 packages, 7 ounces each)
1 lemon, sliced
1 tablespoon mixed whole spices
   Curry Dip *(recipe follows)*

1. Cook lobster tails with lemon and mixed whole spices in boiling salted water, following label directions; drain.
2. When shells are cool enough to handle, cut with scissors through thick membrane on each side where it joins to hard shell; remove. Peel hard shells back with one hand, pulling lobster meat out with the other.
3. Place meat on serving plates; serve with CURRY DIP.

Calorie-counter's serving: 3 lobster tails and ¼ cup dip.

CURRY DIP

Makes 1½ cups

1 large onion, chopped (1 cup)
1 cup water
1 tablespoon curry powder
1 envelope instant chicken broth
   OR: 1 chicken-bouillon cube
¼ teaspoon salt
¼ teaspoon ground ginger
1 can (about 8 ounces) diet-pack
   applesauce
   Granulated, liquid, or tablet
    no-calorie sweetener
2 teaspoons lemon juice

1. Cook onion, stirring often, in ½ cup of the water in a small saucepan 10 minutes, or until onion is soft.
2. Stir in curry powder; cook 1 minute. Stir in chicken broth or bouillon cube, salt, ginger, applesauce, remaining ½ cup water, and your favorite no-calorie sweetener, using the equivalent of 4 teaspoons sugar.
3. Heat to boiling, crushing bouillon cube, if using, with a spoon; simmer, stirring often, 5 minutes, or until thick. Just before serving, stir in lemon juice. Serve warm or chilled. (If using dip for another fish treat, count 30 calories for each ¼ cup.)

BOUILLABAISSE SALAD

Makes 8 servings, 228 calories each

1 bag (1½ pounds) frozen deveined
   shelled raw shrimps
   OR: 2 cans (about 5 ounces each)
   deveined shrimps
2 slices lemon
1 teaspoon salt
½ teaspoon shrimp spice
¾ cup bottled low-calorie French dressing
1 pound fresh sea scallops
   OR: 1 pound frozen sea scallops
1 slice onion
1 head romaine
1 can (about 9 ounces) tuna, drained
   and flaked into large chunks
1 large tomato, cut in wedges
1 large cucumber, sliced thin
2 medium-size carrots, pared and
   grated
1 tablespoon lemon juice
   Granulated or liquid no-calorie
   sweetener

1. Cook frozen shrimps until tender, following the package directions, using about-1-inch depth of water, seasoned with 1 slice of the lemon, ½ teaspoon of the salt, and shrimp spice in medium-size frying pan; drain shrimps well. Place in a medium-size bowl; drizzle with 1 tablespoon of the French dressing; toss to mix; chill. (If using canned shrimps, drain and rinse under cold

water, then toss with dressing and chill.)
2. Drop fresh scallops into an about-1-inch depth of water seasoned with onion and remaining lemon slice and salt in a medium-size frying pan; heat to boiling; cover. Remove from heat; let stand 5 minutes; drain. Place in a medium-size bowl; drizzle with 1 tablespoon of the French dressing; toss to mix; chill. (If using frozen scallops, cook, following label directions, then toss with dressing and chill.)
3. When ready to serve, set a few whole romaine leaves aside; break remaining into bite-size pieces in a large salad bowl; place whole leaves, spoke fashion, on top. Pile shrimps, scallops, and tuna in separate mounds around edge; drizzle 2 tablespoons French dressing over tuna. Tuck tomato wedges and some of the cucumber slices around sea foods. Arrange remaining cucumber slices in a ring in center.
4. Season carrots with lemon juice and your favorite no-calorie sweetener, using the equivalent of 1 teaspoon sugar, in a small bowl; pile into cucumber ring. Garnish scallops with a sprinkling of paprika, and tuna with fresh dill, if you wish, and serve with remaining French dressing.

Calorie-counter's serving: 8 shrimps, 3 scallops, 1 heaping tablespoon tuna, ⅛ of the vegetables, and 1 tablespoon dressing.

Eggs and cheese

BAKED EGG RAMEKINS

Bake at 325° for 20 minutes.
Makes 4 servings, 91 calories each

½ cup skim milk
4 eggs
   Salt and pepper

1. Butter 4 small custard cups very lightly; spoon 2 tablespoons of the skim milk into each.
2. Break each egg into a cup, then slide into custard cup; sprinkle with salt and pepper.
3. Bake in slow oven (325°) 20 minutes, or until eggs are cooked as you like them. Serve in cups.

Calorie-counter's serving: 1 egg.

STRAWBERRY OMELET

Bake at 350° for 5 minutes.
Makes 4 servings, 146 calories each

- 2 cups frozen unsweetened whole strawberries (from a bag or carton)
- 1 tablespoon sugar
- 4 eggs, separated
- ½ teaspoon salt
- 1 tablespoon lemon juice
- 1 tablespoon butter or margarine

1. Toss strawberries with sugar in a medium-size bowl; let stand about two hours to thaw.
2. When ready to prepare omelet, beat egg whites until they stand in firm peaks in a large bowl.
3. Beat egg yolks with salt until fluffy-thick in a medium-size bowl; beat in lemon juice. Fold into egg whites until no streaks of yellow remain.
4. Melt butter or margarine in a large frying pan with ovenproof handle; tilt pan to coat bottom and side. Pour in egg mixture.
5. Cook over low heat 5 minutes, or until mixture is set on the bottom, then bake in moderate oven (350°) 5 minutes, or until puffy and lightly golden on top.
6. Loosen omelet around edge with a knife; lift onto a heated large serving plate. Spoon about half of the strawberry mixture over half of the omelet; lift other half of omelet with a wide spatula and fold over filling. Spoon remaining strawberries on top. Serve hot.

Calorie-counter's serving: ¼ of the omelet and ½ cup strawberry mixture.

DOUBLE-BOILER CHEESE SOUFFLE

Makes 4 servings, 316 calories each

- 1 tablespoon butter or margarine
- 2 tablespoons flour
- ½ teaspoon dry mustard
- ½ teaspoon salt
- ⅛ teaspoon pepper
- 1 cup skim milk
- 1 cup grated Cheddar cheese (4 ounces)
- 4 eggs, separated
- Green-pea Sauce (recipe follows)

1. Melt butter or margarine in a medium-size saucepan. Stir in flour, mustard, salt, and pepper; cook, stirring constantly, until bubbly. Stir in milk; continue cooking and stirring until sauce thickens and boils 1 minute; remove from heat.
2. Stir in cheese until melted; let cool while beating eggs.
3. Beat the egg whites just until they form soft peaks in medium-size bowl.
4. Beat egg yolks until creamy-thick in a large bowl; stir in cooled cheese sauce slowly. Fold in egg whites until no streaks of white remain.
5. Pour into the top of an ungreased 8-cup double boiler with tight-fitting cover; cover.
6. Cook over gently boiling water 60 minutes, or until a knife inserted in center comes out clean. (No peeking during cooking and souffle will puff up high and light.) Serve at once with GREEN-PEA SAUCE.

Calorie-counter's serving: ¼ of the souffle and ⅓ cup sauce.

GREEN-PEA SAUCE

Makes about 2 cups

- 1 package (10 ounces) frozen green peas
- 2 teaspoons flour
- ⅛ teaspoon pepper
- ⅔ cup skim milk

1. Cook peas, following label directions; drain.
2. Sprinkle flour and pepper over peas; stir in milk. Cook, stirring constantly and carefully so as not to mash peas, until mixture thickens slightly and boils 1 minute.

BACON-AND-EGG BUNS

Makes 4 servings, 202 calories each

- 4 slices bacon, halved
- 4 eggs
- Salt and pepper
- 2 split hamburger buns, toasted
- 2 teaspoons butter or margarine

1. Saute bacon until crisp in a medium-size frying pan; remove and drain well on paper toweling.
2. While bacon cooks, pour just enough water into a second medium-size frying pan to cover bottom; break eggs, one at a time, into a cup and slip into pan; sprinkle with salt and pepper; cover.
3. Steam slowly just until eggs are done as you like them.
4. Spread each bun half with ½ teaspoon butter or margarine; top with a "fried" egg and two pieces of bacon.

Calorie-counter's serving: 1 bun half, 1 egg, and 1 slice bacon.

ASPARAGUS ROULADE

Bake at 325° for 45 minutes.
Makes 6 servings, 338 calories each

- 6 tablespoons (¾ stick) butter or margarine
- ¾ cup sifted regular flour
- 1 teaspoon dry mustard
- ½ teaspoon salt
- 3½ cups skim milk
- 4 eggs, separated
- 1 package (10 ounces) frozen cut asparagus
- 4 slices process Swiss cheese (half an 8-ounce package), cut in small pieces

1. Grease a jelly-roll pan, 15x10x1; line with waxed paper; grease paper and dust lightly with flour.
2. Melt butter or margarine in a medium-size saucepan; blend in flour, mustard, and salt; stir in 3 cups of the milk. Cook, stirring constantly, until mixture boils 1 minute and is very thick. Measure 1 cup sauce into a small saucepan; stir in remaining ½ cup milk and set aside for Step 6.
3. Beat egg whites until they form soft peaks in a medium-size bowl. Beat egg yolks slightly in a large bowl; beat in remaining hot sauce, a spoonful at a time, until thoroughly blended. Fold in beaten egg whites until no streaks of white remain. Spread evenly in prepared pan.
4. Bake in slow oven (325°) 45 minutes, or until golden and top springs back when pressed with fingertip.
5. While omelet bakes, cook asparagus, following label directions; drain well.
6. Blend cheese into the 1½ cups sauce in saucepan; heat slowly, stirring constantly, until cheese melts and sauce is smooth.
7. Remove baked omelet from pan this way: Loosen around edges with a spatula; cover with waxed paper or foil, then place a large cooky sheet or tray on top and quickly turn upside down. Lift off pan; peel off waxed paper.
8. Spoon cooked asparagus in a single layer over omelet; drizzle with about ½ cup of the hot cheese sauce. Starting at a 10-inch end, roll up, jelly-roll fashion, lifting waxed paper or foil as you go to steady and guide roll.
9. Cut into 6 slices with a sharp knife; place on serving plates. Top with remaining cheese sauce; garnish each with a sliced cherry tomato and water cress, if you wish.

Calorie-counter's serving: 1 slice roulade, 3 tablespoons sauce, and 1 cherry tomato.

TOMATO-CHEESE PUFF

Bake at 300° for 50 minutes.
Makes 6 servings, 184 calories each

1 can condensed tomato soup
1 cup grated Cheddar cheese (4 ounces)
6 eggs, separated

1. Combine tomato soup and cheese in a medium-size saucepan; heat slowly, stirring often, until cheese melts and sauce is well-blended; let cool while beating eggs.
2. Beat egg whites until they form soft peaks in a large bowl.
3. Beat egg yolks until creamy-thick in a second large bowl; blend in cooled tomato mixture; fold in beaten egg whites until no streaks of white remain. Pour into an ungreased 8-cup souffle or straight-side baking dish. Gently cut a deep circle in mixture about 1 inch in from edge with a rubber spatula. (This gives souffle its double-puffed top.)
4. Bake in slow oven (300°) 50 minutes, or until puffy-firm and golden on top. Serve at once.

Calorie-counter's serving: 1/6 of the souffle.

TRIPLE-CHEESE RAMEKINS

Bake at 350° for 30 minutes.
Makes 4 servings, 301 calories each

½ cup skim milk
2 tablespoons butter or margarine
1½ cups soft bread crumbs
   Dash of cayenne
4 eggs, separated
½ cup grated Swiss cheese
⅓ cup grated Parmesan cheese
2 tablespoons crumbled blue cheese

1. Heat skim milk with butter or margarine just until butter melts in a small saucepan; stir in bread crumbs and cayenne; let cool while beating eggs.
2. Beat egg whites just until they form soft peaks in a medium-size bowl. Beat egg yolks until creamy-thick in a large bowl; stir in cheeses and crumb mixture; fold in beaten egg whites. Spoon into 4 ungreased 6-ounce custard cups; set in a shallow pan for easy handling.
3. Bake in moderate oven (350°) 30 minutes, or until puffed and golden. Serve at once.

Calorie-counter's serving: 1 ramekin.

Vegetables

SKILLET SQUASH

Makes 6 servings, 30 calories each

1 tablespoon vegetable oil
2 small yellow squashes, trimmed and sliced
2 small zucchini, trimmed and sliced
1 teaspoon salt
¼ teaspoon pepper
¼ cup water

1. Heat vegetable oil in a large frying pan; stir in squashes. Saute, stirring lightly, 3 minutes, or just until shiny-moist.
2. Sprinkle with salt and pepper; pour in water; cover. Cook 10 minutes, or just until crisply tender.

Calorie-counter's serving: ½ cup.

LEMON BROCCOLI

Makes 6 servings, 22 calories each

1 bunch broccoli (about 1½ pounds)
1 tablespoon lemon juice
1 tablespoon water
   Granulated, liquid, or tablet no-calorie sweetener

1. Trim outer leaves and tough ends of broccoli; split any thick stalks, then cut stalks and flowerets into about-3-inch lengths.
2. Cook, covered, in boiling salted water in a medium-size saucepan 12 minutes, or just until crisply tender; drain carefully. Spoon into a heated serving bowl.
3. Mix lemon juice, water, and your favorite no-calorie sweetener, using the equivalent of 1 teaspoon sugar, in a cup; drizzle over broccoli.

Calorie-counter's serving: ¾ cup.

SPRING BROCCOLI

Makes 6 servings, 35 calories each

1 bunch broccoli (about 1½ pounds)
2 envelopes instant beef broth
   OR: 2 beef-flavor bouillon cubes
1½ cups boiling water
30 thin pretzel sticks, broken

1. Trim outer leaves and tough ends of broccoli; split large stalks lengthwise.
2. Dissolve beef broth or bouillon cubes in water in a medium-size

frying pan; place broccoli in pan; cover.
3. Cook 12 minutes, or just until crisply tender and liquid is almost absorbed. Spoon into a heated serving bowl. Just before serving, sprinkle pretzels over top so they'll stay snappy-crisp.

Calorie-counter's serving: ¾ cup broccoli plus 5 pretzel sticks.

GREEN-BEAN MINGLE

Makes 4 servings, 29 calories each

1 package (9 ounces) frozen French-style green beans
2 cups diced celery
1 teaspoon salt
½ teaspoon seasoned salt
½ cup water

1. Combine green beans, celery, salt, seasoned salt, and water in a medium-size saucepan; cover.
2. Heat to boiling, then simmer 10 minutes, or just until vegetables are tender; drain. Sprinkle with more seasoned salt, if you wish.

Calorie-counter's serving: ¾ cup.

DILLED ZUCCHINI

Makes 6 servings, 42 calories each

6 small zucchini
1 tablespoon butter or margarine
1 teaspoon salt
1 teaspoon dill weed
¼ cup water

1. Trim zucchini; quarter each lengthwise, then cut in 3-inch-long sticks.
2. Heat butter or margarine, salt, dill weed, and water to boiling in a large saucepan; stir in zucchini; cover.
3. Cook 15 minutes, or until crisply tender.

Calorie-counter's serving: 1 cup.

ZUCCHINI STICKS

Makes 6 servings, 10 calories each

4 medium-size zucchini
1 teaspoon celery salt
¼ cup water

1. Trim zucchini; quarter each lengthwise, then cut into 3-inch-long sticks.
2. Combine with celery salt and water in a medium-size frying pan; cover.
3. Cook 15 minutes, or until zucchini is crisply tender.

Calorie-counter's serving: ½ cup.

SALAD-VEGETABLE TRAY

Makes 4 servings, 51 calories each

1 package (10 ounces) frozen broccoli
   spears
4 medium-size carrots, pared and
   sliced thin
4 tablespoons bottled low-calorie Italian
   salad dressing
½ pound mushrooms, washed and
   trimmed

1. Cook broccoli, following label directions; drain. Cook carrots, covered, in a small amount of boiling slightly salted water in a small saucepan, 10 minutes, or just until crisply tender; drain.
2. Place broccoli and carrots in separate pie plates; drizzle 2 tablespoons salad dressing over each; cover. Chill at least an hour to season and blend flavors.
3. When ready to serve, arrange broccoli and carrots in rings on a tray or shallow platter. Slice mushrooms; pile in center; sprinkle lightly with salt, if you wish.

Calorie-counter's serving: ½ cup broccoli, ⅓ cup carrots, and ¾ cup mushrooms.

SALAD-VEGETABLE SAUTE

Makes 6 servings, 49 calories each

1 tablespoon vegetable oil or peanut oil
3 cups thinly sliced celery
2 cups cut green beans
4 cups coarsely chopped Chinese
   cabbage
2 cups coarsely chopped spinach leaves
1 teaspoon salt
¼ teaspoon pepper
¼ cup water

1. Heat vegetable oil or peanut oil in a large frying pan. Stir in celery and green beans; saute, stirring constantly, 2 to 3 minutes, or just until shiny-moist.
2. Add cabbage and spinach; toss lightly to mix well. Sprinkle with salt and pepper; pour in water; cover.
3. Cook 10 minutes, or just until vegetables are crisply tender.

Calorie-counter's serving: ¾ cup.

WHITE-WHITE CAULIFLOWER

Makes 6 servings, 30 calories each

1 medium-size head cauliflower
1 cup water
1 tablespoon lemon juice
1 teaspoon salt

1. Cut off thick green leafy stems from cauliflower. (Save stems to

trim, dice, and cook for another meal.) Wash cauliflower and separate into 6 large flowerets.
2. Heat water, lemon juice, and salt to boiling in a large saucepan; add cauliflowerets; cover.
3. Cook 15 minutes, or just until crisply tender; drain well. (To keep cauliflower snowy-white, do not lift cover during cooking.)
4. Serve plain, or sprinkle lightly with seasoned salt, if you wish.

Calorie-counter's serving: 1 floweret.

SESAME ASPARAGUS

Makes 6 servings, 24 calories each

2 packages (10 ounces each) frozen
   asparagus spears
1 tablespoon sesame seeds

1. Cook asparagus, following label directions; drain.
2. While asparagus cooks, toast sesame seeds over low heat in a small frying pan, shaking pan often, just until golden; sprinkle evenly over asparagus.

Calorie-counter's serving: 8 asparagus spears and ½ teaspoon sesame seeds.

PARSLIED CARROTS

Makes 6 servings, 46 calories each

10 medium-size carrots
1 tablespoon chopped parsley

1. Pare carrots and cut diagonally in thin slices.
2. Cook, covered, in boiling salted water in a medium-size saucepan 10 minutes, or until tender; drain.
3. Sprinkle with parsley; toss to mix.

Calorie-counter's serving: ⅔ cup.

SAUCEPAN RISOTTO

Makes 4 servings, 141 calories each

½ cup wild rice
1 medium-size onion, chopped (½ cup)
1 envelope instant chicken broth
   OR: 1 chicken-bouillon cube
1½ cups water
⅓ cup uncooked white rice

1. Combine wild rice, onion, chicken broth or bouillon cube, and water in a small saucepan; cover.
2. Heat to boiling; simmer 15 minutes; stir in white rice. Simmer 15 minutes longer, or until rices are tender and liquid is absorbed. Fluff up with a fork before serving.

Calorie-counter's serving: ¾ cup.

TOP-HAT TOMATO CUPS

Bake at 400° for 25 minutes.
Makes 6 servings, 111 calories each

6 medium-size firm tomatoes
1½ cups frozen peas (from a 2-pound
   bag)
¼ cup water
2 tablespoons butter or margarine
¼ cup sifted regular flour
⅛ teaspoon salt (for batter)
1 egg
1 teaspoon sugar
½ teaspoon salt (for tomatoes)
¼ teaspoon oregano

1. Cut off tops of tomatoes; scoop out insides with a teaspoon. Turn cups upside down to drain. (Use pulp to season soup or stew.)
2. Cook peas, following label directions; drain. Keep hot.
3. Heat water and butter or margarine to boiling in a small saucepan. Add flour and the ⅛ teaspoon salt all at once; stir vigorously with a wooden spoon about 2 minutes, or until batter forms a thick smooth ball that follows spoon around pan. Remove from heat at once; cool slightly.
4. Beat in egg until mixture is thick and shiny-smooth.
5. Sprinkle tomato cups with sugar, the ½ teaspoon salt, and oregano; fill with hot cooked peas.
6. Spread about 1 tablespoon batter over peas in each tomato, then spoon remaining batter, dividing evenly, in a mound on top. (This gives the "top-hat" effect.)
7. Bake in hot oven (400°) 25 minutes, or until topping is puffed and lightly golden.

Calorie-counter's serving: 1 stuffed tomato.

BAKED TOMATO MOONS

Bake at 350° for 15 minutes.
Makes 6 servings, 23 calories each

3 large firm tomatoes
2 tablespoons bottled low-calorie French
   dressing

1. Cut each tomato in half. (To make a fancy fluted edge, mark a guideline around middle of each tomato with a wooden pick, then make even saw-tooth cuts into tomato above and below the line all the way around. Pull halves apart gently.)
2. Arrange, cut sides up, in a shallow baking pan; brush each with 1 teaspoon of the French dressing.
3. Bake in moderate oven (350°) 15 minutes, or just until bubbly on top.

Calorie-counter's serving: 1 tomato half.

133

POTATO-SPINACH NESTS

Makes 6 servings, 113 calories each

6 small potatoes (about ¾ pound)
2 pounds fresh spinach
Salt
1 teaspoon lemon juice

1. Scrub potatoes well. Cook in boiling salted water in a medium-size saucepan 20 minutes, or until tender. Drain, then shake in pan over low heat just until skins start to burst.
2. While potatoes cook, remove stems from spinach; wash leaves well; drain slightly. Pile into a large frying pan; sprinkle lightly with salt; cover. (No need to add any water.)
3. Heat slowly until steam appears, then steam 3 minutes, or just until leaves wilt; drain well. Sprinkle with lemon juice; toss lightly.
4. Spoon spinach onto heated serving plates. Peel skin from potatoes; press each potato through a ricer onto spinach on each plate.

Calorie-counter's serving: ½ cup spinach and 1 potato.

SNOWCAP CARROT NESTS

Makes 4 servings, 79 calories each

10 medium-size carrots, pared and sliced thin
1 teaspoon salt
½ teaspoon marjoram
½ cup water
2 medium-size potatoes, pared and cut up

1. Combine carrots with salt, marjoram, and water in a medium-size saucepan; cover.
2. Simmer 20 minutes, or until tender; drain, then shake pan over low heat to dry slices.
3. Cook potatoes, covered, in a small amount of boiling salted water in a small saucepan 15 minutes, or until tender; drain, then shake pan over low heat the same as carrots.
4. Put carrots through a ricer; spoon into rings on serving plates. Repeat ricing with potatoes; spoon into carrot rings.

Calorie-counter's serving: ½ cup carrots and ¼ cup potatoes.

TOMATOES VINAIGRETTE

Makes 6 servings, 30 calories each

2 cans (about 1 pound each) peeled whole tomatoes
2 tablespoons cider vinegar
Granulated, liquid, or tablet no-calorie sweetener
½ teaspoon dill weed
Salt and pepper
1 small white onion

1. Empty tomatoes into a shallow pan; carefully lift out tomatoes and place in a serving dish or individual bowls.
2. Mix vinegar with your favorite no-calorie sweetener, using the equivalent of 1½ teaspoons sugar, in a cup. Spoon over tomatoes; sprinkle with dill weed and salt and pepper.
3. Peel onion, slice, and separate into rings; place on top of each tomato.

Calorie-counter's serving: 1 tomato.

TOMATOES GARNI

Makes 4 servings, 72 calories each

2 cans (about 1 pound each) peeled whole tomatoes
1 small onion, peeled and sliced
¼ cup chopped celery
¼ cup chopped green pepper
1 teaspoon salt
⅛ teaspoon pepper
Granulated or liquid no-calorie sweetener
1 slice bread, toasted and cut into tiny cubes

1. Empty tomatoes carefully into a medium-size frying pan.
2. Stir onion, celery, green pepper, salt, and pepper into frying pan; sweeten with your favorite no-calorie sweetener, using the equivalent of 1 teaspoon sugar. Heat just to boiling.
3. Lift out four of the prettiest tomatoes with a slotted spoon and place each in an individual serving bowl; spoon remaining over top. Sprinkle evenly with toasted bread cubes.

Calorie-counter's serving: 1 bowlful.

ARTICHOKE FLOWERS

Makes 6 servings, 40 calories each

6 medium-size artichokes
6 whole allspice
1 bay leaf
1 teaspoon salt
1 tablespoon olive oil

1. Wash artichokes, cut stems, and snip about 1 inch from tips of leaves with scissors. Stand artichokes upright in a large saucepan; add all-

spice, bay leaf, salt, olive oil, and enough water to half fill pan; cover.
2. Cook 40 minutes, or until tender when pierced with a fork. Lift out and set on paper toweling to drain well. Serve plain, as the olive oil and spice give an inviting flavor.

Calorie-counter's serving: 1 artichoke.

ARTICHOKE HEARTS ITALIANO

Makes 6 servings, 24 calories each

2 packages (9 ounces each) frozen artichoke hearts
2 tablespoons bottled low-calorie Italian salad dressing

1. Cook artichoke hearts, following label directions; drain well.
2. Toss with salad dressing.

Calorie-counter's serving: ½ cup.

STEAMED CELERY CABBAGE

Makes 6 servings, 15 calories each

1 medium-size head Chinese cabbage
1 teaspoon salt
1 teaspoon celery seeds

1. Shred cabbage fine; wash; drain.
2. Place in a large frying pan. (No need to add any water.) Sprinkle with salt and celery seeds; cover.
3. Steam 5 minutes, or just until crisply tender. Drain well before serving.

Calorie-counter's serving: 1 cup.

SPRING CARROTS

Makes 4 servings, 23 calories each

4 medium-size carrots, pared
1 tablespoon chopped fresh mint

1. Cut carrots into 2-inch-long sticks.
2. Cook in a small amount of boiling salted water in a medium-size saucepan 10 minutes, or just until crisply tender; drain. Sprinkle with mint.

Calorie-counter's serving: ⅓ cup.

ASPARAGUS PIQUANT

Makes 6 servings, 29 calories each

2 packages (10 ounces each) frozen asparagus spears
2 tablespoons bottled low-calorie French dressing

1. Cook asparagus, following label directions; drain.
2. Drizzle with French dressing.

Calorie-counter's serving: 8 asparagus spears and 1 teaspoon dressing.

HOMINY TIMBALES

Makes 4 servings, 94 calories each

- 2½ cups water
- ½ cup hominy grits (from a 1-pound, 8-ounce package)
- ½ teaspoon salt
- 2 teaspoons butter or margarine

1. Heat water to boiling in a small saucepan; stir in hominy grits and salt; cover.
2. Cook, stirring several times, 40 minutes, or until very thick. Spoon into four *very lightly* buttered 5-ounce custard cups; let stand 10 minutes, then unmold.
3. Top each with ½ teaspoon butter or margarine. Garnish with parsley, if you wish.

Calorie-counter's serving: 1 timbale.

ZUCCHINI FANS

Makes 6 servings, 18 calories each

- 6 medium-size zucchini
- ½ teaspoon salt
- 1 teaspoon mixed salad herbs
- ½ cup water

1. Trim zucchini; halve each crosswise. Make 4 or 5 cuts in each half, starting at wide end and cutting almost to tip. Combine with salt, herbs, and water in a medium-size frying pan; cover.
2. Cook 15 minutes, or until crisply tender; drain.
3. Place on heated serving plates; spread cuts to form a fan.

Calorie-counter's serving: 2 fans.

SPINACH MIMOSA

Makes 4 servings, 62 calories each

- 2 packages (10 ounces each) frozen chopped spinach
- 1 tablespoon flour
- ½ teaspoon salt
- ¼ teaspoon nutmeg
- ¼ cup water
- 1 hard-cooked egg, shelled

1. Place blocks of frozen spinach, side by side, in a medium-size frying pan. Sprinkle with flour, salt, and nutmeg; pour in water.
2. Heat slowly, breaking up spinach with a fork, just until thawed, then cook 1 minute, or until hot.
3. Spoon into mounds on serving plates; press hard-cooked egg through a sieve on top. Garnish each with a carrot curl and water cress, if you wish.

Calorie-counter's serving: ¾ cup spinach and ¼ egg.

Salads

GREEN SALAD PIQUANT

Makes 6 servings, 20 calories each

- ½ medium-size head iceberg lettuce, broken into bite-size pieces
- 1 cup thinly sliced celery
- 6 small radishes, trimmed and sliced thin
- 1 tablespoon capers, drained
- 2 tablespoons bottled low-calorie French dressing

Combine lettuce, celery, radishes, and capers in a salad bowl; drizzle dressing over; toss to mix.

Calorie-counter's serving: ¾ cup.

ORIENTAL CABBAGE TOSS

Makes 4 servings, 46 calories each

- 6 cups shredded Chinese cabbage
- 1 cup diced celery
- ½ cup diced green pepper
- ¼ cup bottled low-calorie blue-cheese dressing

Combine cabbage, celery, and green pepper in a salad bowl; toss with blue-cheese dressing; cover. Chill at least an hour to blend flavors.

Calorie-counter's serving: 1¾ cups.

MUSHROOM-ASPIC MOLDS

Makes 6 servings, 25 calories each

- 1 can (3 or 4 ounces) sliced mushrooms
- 1 envelope unflavored gelatin
- 1½ cups tomato juice
- ½ teaspoon celery salt
- ½ teaspoon basil

1. Pour mushrooms and liquid into a medium-size bowl; sprinkle gelatin over to soften.
2. Simmer tomato juice, celery salt, and basil in a small saucepan 5 minutes; stir into mushroom mixture until gelatin dissolves.
3. Chill 20 minutes, or until mixture starts to thicken; stir, then spoon into 6 individual molds or custard cups. Chill several hours, or until firm.
4. Unmold onto salad plates; serve plain or garnish with water cress and sliced cucumbers, if you wish.

Calorie-counter's serving: 1 mold.

BOUQUET SALADS

Makes 6 servings, 40 calories each

- 12 large romaine leaves
- 3 cups grated pared raw carrots (about 7 medium-size)
- 3 cups sliced celery
- 3 stalks Belgian endive, halved lengthwise
- 2 tablespoons bottled low-calorie French dressing

1. Trim coarse ends of romaine leaves; arrange 2 leaves on each of 6 salad plates.
2. Pile carrots and celery, dividing evenly, in separate mounds on top; place a spear of endive between mounds. Drizzle each with 1 teaspoon French dressing.

Calorie-counter's serving: 1 salad with 1 teaspoon dressing.

TOMATO-BEAN CUPS

Makes 6 servings, 57 calories each

- 1 package (9 ounces) frozen cut green beans
- 3 tablespoons bottled low-calorie chef's dressing
- 6 medium-size firm ripe tomatoes
- 6 leaves iceberg lettuce

1. Cook green beans, following label directions; drain; place in a small bowl. Drizzle with dressing; toss lightly to mix.
2. Cut a slice from top of each tomato; hollow out insides, saving for soup; turn tomato cups upside down on paper toweling to drain.
3. Spoon beans into tomato cups; replace tops; place in a pie plate. Chill at least an hour to season.
4. Serve on lettuce-lined salad plates.

Calorie-counter's serving: 1 stuffed tomato.

DOUBLE GREEN SALADS

Makes 6 servings, 17 calories each

- 1 head Boston or butter lettuce
- 1 package (10 ounces) frozen asparagus spears, cooked, drained, and chilled
- 1 lemon, cut in 6 slices

1. Trim any coarse outer leaves from lettuce; cut out core. Separate leaves, wash, and dry. Arrange in 6 individual salad bowls; tuck asparagus spears into each, dividing evenly.
2. Serve with lemon slices to squeeze over.

Calorie-counter's serving: 1 salad.

BERRY SALAD BOWL

Makes 4 servings, 31 calories each

6 cups broken mixed salad greens
1 cup strawberries, washed, hulled, and halved
¼ cup Creamy Cooked Dressing (recipe follows)

1. Place greens in a large shallow salad bowl; top with strawberries.
2. Just before serving, drizzle dressing over; toss lightly to coat well.

Calorie-counter's serving: 1 cup.

CREAMY COOKED DRESSING

Makes 2 cups

1½ teaspoons (from 1 envelope) unflavored gelatin
1½ cups skim milk
1 teaspoon salt
Granulated or liquid no-calorie sweetener
2 egg yolks
2 teaspoons dry mustard
2 tablespoons cider vinegar
2 tablespoons lemon juice

1. Sprinkle gelatin over milk in top of a small double boiler; stir in salt and your favorite no-calorie sweetener, using the equivalent of 6 teaspoons sugar. Heat, stirring constantly, over hot water until gelatin dissolves.
2. Beat egg yolks slightly in a small bowl; stir in a generous ½ cup of the hot mixture, then stir back into remaining mixture in top of double boiler. Cook, stirring constantly, 10 minutes, or until thick; remove from heat.
3. Stir in mustard until completely blended, then *very slowly* stir in vinegar and lemon juice; cover; chill. Store leftover dressing in a covered jar in the refrigerator.

PINEAPPLE SALAD BOWL

Makes 6 servings, 41 calories each

6 cups broken salad greens
1 can (about 9 ounces) diet-pack pineapple tidbits, drained
3 slices Bermuda onion, peeled and separated into rings
2 tablespoons bottled low-calorie blue-cheese dressing
2 tablespoons skim milk

1. Place greens in a large salad bowl; top with pineapple and onion.
2. Mix blue-cheese dressing and milk in a cup; drizzle over salad mixture; toss lightly to mix.

Calorie-counter's serving: 1/6 of the salad.

GARDEN RELISH PLATES

Makes 4 servings, 9 calories each

2 stalks Belgian endive
12 radishes

1. Quarter endive; cut each quarter into thin strips almost to core end. Place in a bowl of ice and water until tips curl.
2. Trim radishes; cut four thin "petals" in each from tip almost to stem; fold "petals" back carefully so as not to break; cut center part into eighths. Chill in a bowl of ice and water.
3. When ready to serve, drain both vegetables well; arrange on individual salad plates.

Calorie-counter's serving: ½ stalk endive and 3 radishes.

RELISH TOMATOES

Makes 6 servings, 46 calories each

6 medium-size tomatoes, peeled and sliced ½ inch thick
⅓ cup bottled low-calorie Italian dressing
¼ cup finely chopped celery
¼ cup finely chopped parsley

1. Place tomatoes in a shallow bowl.
2. Combine remaining ingredients in a cup; pour over tomatoes; chill 30 minutes to season.

Calorie-counter's serving: 1 tomato with 2 tablespoons dressing.

RELISH RUFFLES

Makes 6 servings, 32 calories each

2 small carrots
6 whole pimientos (from a 7-ounce can)
2 stalks celery
6 small leaves Boston lettuce
6 pitted ripe olives

1. Pare carrots and halve lengthwise. Shave into long paper-thin strips with a vegetable parer; roll each strip around finger; slide off into a bowl of ice water. Let stand to curl and crisp.
2. Place pimientos flat on a cutting board; carefully make even sawtooth cuts all around edge of each with a sharp knife. Cut celery into thin slices.
3. When ready to serve, place each pimiento on a lettuce leaf on a serving plate; tuck celery slices and olives into centers. Drain carrot curls; arrange around edges.

Calorie-counter's serving: 1 pimiento, ⅓ stalk celery, 1 olive, 4 carrot curls, and 1 lettuce leaf.

APPLE-CHEESE WHIRL

Makes 4 servings, 58 calories each

2 medium-size apples
4 long thin slices process American cheese spread, cut from an 8-ounce package
4 leaves iceberg lettuce

1. Quarter apples; core and slice thin.
2. Roll cheese slices, jelly-roll fashion. (Tip: Cheese is easy to turn into "curls" if you let block stand at room temperature first to soften, then shave off paper-thin slices with a vegetable parer.)
3. Arrange cheese and apple slices on lettuce-lined serving plates. Serve plain.

Calorie-counter's serving: ½ apple, 1 cheese curl, and 1 lettuce leaf.

LOTUS BLOSSOM SALADS

Makes 6 servings, 67 calories each

1 head romaine
1 large red apple
1 can (about 11 ounces) diet-pack mandarin-orange segments, drained
6 tablespoons bottled low-calorie blue-cheese dressing

1. Separate romaine leaves; wash and dry well. Break large outer leaves into bite-size pieces and divide among 6 individual salad bowls; tuck small leaves evenly around the edges.
2. Cut apple into sixths, core, and slice thin. Cut 3 slices into small wedges for flower centers, then arrange remaining, overlapping, in salad bowls. Arrange mandarin-orange segments in rings next to apples; stand apple wedges in center. Drizzle 1 tablespoon dressing over each.

Calorie-counter's serving: 1 bowl.

MUSHROOM CHIP SALAD BOWL

Makes 6 servings, 23 calories each

½ teaspoon seasoned salt
⅛ teaspoon seasoned pepper
½ teaspoon sugar
2 tablespoons wine vinegar or cider vinegar
1 tablespoon vegetable oil
6 large fresh mushrooms
6 cups broken mixed salad greens

1. Combine seasoned salt and pepper, sugar, wine vinegar or cider vinegar, and vegetable oil in the bottom of a large salad bowl.
2. Wash mushrooms and trim, then slice thin. Place along with greens in bowl. Toss with dressing to coat.

Calorie-counter's serving: 1¾ cups.

RELISH ASPARAGUS PLATES .

Makes 6 servings, 26 calories each

1 package (10 ounces) frozen asparagus
    spears
6 tablespoons bottled low-calorie
    Italian dressing
3 small stalks Belgian endive
½ head Boston lettuce

1. Cook asparagus, following label directions; drain. Place in a pie plate; drizzle dressing over. Chill at least 30 minutes to season.
2. When ready to serve, split each stalk of endive in half lengthwise; separate lettuce leaves. Place half an endive and 2 lettuce leaves on each of 6 salad plates; arrange asparagus at sides. Drizzle any remaining dressing in pie plate over all. Garnish with water cress, if you wish.

Calorie-counter's serving: 1 salad plate.

CREAMY COLESLAW

Makes 6 servings, 67 calories each

8 cups finely shredded cabbage
    (about 2 pounds)
2 tablespoons sugar
2 tablespoons lemon juice
2 tablespoons low-calorie whipped
    dressing
2 tablespoons light or table cream
¼ teaspoon salt
⅛ teaspoon pepper

1. Place cabbage in a large bowl; sprinkle with sugar; toss lightly; cover. Chill at least 30 minutes to crisp and mellow cabbage.
2. Just before serving, blend lemon juice with dressing, cream, salt, and pepper in a cup; pour over cabbage; toss until shreds are evenly coated.

Calorie-counter's serving: 1 cup.

ORANGE-PEAR ROSETTES

Makes 4 servings, 94 calories each

½ wedge (1⅓ ounces) Camembert cheese
2 tablespoons cream-style cottage
    cheese
2 medium-size fresh ripe pears
4 leaves iceberg lettuce
1 can (about 11 ounces) diet-pack
    mandarin-orange segments, drained
Grated orange rind

1. Mash Camembert cheese in a small bowl; blend in cottage cheese; chill.
2. Just before serving, halve pears lengthwise and core.
3. Place a half on each of four lettuce-lined serving plates; spoon cheese

mixture into hollows. Arrange six mandarin-orange segments, petal fashion, around cheese in each; sprinkle with grated orange rind. (Save any remaining mandarin-orange segments for another day.)

Calorie-counter's serving: 1 pear half, 6 mandarin-orange segments, 1 rounded teaspoonful cheese mixture, and 1 lettuce leaf.

BLOSSOM SALADS

Makes 6 servings, 39 calories each

6 small heads Bibb lettuce
18 cherry tomatoes
½ pound fresh peas, shelled
4 tablespoons bottled low-calorie
    blue-cheese dressing

1. Trim each head of lettuce, then wash under cold water, spreading leaves to resemble a flower; drain well.
2. Place each head in an individual salad bowl. Quarter 2 of the tomatoes for each salad and tuck sections among leaves. Cut remaining tomatoes into eighths almost to stem end; spread cuts slightly; place in centers of salads.
3. Sprinkle with fresh peas, then drizzle with blue-cheese dressing.

Calorie-counter's serving: 1 salad.

RAINBOW SALAD PLATES

Makes 6 servings, 46 calories each

1 can (1 pound) diced beets, drained
2 cups diced pared carrots, cooked
2 tablespoons bottled low-calorie
    Italian dressing
1 small cucumber, sliced thin
¼ teaspoon salt
⅛ teaspoon ground ginger
2 tablespoons lemon juice
    Granulated or liquid no-calorie
    sweetener
6 lettuce leaves

1. Place beets and carrots in separate small bowls. Drizzle each with 1 tablespoon of the Italian dressing; toss lightly to mix. Chill at least an hour to season.
2. Place cucumber in a small bowl; sprinkle with salt, ginger, and lemon juice; stir in your favorite no-calorie sweetener, using the equivalent of 3 teaspoons sugar. Chill at least an hour to season.
3. When ready to serve, pile beets, carrots, and cucumber in separate mounds on lettuce-lined serving plates.

Calorie-counter's serving: ⅓ cup beets, ⅓ cup carrots, ¼ cup cucumber, and 1 lettuce leaf.

RUFFLED TOMATO CUPS

Makes 6 servings, 24 calories each

6 firm ripe tomatoes
2 celery hearts, cut lengthwise
    in thin sticks
    Lettuce and chicory leaves
2 tablespoons chopped parsley
2 tablespoons bottled low-calorie Italian
    dressing
1 small stalk celery, cut in julienne
    strips
6 pitted large ripe olives

1. Peel tomatoes; scoop out insides; turn cups upside down to drain. (Save pulp to use for soup or stew.)
2. Fill each cup with celery hearts and several snips of lettuce and chicory leaves.
3. Mix parsley and salad dressing in a cup; drizzle over tomatoes. Thread celery strips through olives; lay across tops.

Calorie-counter's serving: 1 salad.

ORANGE CARTWHEEL SALADS

Makes 4 servings, 41 calories each

½ medium-size head iceberg lettuce
2 medium-size seedless oranges
¼ cup lemon juice
1 teaspoon dill weed
    Granulated or liquid no-calorie
    sweetener

1. Cut lettuce into 4 slices; place on salad plates.
2. Pare oranges; cut each into 8 slices; arrange 4 each on top of lettuce on each plate.
3. Mix lemon juice, dill weed, and your favorite no-calorie sweetener, using the equivalent of 2 teaspoons sugar, in a cup; drizzle over oranges.

Calorie-counter's serving: 1 slice lettuce, 4 slices orange, and 1 tablespoon dressing.

RING-A-LING SALAD BOWL

Makes 6 servings, 41 calories each

6 cups broken mixed salad greens
1 can (1 pound) julienne beets, drained
1 small onion, peeled, sliced thin,
    and separated into rings
3 tablespoons bottled low-calorie chef's
    dressing

Combine greens, beets, and onion rings in a large salad bowl; drizzle dressing over; toss to mix well.

Calorie-counter's serving: 1¼ cups.

DILL MUSHROOMS

Makes 6 servings, 10 calories each

2 cans (3 or 4 ounces each) mushroom caps
½ cup white vinegar
Granulated, liquid, or tablet no-calorie sweetener
1 teaspoon salt
½ teaspoon dill weed

1. Pour mushrooms and liquid into a small bowl. Stir in vinegar, your favorite no-calorie sweetener, using the equivalent of 4 teaspoons sugar, salt, and dill weed; toss lightly to mix; cover.
2. Chill several hours or overnight to season; drain before serving.
Calorie-counter's serving: ¼ cup.

VITAMIN RELISH

Makes 4 servings, 25 calories each

3 cups finely chopped cabbage
1 medium-size cucumber, pared and chopped
½ cup chopped green pepper
2 pimientos, chopped
Granulated, liquid, or tablet no-calorie sweetener
1 teaspoon salt
1 tablespoon lemon juice
1 tablespoon water

1. Combine cabbage, cucumber, green pepper, and pimientos in a medium-size bowl.
2. Mix your favorite no-calorie sweetener, using the equivalent of 3 teaspoons sugar, salt, lemon juice, and water in a cup; pour over vegetables. Toss to mix; cover. Chill at least an hour to season.
Calorie-counter's serving: 1 cup.

LETTUCE WEDGES WITH DANISH DRESSING

Makes 4 servings, 66 calories each

½ cup cream-style cottage cheese
1 tablespoon crumbled blue cheese
1 tablespoon skim milk
1 small head iceberg lettuce, quartered

1. Combine cottage cheese, blue cheese, and skim milk in an electric-blender container; cover. Beat until smooth; chill. (Or beat all ingredients together with an electric beater. Dressing may not be as smooth, but it will taste just as good.)
2. When ready to serve, place lettuce wedges on salad plates; spoon dressing over each.
Calorie-counter's serving: 1 lettuce wedge with 2 tablespoons dressing.

CUCUMBER-COOL RELISH-SALAD

Makes 4 servings, 27 calories each

1 small cucumber, pared and sliced
1 cup cherry tomatoes, washed, stemmed, and halved
4 green onions, trimmed and sliced
2 tablespoons cider vinegar
2 tablespoons water
2 teaspoons chopped fresh dill
1 teaspoon salt
¼ teaspoon pepper
Granulated or liquid no-calorie sweetener
4 leaves Boston lettuce

1. Combine cucumber, tomatoes, and green onions in a medium-size bowl. Stir in vinegar, water, dill, salt, pepper, and your favorite no-calorie sweetener, using the equivalent of 6 teaspoons sugar; toss lightly to mix. Chill at least an hour to season.
2. When ready to serve, place a lettuce leaf on each of 4 salad plates to form a cup; spoon cucumber mixture into lettuce. Garnish each with a sprig of fresh dill, if you wish.
Calorie-counter's serving: 1 salad.

HOT SPINACH SALAD

Makes 4 servings, 37 calories each

1 package (10 ounces) fresh spinach
2 tablespoons lemon juice
1 teaspoon vegetable oil
¼ teaspoon salt
¼ teaspoon Worcestershire sauce
Granulated, liquid, or tablet no-calorie sweetener

1. Remove stems from spinach; wash leaves well; drain. Place in a large saucepan, without adding any water; cover.
2. Steam 2 to 3 minutes, or just until leaves wilt; drain any liquid from pan.
3. Combine lemon juice, vegetable oil, salt, Worcestershire sauce, and your favorite no-calorie sweetener, using the equivalent of 1 teaspoon sugar, in a cup; pour over spinach; toss to coat leaves well.
Calorie-counter's serving: ½ cup.

Desserts

BAKED APRICOT SOUFFLE

Bake at 350° for 40 minutes.
Makes 6 servings, 98 calories each

1 can (8 ounces) diet-pack apricot halves, drained
2 eggs
Dash of salt
⅓ cup sugar
1 tablespoon lemon juice
Golden Sauce (recipe follows)

1. Press apricot halves through a sieve into a small bowl; set aside for Step 3.
2. Separate eggs, placing whites in a medium-size bowl and yolks in a cup for making sauce.
3. Beat egg whites with salt until foamy-white and double in volume; sprinkle in sugar, 1 tablespoon at a time, beating all the time until sugar dissolves completely and meringue stands in firm peaks. Fold in sieved apricots and lemon juice.
4. Pour into a buttered 4-cup mold or baking dish; set in a shallow baking pan; place on oven shelf. Pour boiling water into pan to a depth of about an inch.
5. Bake in moderate oven (350°) 40 minutes, or until firm on top when lightly pressed with fingertip. Remove from pan of water.
6. Spoon from mold into serving dishes, or unmold this way: Cool in mold on a wire rack 5 minutes, or until souffle settles slightly. Loosen around edge with a sharp-tip, thin-blade knife; cover mold with a serving dish; turn upside down, then gently lift off mold. Serve warm with GOLDEN SAUCE.

GOLDEN SAUCE—Beat saved 2 egg yolks with 1 cup skim milk and your favorite no-calorie sweetener, using the equivalent of 9 teaspoons sugar, until blended in the top of a small double boiler. Cook, stirring constantly, over simmering water 10 minutes, or until mixture coats a metal spoon; remove from heat. Stir in 1 teaspoon vanilla and ¼ teaspoon lemon extract; serve warm. Makes 1¼ cups.
Calorie-counter's serving: 1/6 of the souffle plus 3 tablespoons sauce.

138

BAKED VANILLA PUFF

Bake at 350° for 45 minutes.
Makes 6 servings, 109 calories each

- 5 teaspoons butter or margarine
- 3 tablespoons flour
- ¼ teaspoon salt
- ¾ cup skim milk
- 1½ teaspoons vanilla
- Granulated or liquid no-calorie sweetener
- 3 eggs, separated
- 2 tablespoons sugar

1. Melt butter or margarine in a medium-size saucepan; blend in flour and salt. Stir in milk, vanilla, and your favorite no-calorie sweetener, using the equivalent of 6 teaspoons sugar.
2. Cook, stirring constantly, over low heat until sauce thickens and boils 1 minute; cool.
3. Beat egg whites until foamy-white and double in volume in a medium-size bowl; sprinkle in sugar, 1 tablespoon at a time, beating all the time until sugar completely dissolves and meringue stands in firm peaks.
4. Beat egg yolks well in a large bowl; stir in cooled sauce slowly; fold in meringue.
5. Pour into an ungreased 4-cup souffle dish; cut a deep circle in mixture about 1 inch in from edge with knife.
6. Set dish in a baking pan; place on oven shelf; pour boiling water into pan to depth of about an inch.
7. Bake in moderate oven (350°) 45 minutes, or until puffy-firm and golden. Serve at once.

Calorie-counter's serving: 1/6 of the puff.

APRICOT TRIFLE

Makes 6 servings, 128 calories each

- 1 envelope low-calorie vanilla-flavor pudding mix (2 to a package)
- 2 cups skim milk
- 1 can (1 pound) diet-pack apricot halves
- ½ teaspoon rum flavoring or extract
- 12 vanilla wafers
- 6 teaspoons low-sugar apple jelly

1. Prepare pudding mix with skim milk, following label directions; chill.
2. Drain syrup from apricot halves and measure ¼ cup; stir in rum flavoring or extract. Set apricots aside for Step 4.
3. Place 1 vanilla wafer in each of six serving dishes; drizzle 2 teaspoons rum syrup over each; let stand 5

minutes. Spoon half of the chilled pudding, dividing evenly, on top.
4. Set aside 6 of the apricot halves for topping; place remaining over pudding layers; add a second cooky; top with remaining pudding.
5. Garnish each with a saved apricot half, cut side up; spoon jelly into centers.

Calorie-counter's serving: 1 dessert dish.

RASPBERRY FLOATING ISLAND

Makes 6 servings, 125 calories each

- 1 envelope low-calorie vanilla-flavor pudding mix (2 to a package)
- 3 cups skim milk
- 1 teaspoon vanilla
- ¼ teaspoon lemon extract or almond extract
- ¼ cup cream for whipping
- Granulated or liquid no-calorie sweetener
- 1 pint raspberries

1. Prepare pudding mix with the 3 cups milk, following label directions; pour into a small bowl. Stir in vanilla and lemon or almond extract; cover; chill.
2. Just before serving, combine cream and your favorite no-calorie sweetener, using the equivalent of 1 teaspoon sugar, in a small bowl; beat until stiff.
3. Spoon pudding into six dessert dishes; top each with whipped cream and raspberries.

Calorie-counter's serving: 1 dessert dishful, with a generous tablespoon of whipped cream and ⅓ cup raspberries.

GINGER FRUIT COMPOTE

Makes 6 servings, 98 calories each

- 6 medium-size oranges
- ¼ small ripe pineapple, cut lengthwise
- 1 cup no-calorie ginger ale

1. Pare oranges and section into a medium-size bowl.
2. Cut core from pineapple; slice fruit into ¼-inch-thick fan-shape pieces, then pare. Place in bowl with oranges; chill until serving time.
3. Spoon into 6 dessert dishes, dividing evenly; pour ginger ale over. Garnish each with a sprig of mint, if you wish.

Calorie-counter's serving: 1 dessert dish, or about 1 cupful.

LEMON-LIME CROWN

Bake at 350° for 35 minutes.
Makes 6 servings, 90 calories each

- 4 eggs, separated
- ¼ teaspoon salt
- 4 tablespoons sugar
- 1 teaspoon grated lemon rind
- ½ teaspoon grated lime rind
- 2 tablespoons lemon juice
- 1 tablespoon lime juice

1. Beat egg whites with salt until foamy-white and double in volume in a large bowl. Sprinkle in 2 tablespoons of the sugar *very slowly,* beating all the time until meringue forms soft peaks.
2. Beat egg yolks until creamy-thick in a medium-size bowl; beat in remaining 2 tablespoons sugar, then remaining ingredients, beating about 1 minute longer, or until slightly thick. Fold into beaten egg whites until no streaks of yellow remain.
3. Spoon into an ungreased 4-cup souffle dish or straight-side baking dish; set dish in a shallow pan. Place pan on oven shelf; pour boiling water into pan to depth of about an inch.
4. Bake in moderate oven (350°) 35 minutes, or until puffy-firm and golden on top. Serve at once.

Calorie-counter's serving: 1/6 of the baked puff.

RASPBERRY SPARKLE

Makes 8 servings, 24 calories each

- 1 package (2 envelopes) low-calorie raspberry-flavor gelatin
- 2 cups boiling water
- Ice cubes
- ½ cup plain yogurt (half an 8-ounce container)
- 4 teaspoons low-calorie raspberry jam

1. Dissolve gelatin in boiling water in a 4-cup measure. Add enough ice cubes to bring liquid to 4-cup level; stir until almost all of the ice melts and gelatin is just starting to set. (Remove any small pieces of unmelted ice.)
2. Spoon gelatin into 8 parfait glasses or dessert dishes, dividing evenly; top each with 1 tablespoon yogurt. (It will sink in slightly.) Chill until firm.
3. When ready to serve, place ½ teaspoon jam on top of yogurt in each glass.

Calorie-counter's serving: 1 parfait glass.

139

*What an array of sweets—all special for waistline-trimmers!
Cake fans have two choices: Cheery Cherry Roll (recipe on
page 151) and Whitecap Cheesecake (recipe on page 153).   Sunshine
Fruit Cup (recipe on page 142), the Harlequin Parfait (recipe
on page 145), and even homemade Pineapple Sherbet in an Orange*

Cheery Cherry Roll   *Whitecap Cheesecake*

Cup (recipe on page 145) *are unbelievably low in calories*

Total calories per serving: Cheery Cherry Roll—135; Whitecap Cheesecake—130; Sunshine Fruit Cup—96; Harlequin Parfait—12; Pineapple Sherbet in Orange Cup—165

Sunshine Fruit Cup   *Harlequin Parfait*   *Pineapple Sherbet in Orange Cup*

STRAWBERRY CROWN

Makes 6 servings, 53 calories each

1 envelope unflavored gelatin
½ cup cold water
1 envelope low-calorie strawberry-flavor gelatin (2 to a package)
2½ cups boiling water
2 cups (1 pint) strawberries
1 cup (8-ounce carton) vanilla-flavor yogurt

1. Soften unflavored gelatin in cold water in a small saucepan; heat, stirring constantly, just until gelatin dissolves; remove from heat.
2. Dissolve strawberry-flavor gelatin in boiling water in a large bowl; stir in plain gelatin mixture; pour ½ cup into a 6-cup mold. Chill 15 minutes, or just until syrupy. Let remaining gelatin in bowl stand at room temperature to cool.
3. While gelatin in mold chills, set aside 12 strawberries for garnish, then hull remaining. Arrange 6 berries in a ring in gelatin in mold; spoon 2 tablespoons more gelatin mixture over berries.
4. Beat yogurt into cooled gelatin mixture in bowl; chill along with layer in mold just until syrupy and layer is sticky-firm.
5. Slice remaining hulled strawberries and fold into yogurt mixture; spoon over sticky-firm layer in mold. Chill several hours, or until firm.
6. When ready to serve, run a sharp-tip, thin-blade knife around top of mold, then dip mold *very quickly* in and out of a pan of hot water. Cover mold with a serving plate; turn upside down, then gently lift off mold. Garnish with saved whole strawberries.

Calorie-counter's serving: 1/6 of the mold plus 2 strawberries.

COFFEE SPARKLE

Makes 6 servings, 39 calories each

2 envelopes unflavored gelatin
½ cup cold water
3½ cups freshly brewed strong coffee
Granulated or liquid no-calorie sweetener
½ teaspoon vanilla
Dash of salt
Dieter's Whipped Cream (recipe follows)

1. Soften gelatin in water in a medium-size saucepan; heat, stirring constantly, until gelatin dissolves; stir in coffee. Sweeten with your favorite no-calorie sweetener, using the equivalent of 16 teaspoons (⅓

cup) sugar; stir in vanilla and salt.
2. Pour into shallow pan, 8x8x2; chill 2 hours, or until firm. Break gelatin up with a fork or press through a potato ricer into a medium-size bowl.
3. Spoon into 6 parfait glasses, dividing evenly; top each with 1 tablespoon DIETER'S WHIPPED CREAM. Garnish with an orange twist, if you wish. (To make, cut 6 thin ribbons from rind of an orange; tie each in a loose knot.)

DIETER'S WHIPPED CREAM — Beat 3 tablespoons cream for whipping until stiff in a small bowl. Serve plain or sweeten to taste with your favorite liquid no-calorie sweetener. Makes about ⅓ cup.

Calorie-counter's serving: 1 parfait glass.

ANGEL LIME PIE

Bake shell at 350° for 10 minutes.
Makes 8 servings, 97 calories each

6 tablespoons zwieback crumbs (about 5 slices)
2 teaspoons brown sugar
¼ teaspoon cinnamon
2 tablespoons butter or margarine, melted
1 envelope low-calorie lime-flavor gelatin (2 to a package)
2 tablespoons granulated sugar
1 cup boiling water
½ cup instant nonfat dry milk
½ cup ice water
1 tablespoon lemon juice

1. Mix zwieback crumbs with brown sugar and cinnamon in a small bowl; blend in melted butter or margarine. Press evenly over bottom and side of an 8-inch pie plate.
2. Bake in moderate oven (350°) 10 minutes, or until lightly browned; cool completely on a wire rack.
3. Dissolve gelatin and granulated sugar in boiling water in a bowl; chill about an hour, or until as thick as unbeaten egg white.
4. Sprinkle nonfat dry milk powder over ice water in a chilled large bowl; beat with an electric beater at high speed 3 minutes, or until soft peaks form. Add lemon juice; continue beating 3 minutes, or until mixture stands in firm peaks. Fold in thickened gelatin mixture until no streaks of green remain; spoon into cooled crust.
5. Chill several hours, or until firm. Just before serving, garnish with a few seedless grapes, if you wish. Cut into 8 even wedges.

Calorie-counter's serving: 1 wedge with 1 grape.

CARDAMOM CUP SOUFFLES

Bake at 325° for 30 minutes.
Makes 8 servings, 63 calories each

¼ cup sugar
4 eggs, separated
½ teaspoon baking powder
¼ teaspoon salt
¼ teaspoon ground cardamom
1 teaspoon grated lemon rind
3 tablespoons lemon juice

1. Butter 8 half-cup souffle dishes, then make a 2-inch stand-up collar for each this way: Fold a piece of foil 6 inches wide and 11 inches long in half lengthwise; butter lightly and wrap around dish, overlapping ends; fasten with a paper clip. Sprinkle cups and collars lightly with about 1 tablespoon of the sugar, tapping out any excess.
2. Beat egg whites with baking powder, salt, and cardamom just until they form soft peaks in a medium size bowl.
3. Beat egg yolks well in a large bowl; beat in remaining sugar, 1 tablespoon at a time, until very thick, then stir in lemon rind and juice. Fold in beaten egg-white mixture until no streaks of white remain.
4. Spoon into prepared cups, dividing evenly. Set cups, not touching, in a shallow baking pan; place on oven shelf. Pour boiling water into pan to depth of about an inch.
5. Bake in slow oven (325°) 30 minutes, or until puffy-light and firm in center. Carefully peel off collars; serve at once.

Calorie-counter's serving: 1 souffle.

SUNSHINE FRUIT CUP

Makes 6 servings, 96 calories each

4 medium-size oranges
2 medium-size grapefruits
Granulated or liquid no-calorie sweetener
12 seedless grapes
6 small thin pieces crystallized ginger

1. Pare oranges and grapefruits; section into a medium-size bowl, squeezing juice from membranes into bowl. Sweeten to taste with your favorite no-calorie sweetener.
2. Spoon into 6 serving dishes, dividing evenly. Garnish each with two grapes and a piece of ginger threaded onto a wooden pick, kebab style.

Calorie-counter's serving: 1 dishful.

RIBBON-CANDY PUFF

Makes 8 servings, 93 calories each

1 envelope low-calorie lime-flavor
   gelatin (2 to a package)
1 envelope low-calorie cherry-flavor
   gelatin (2 to a package)
3 cups boiling water
1 envelope low-calorie whipped
   dessert topping mix (2 to a
   package)
3 squares sweet cooking chocolate
   (from a 4-ounce package)

1. Dissolve each flavor gelatin in 1½ cups of boiling water in separate large bowls; cool at room temperature about 30 minutes.
2. Measure out 1 cup lime-gelatin; set aside. Place bowl of remaining lime-gelatin in a pan of ice and water; beat until double in volume and mixture forms soft peaks. Spoon into 10-cup mold; chill until sticky-firm.
3. Repeat beating with cherry-gelatin, then the saved 1-cup lime-gelatin, layering and chilling each in mold to make three layers. Chill several hours, or overnight, until firm.
4. Prepare the topping, following label directions; refrigerate. Shave the chocolate into paper-thin strips with vegetable parer.
5. To unmold gelatin, run a sharp-tip, thin-blade knife around top; tip mold, then tap gently to release gelatin from side. Cover mold with serving plate and turn both over together; lift out mold.
6. Just before serving, frost gelatin with whipped topping; sprinkle with the chocolate; cut into 8 wedges.

Calorie-counter's serving: 1 wedge.

JELLIED AMBROSIA CUPS

Makes 8 servings, 54 calories each

2 envelopes unflavored gelatin
2 bottles (16 ounces each)
   low-calorie ginger ale
2 tablespoons lemon juice
1 can (about 11 ounces) mandarin-
   orange segments, drained
1 can (8 ounces) diet-pack sliced
   peaches, drained
½ cup sliced green grapes
2 tablespoons flaked coconut

1. Soften gelatin in ½ cup of the ginger ale in a small saucepan. Heat, stirring constantly, just until gelatin dissolves.
2. Stir into remaining ginger ale and lemon juice in a medium-size bowl; chill 50 minutes, or until as thick as unbeaten egg white.
3. Fold in drained mandarin-orange segments, sliced peaches, and

grapes; spoon into eight goblets or sherbet dishes. Chill one hour, or until firm. Just before serving, spoon coconut in a cone on top.

Calorie-counter's serving: ¾ cup gelatin mixture and ¾ teaspoon coconut.

ANGEL FLUFF

Makes 6 servings, 74 calories each

1 envelope unflavored gelatin
3 tablespoons brown sugar
½ cup water
1 small can evaporated milk (⅔ cup)
1 tablespoon rum flavoring or extract
1 egg white
¼ cup corn flakes, crushed

1. Soften gelatin with 2 tablespoons of the brown sugar in water in a small saucepan. Heat slowly, stirring constantly, just until gelatin and sugar dissolve; remove from heat. Stir in evaporated milk and rum flavoring or extract.
2. Pour into a medium-size bowl; chill 30 minutes, or just until as thick as unbeaten egg white.
3. Beat egg white with remaining 1 tablespoon brown sugar until meringue stands in firm peaks in a small bowl.
4. Beat thickened gelatin mixture until fluffy; fold in meringue; spoon into 6 custard cups. Sprinkle corn flakes over top. Chill several hours, or until firm. Serve in cups.

Calorie-counter's serving: 1 custard cup.

FRUITS SCANDIA

Makes 6 servings, 81 calories each

3 tablespoons quick-cooking tapioca
1½ cups water
2 cups orange juice
¼ teaspoon ground cardamom
   Granulated, liquid, or tablet
   no-calorie sweetener
1 medium-size seedless orange, pared
   and sectioned
1 medium-size seedless grapefruit,
   pared and sectioned
1 small banana, peeled and sliced

1. Combine tapioca and water in a small saucepan; let stand 5 minutes, then heat, stirring constantly, to a full rolling boil.
2. Pour into a medium-size bowl; stir in orange juice, cardamom, and your favorite no-calorie sweetener, using the equivalent of 3 teaspoons sugar; chill.
3. Just before serving, stir in fruits.

Calorie-counter's serving: ¾ cup.

APRICOT-RASPBERRY SNOW

Makes 6 servings, 25 calories each

1 envelope low-calorie raspberry-
   flavor gelatin (2 to a package)
1½ cups boiling water
2 egg whites
6 diet-pack apricot halves (from an
   8-ounce can)
1 teaspoon flaked coconut

1. Dissolve gelatin in boiling water in large bowl; chill 50 minutes, or until as thick as unbeaten egg white.
2. Set bowl in a pan of ice and water; add unbeaten egg whites. Beat with electric beater at high speed, or vigorously with a rotary beater, until mixture mounds lightly on a spoon. Pour into an 8-cup mold; chill several hours, or until firm.
3. To unmold, run a sharp-tip thin-blade knife around top of mold, then dip mold *very quickly* in and out of a pan of hot water. Cover mold with a serving plate; turn upside down; carefully lift off mold. Decorate with a crown of apricot halves; sprinkle coconut in center.

Calorie-counter's serving: 1/6 of mold and 1 apricot half.

DAPPLE APPLE BAKE

Bake at 400° for 30 minutes.
Makes 8 servings, 112 calories each

4 medium-size apples, pared,
   quartered, cored, and sliced
   Granulated or liquid no-calorie
   sweetener
1 tablespoon lemon juice
¼ teaspoon cinnamon
½ cup graham-cracker crumbs
½ cup zwieback crumbs
1 tablespoon butter or margarine,
   melted
¾ cup hot water

1. Place apples in a 6-cup shallow baking dish; sweeten with your favorite no-calorie sweetener, using the equivalent of 24 teaspoons (½ cup) sugar. Sprinkle with lemon juice and cinnamon; toss to mix.
2. Toss graham-cracker and zwieback crumbs with melted butter or margarine in a small bowl; sprinkle over apple mixture. Pour in hot water; cover.
3. Bake in hot oven (400°) 15 minutes; uncover. Bake 15 minutes longer, or until apples are tender. Serve warm.

Calorie-counter's serving: ½ cup.

DIET-LIGHT SPONGECAKE

Bake at 325° for 55 minutes.
Makes 12 servings, 125 calories each

1⅓ cups sifted cake flour
1½ teaspoons baking powder
¼ teaspoon salt
3 eggs, separated
1 cup granulated sugar
½ teaspoon vanilla
½ teaspoon lemon extract
⅓ cup boiling water
1 tablespoon 10X (confectioners'
powdered) sugar

1. Measure cake flour, baking powder, and salt into sifter.
2. Beat egg whites until foamy-white and double in volume in a large bowl; sprinkle in ½ cup of the sugar, 1 tablespoon at a time, beating all the time, until meringue forms soft peaks.
3. Beat egg yolks with vanilla and lemon extract until fluffy-thick in a medium-size bowl; beat in remaining ½ cup sugar, 1 tablespoon at a time. Stir in boiling water; beat vigorously 3 minutes, or until mixture is creamy-thick and forms soft peaks.
4. Fold egg-yolk mixture into egg-white mixture until no streaks of yellow or white remain. Sift flour mixture, ¼ at a time, over top; gently fold in. Pour into an ungreased 9-inch tube pan.
5. Bake in slow oven (325°) 55 minutes, or until top springs back when lightly pressed with fingertip.
6. Hang cake in pan upside down on a bottle; cool completely. Loosen around edge and tube with a knife; turn out, then turn right side up onto a serving plate. Sprinkle top with 10X sugar. Slice cake into 12 wedges.

Calorie-counter's serving: 1 wedge or 1/12 of cake.

PEACH CORDIAL

Makes 4 servings, 106 calories each

¼ cup light corn syrup
5 teaspoons frozen concentrate for
orange juice (from a 6-ounce can)
1 tablespoon water
4 drops bottled aromatic bitters
4 medium-size peaches

1. Mix corn syrup, concentrate for orange juice, water, and bitters in a cup; chill.
2. When ready to serve, peel peaches, then pit and slice; place in dessert dishes; top with orange syrup. Garnish with mint, if you wish.

Calorie-counter's serving: 1 peach plus 5 teaspoons syrup.

DAFFODIL RING

Bake at 325° for 30 minutes.
Makes 10 servings, 113 calories each

¾ cup sifted cake flour
½ teaspoon salt
3 eggs, separated
½ teaspoon cream of tartar
⅔ cup sugar
1 teaspoon vanilla
3 tablespoons hot water
1 teaspoon orange extract
1 tablespoon 10X (confectioners'
powdered) sugar
1 can (1 pound) diet-pack
apricot halves

1. Sift flour and salt onto waxed paper.
2. Beat egg whites with cream of tartar until foamy-white and double in volume in a large bowl. Sprinkle in ⅓ cup of the granulated sugar, 1 tablespoon at a time, beating all the time until meringue stands in firm peaks; beat in vanilla. (Set remaining ⅓ cup sugar aside for Step 4.)
3. Sprinkle 2 tablespoons of the flour mixture over meringue; fold in completely. Repeat with 4 tablespoons more flour mixture. (Set remaining 6 tablespoons flour aside for Step 5.)
4. Beat egg yolks with hot (*not boiling*) water until very thick and light lemon color in a medium-size bowl. Sprinkle in remaining ⅓ cup granulated sugar, 1 tablespoon at a time, beating all the time until mixture is creamy-thick; beat in orange extract.
5. Sprinkle 2 tablespoons of the remaining flour mixture over top of egg-yolk mixture; fold in completely. Repeat with remaining flour mixture.
6. Spoon batters, alternating spoonfuls of white and yellow, into an ungreased 9-inch ring mold. (Do not stir batters in pan.)
7. Bake in slow oven (325°) 30 minutes, or until golden and top springs back when pressed with fingertip.
8. Turn cake in pan upside down on a wire rack; cool completely. When ready to unmold, loosen around edge and center with a knife; invert onto a serving plate. Sprinkle 10X sugar over top. Spoon apricot halves into a small bowl; set in center of cake.

Calorie-counter's serving: 1 wedge or 1/10 of cake plus 2 apricot halves.

APRICOT SPONGE TORTE

Bake at 325° for 30 minutes.
Makes 8 servings, 106 calories each

⅓ cup sifted cake flour
½ teaspoon baking powder
Dash of salt
2 eggs
¼ cup sugar
½ teaspoon vanilla
½ teaspoon almond extract
1 can (about 1 pound) whole
peeled apricots
1 teaspoon cornstarch
1 tablespoon water

1. Sift cake flour, baking powder, and salt onto waxed paper.
2. Beat eggs until foamy in a large bowl; beat in sugar gradually until mixture forms soft peaks. (Beating will take about 10 minutes in all with an electric beater.) Stir in vanilla and almond extract; fold in flour mixture. Pour into a greased 8-inch layer-cake pan with removable bottom.
3. Bake in slow oven (325°) 25 minutes. While cake bakes, drain syrup from apricots into a cup. Blend cornstarch with water in a small saucepan; stir in ½ cup of the apricot syrup. Cook, stirring constantly, until sauce thickens and boils 3 minutes.
4. Remove almost-baked cake from oven; arrange drained apricots on top; spoon half of the hot sauce over; return to oven.
5. Bake 5 minutes longer, or until cake pulls away from side of pan. Spoon remaining sauce over apricots to glaze.
6. Cool cake in pan on a wire rack 5 minutes; remove, leaving cake on its metal base. Cut into 8 wedges. Serve warm.

Calorie-counter's serving: 1 wedge.

BANANA WHIZZ

Makes 6 servings, 75 calories each

2 cans (10 ounces each) banana-flavor
dietary drink for weight control
2 teaspoons instant coffee

1. Mix dietary drink and instant coffee in a medium-size bowl; pour into an ice-cube tray. Freeze 1 hour, or until almost firm in middle.
2. Spoon into an electric-blender container; cover; beat until frothy-light but still icy. (Or spoon into a bowl and beat with an electric mixer.) Pour into 6 juice glasses, dividing evenly.

Calorie-counter's serving: A scant ½ cup.

HARLEQUIN PARFAITS

Makes 6 servings, 12 calories each

1 envelope low-calorie lime-flavor
   gelatin (2 to a package)
4 cups boiling water
1 envelope low-calorie raspberry-
   flavor gelatin (2 to a package)

1. Dissolve lime-flavor gelatin in 2 cups of the boiling water in 2-cup measure. Dissolve raspberry-flavor gelatin in remaining 2 cups boiling water in a small bowl.
2. Pour 1 cup of the lime-flavor gelatin into 6 parfait glasses; chill until firm. Keep remaining gelatins at room temperature for other layers.
3. When gelatin in glasses has set, spoon out 1 cup raspberry-flavor gelatin and set aside for top layers. Place bowl of remaining raspberry-flavor gelatin in a pan of ice and water; beat until mixture forms soft peaks. Spoon over firm lime layers in glasses. Chill until firm.
4. Spoon remaining lime-flavor gelatin over firm raspberry layers; chill again until firm.
5. Beat the saved 1 cup raspberry-flavor gelatin over ice and water until it forms soft peaks; spoon on top. Chill until serving time.

Calorie-counter's serving: 1 parfait glass.

PINEAPPLE SHERBET IN ORANGE CUPS

Makes 6 servings, 165 calories each

2 cups buttermilk
1 can (6 ounces) frozen concentrated
   pineapple juice, thawed
   Granulated or liquid no-calorie
   sweetener
6 small oranges, peeled
6 whole strawberries, washed and hulled

1. Combine buttermilk and concentrated pineapple juice in a medium-size bowl; sweeten with your favorite no-calorie sweetener, using the equivalent of 48 teaspoons (1 cup) sugar; beat until well-blended. Pour into an ice-cube tray or pan, 8x8x2. Freeze until firm almost to middle.
2. Spoon into a chilled medium-size bowl; beat quickly until fluffy-smooth; return to tray. Freeze 2 to 3 hours longer, or until firm.
3. Separate sections of each orange slightly to form a cup; place in dessert dishes; scoop sherbet into middle. Garnish each with a fresh strawberry.

Calorie-counter's serving: ½ cup sherbet, 1 orange, and 1 strawberry.

JEWEL PARFAITS

Makes 6 servings, 25 calories each

2 envelopes unflavored gelatin
1 bottle (16 ounces) no-calorie cherry-
   flavor carbonated beverage
1 bottle (16 ounces) no-calorie lemon-
   lime–flavor carbonated beverage
1 tablespoon lemon juice
   Green food coloring
1 medium-size banana

1. Soften 1 envelope of the unflavored gelatin in ½ cup of the cherry beverage in a small saucepan; heat over low heat, stirring constantly, just until gelatin dissolves; remove from heat. Stir in remaining cherry beverage.
2. Soften remaining envelope gelatin in ½ cup of the lemon-lime beverage in a second small saucepan; heat over low heat, stirring constantly, just until gelatin dissolves; remove from heat. Stir in remaining beverage, lemon juice, and food coloring to tint green. Chill both mixtures 50 minutes, or until as thick as unbeaten egg white, then keep at room temperature while layering in glasses.
3. Spoon ¼ cup thickened cherry gelatin into each of 3 parfait glasses and ¼ cup thickened lemon-lime gelatin into each of 3 other glasses; chill until firm.
4. Peel banana halfway and cut 6 slices; lay 1 slice on top of firm gelatin in each glass; spoon another 3 tablespoons gelatin mixture in each, alternating colors to those in bottom; chill again until firm.
5. Peel and slice remaining banana; place in glasses; top with remaining gelatin mixtures, dividing evenly and alternating colors again; chill. Just before serving, garnish with more banana slices, arranged cartwheel style, if you wish.

Calorie-counter's serving: 1 parfait.

CARIOCA FLUFF

Makes 6 servings, 88 calories each

1 envelope unflavored gelatin
2 cups skim milk
1 square unsweetened chocolate
⅛ teaspoon cinnamon
   Granulated, liquid, or tablet
   no-calorie sweetener
¼ teaspoon vanilla
3 tablespoons cream, whipped

1. Soften gelatin in milk in the top of a small double boiler; add chocolate and cinnamon. Heat, stirring often, over simmering water until chocolate melts and gelatin dissolves; remove from heat.

2. Sweeten with your favorite no-calorie sweetener, using the equivalent of 3 teaspoons sugar; stir in vanilla. Chill 1 hour, or until as thick as unbeaten egg white.
3. Fill bottom of double boiler with ice and water; set top over bottom; beat mixture until fluffy-light and double in volume.
4. Spoon into 6 individual molds or custard cups, dividing evenly. Chill until firm.
5. Unmold onto dessert plates or serve in cups. Garnish each with a dollop of whipped cream.

Calorie-counter's serving: 1 mold plus 1 tablespoon unsweetened whipped cream.

LEMON-LIME ROYALE

Makes 6 servings, 45 calories each

1 envelope low-calorie lemon-flavor
   gelatin (2 to a package)
2 cups boiling water
6 thin slices fresh lime
1 medium-size grapefruit
2 oranges

1. Dissolve gelatin in boiling water in medium-size bowl; chill until as thick as unbeaten egg white.
2. Spoon into 6 parfait glasses, dividing evenly. Carefully stand a lime slice in center of gelatin in each glass; chill until firm.
3. Pare grapefruit and oranges and section into a small bowl; chill. When ready to serve, drain off juices and save for breakfast beverage. Spoon fruits on top of gelatin, dividing evenly. Garnish with a thin orange slice, if you wish.

Calorie-counter's serving: 1 parfait glass.

SPRING FRUIT COUPE

Makes 6 servings, 50 calories each

1 pint strawberries, washed
1 tablespoon sugar
2 cups diced pared fresh pineapple

1. Set aside 6 whole strawberries for garnish. Hull and slice remaining into a small bowl; sprinkle with half of the sugar. Sprinkle remaining sugar over pineapple in a second small bowl. Chill both fruits until serving time.
2. Spoon strawberries into 6 dessert dishes; top each with a mound of pineapple; garnish with saved strawberries.

Calorie-counter's serving: 1 dessert dishful.

145

Refreshing orange and grapefruit sections and tangy low-calorie gelatin layered into a tall glass create this shimmering Lemon-lime Royale (recipe on page 145). And what a boon to good health, for fresh citrus fruits are always on the right side of dieters—nondieters, too

Even on a diet, chocolate lovers can have a smidgen of their favorite atop Choco-chip Pear Velvet (recipe on page 150). The Strawberry Wonder Torte (recipe on page 148) with its rosy berry filling stands six layers high, and fruit-crowned Banana Bounty Pie (recipe on page 153) boasts a creamy filling peaked with shreds of toasty coconut

Total calories per serving: 45

Total calories per serving: Choco-chip Pear Velvet — 120; Strawberry Wonder Torte—100; Banana Bounty Pie—173

Lemon-lime Royale

Choco-chip Pear Velvet   Strawberry Wonder Torte

This glamorous *Baked Apricot Souffle* (recipe on page 138)—*just sweet and light enough for everyone—will help make weight-off wishes come true. Easy to put together, it puffs up handsomely and unmolds perfectly. A rich lemony custard topper goes right along with each serving for a diet-right dividend*

Total calories per serving: 98

Banana Bounty Pie   **Baked Apricot Souffle**

147

STRAWBERRY WONDER TORTE

Bake at 400° for 10 minutes.
Makes 12 servings, 100 calories each

3/4 cup sifted cake flour
1 teaspoon baking powder
1/4 teaspoon salt
4 eggs
1/2 cup sugar
1 teaspoon vanilla
1/4 teaspoon lemon extract
    Strawberry Filling (recipe follows)
1 tablespoon 10X (confectioners' powdered) sugar

1. Grease bottoms of 3 eight-inch layer-cake pans; line with waxed paper; grease paper.
2. Measure cake flour, baking powder, and salt into sifter.
3. Beat eggs until foamy-light in a large bowl; sprinkle in sugar, 1 tablespoon at a time, beating all the time until mixture is creamy-thick. Beat in vanilla and lemon extract.
4. Sift flour mixture over; fold in until no streaks of white remain.
5. Measure 1 cup of batter into each of the prepared pans; spread to edges to make thin layers. (Cover remaining batter for baking 3 more layers.)
6. Bake in hot oven (400°) 10 minutes, or until centers spring back when lightly pressed with fingertip.
7. Cool on wire racks 5 minutes; loosen around edges with a knife; turn out onto racks; peel off waxed paper; cool completely.
8. Wash pans; grease and line with waxed paper, as in Step 1. Bake and cool 3 more layers with remaining batter, following Steps 5, 6, and 7.
9. Make STRAWBERRY FILLING. Put layers together with about 1/3 cup filling between each on a serving plate. Dust top with 10X sugar. Garnish with a ring of 2 strawberries, hulled and sliced; place 1 hulled whole berry in center. Divide cake into quarters, then cut each quarter into 3 thin wedges.

Calorie-counter's serving: 1 wedge or 1/12 of torte.

STRAWBERRY FILLING

Makes about 2 cups

2 cups (1 pint) strawberries, washed
1 cup water
2 tablespoons cornstarch
    Granulated or liquid no-calorie sweetener
1 teaspoon vanilla

1. Set aside 3 of the prettiest strawberries for garnish; hull and slice remaining berries into a small bowl.
2. Stir water, a little at a time, into cornstarch until smooth in a small saucepan. Stir in sliced berries and your favorite no-calorie sweetener, using the equivalent of 24 teaspoons (1/2 cup) sugar.
3. Cook, stirring constantly and mashing berries well with back of spoon, over low heat until mixture thickens and boils 3 minutes. Remove from heat; stir in vanilla; cool.

GINGER SHRUB

Makes 6 servings, 33 calories each

2 cups no-calorie ginger ale, well-chilled
1/2 pint vanilla-flavor ice milk

Pour 1/3 cup ginger ale into each of 6 small cups or juice glasses; float a generous tablespoon ice milk on each. *Calorie-counter's serving: 1 cup or glass.*

DOLLAR-PANCAKE STACKS

Makes 6 servings, 150 calories each

4 eggs
1 cup skim milk
1/2 cup sifted cake flour
1 tablespoon butter or margarine
3/4 cup cream-style cottage cheese
1 cup (half a pint) fresh blueberries

1. Beat eggs until thick in a medium-size bowl; beat in milk, then flour just until smooth.
2. Heat a large heavy frying pan slowly over low heat. Test temperature by sprinkling in a few drops of water. When drops bounce about, temperature is right. Lightly grease the pan with some of the butter or margarine.
3. Measure 1 tablespoon batter for each pancake into pan. (Wait until one has set before pouring the next one.) Bake until edge appears dry and underside is golden; turn; brown other side. Repeat baking, lightly greasing pan each time, to make 36 pancakes.
4. As pancakes are baked, stack in a pie plate; cover with a colander and set in a warm place.
5. For each serving, divide 2 tablespoons cottage cheese onto 6 pancakes; stack on a serving plate. Top with about 3 tablespoons blueberries. Serve warm.

Calorie-counter's serving: 1 stack of 6 filled pancakes with blueberry topping.

LEMON CHEESECAKE TOWER

Makes 12 servings, 123 calories each

2 eggs, separated
1 cup water
1/4 teaspoon salt
    Granulated or liquid no-calorie sweetener
3 envelopes unflavored gelatin
1/3 cup instant nonfat dry milk
1 teaspoon grated lemon rind
3 tablespoons lemon juice
1 teaspoon vanilla
1 envelope low-calorie, lemon-flavor gelatin (2 to a package)
    Green food coloring
3 cups (1 1/2 pounds) cream-style cottage cheese
1 cup evaporated milk, *well-chilled*

1. Beat egg yolks slightly with water and salt in a small bowl; sweeten with your favorite no-calorie sweetener, using the equivalent of 48 teaspoons (1 cup) sugar.
2. Mix unflavored gelatin and dry milk in the top of a small double boiler; stir in egg-yolk mixture. Cook, stirring constantly, over simmering water 5 minutes, or until gelatin dissolves and mixture coats a metal spoon; remove from heat.
3. Strain into a large bowl; stir in lemon rind, 2 tablespoons of the lemon juice, and vanilla. Chill 30 minutes, or just until as thick as unbeaten egg white. (Set remaining 1 tablespoon lemon juice aside for Step 6.)
4. While gelatin-custard mixture chills, prepare lemon-flavor gelatin, following label directions; tint lightly with a drop or two of green food coloring. Pour into a 10-cup tall mold. Chill 20 minutes, or *just* until sticky-firm.
5. Press cottage cheese through a sieve into a medium-size bowl; stir into thickened gelatin-custard mixture from Step 3.
6. Beat egg whites until they stand in firm peaks in a small bowl. Beat well-chilled evaporated milk with saved 1 tablespoon lemon juice until stiff in a small bowl.
7. Fold beaten egg whites, then whipped milk into gelatin-cheese mixture; pour over *sticky-firm layer* in mold. Chill at least 4 hours, or until firm.
8. To unmold, run a sharp-tip, thin-blade knife around top of mold, then dip mold *very quickly* in and out of a pan of hot water. Cover mold with a serving plate; turn upside down; carefully lift off mold. Garnish with a small cluster of green grapes, if you wish. Cut into 12 wedges.

Calorie-counter's serving: 1 wedge or 1/12 of mold.

A dessert fan's dream come true—that's this diet-right
Lemon Cheesecake Tower (recipe at left). Skim milk,
creamy cottage cheese, and nippy lemon are folded into
whipped evaporated milk for the rich-tasting bottom
layer and low-calorie gelatin makes the shimmery crown

Total calories per serving: 123

CHOCO-CHIP PEAR VELVET

Makes 6 servings, **120 calories each**

- 1 egg, separated
- ½ cup water
  Dash of salt
  Granulated or liquid no-calorie sweetener
- 1 envelope unflavored gelatin
- 3 tablespoons instant nonfat dry milk
- 1 teaspoon vanilla
- 2 containers (8 ounces each) vanilla yogurt
- 1 can (1 pound) diet-pack pear halves, drained and halved
- 1 tablespoon grated sweet cooking chocolate (from a 4-ounce bar)

1. Beat egg yolk slightly in a bowl; beat in water and salt. Sweeten with your favorite no-calorie sweetener, using the equivalent of 24 teaspoons (½ cup) sugar.
2. Mix gelatin and dry milk in the top of a small double boiler; stir in egg-yolk mixture.
3. Cook, stirring constantly, over simmering water, 5 minutes, or until gelatin dissolves and mixture coats a metal spoon. Strain into a large bowl; stir in vanilla.
4. Chill 30 minutes, or just until mixture is as thick as unbeaten egg white, then blend in yogurt until creamy-smooth.
5. Beat egg white until it forms soft peaks in a small bowl; fold into yogurt mixture. Pour into a 4-cup shallow mold or an 8-inch layer-cake pan. Chill 3 to 4 hours, or until firm.
6. To unmold, run a sharp-tip, thin-blade knife around top of mold, then dip mold *very quickly* in and out of a pan of hot water. Invert onto a chilled serving plate; lift off mold. Arrange pear quarters in a ring on top; sprinkle with grated chocolate. Cut into 6 wedges.

Calorie-counter's serving: 1 wedge or 1/6 of the mold.

BOUQUET FRUITS

Makes 6 servings, **100 calories each**

- 2 medium-size grapefruits
- 1 can (1 pound) diet-pack fruits for salad
- 1 can (8 ounces) diet-pack purple plums, drained

1. Pare grapefruits and section into a medium-size bowl. Stir in fruits for salad and plums.
2. Spoon into 6 dessert dishes; garnish each with mint, if you wish.

Calorie-counter's serving: 1 dishful.

DIETER'S CUSTARD PIE

Bake at 450° for 10 minutes, then at 300° for 45 minutes.
Makes 8 servings, **175 calories each**

Low-calorie Pastry (recipe follows)
- 4 eggs
- ¼ teaspoon salt
- ⅛ teaspoon nutmeg
- 1 teaspoon grated lemon rind
- 3 cups skim milk
  Granulated, liquid, or tablet no-calorie sweetener
- 1 teaspoon vanilla

1. Make LOW-CALORIE PASTRY. Roll out to a 12-inch round between two sheets of waxed paper (no flour needed); fit into a 9-inch pie plate. Trim overhang to ½ inch; turn under, flush with rim; flute. Chill while preparing filling.
2. Beat eggs slightly with salt, nutmeg, and lemon rind in a medium-size bowl; stir in skim milk, your favorite no-calorie sweetener, using the equivalent of 16 teaspoons (⅓ cup) sugar, and vanilla.
3. Set pie plate on a cooky sheet; place on rack in oven. Strain custard mixture into prepared shell.
4. Bake in very hot oven (450°) 10 minutes; lower heat to slow (300°). Bake 45 minutes longer, or until center is almost set but still soft. (Do not overbake, for custard will set as it cools.) Cool pie completely on a wire rack. Cut into 8 wedges.

Calorie-counter's serving: 1 wedge or ⅛ of pie.

LOW-CALORIE PASTRY

Makes 1 nine-inch pie shell

- 1 cup sifted regular flour
- ½ teaspoon salt
- 4 tablespoons (½ stick) margarine
- 2½ tablespoons ice water

1. Sift ½ cup of the flour and salt into a medium-size bowl; cut in margarine with a pastry blender until mixture is crumbly, then blend in remaining ½ cup sifted flour until crumbly.
2. Sprinkle ice water over, 1 tablespoon at a time; mix lightly with a fork just until pastry holds together and leaves side of bowl clean.

BUTTERFLY ECLAIRS

Bake at 400° for 30 minutes.
Makes 18 eclairs, **64 calories each**

- ½ cup water
- 4 tablespoons (½ stick) butter or margarine
- ½ cup sifted regular flour
- ⅛ teaspoon salt
- 2 eggs
- 1 package (2 envelopes) low-calorie vanilla-flavor pudding mix
- 2 cups skim milk

1. Heat water and butter or margarine to boiling in a medium-size saucepan. Stir in flour and salt all at once with a wooden spoon; continue stirring vigorously about 2 minutes, or until batter forms a thick smooth ball that follows spoon around pan.
2. Remove from heat; cool slightly; beat in eggs, 1 at a time, until mixture is thick and shiny-smooth.
3. Shape batter, 1 tablespoon at a time, into thin strips, about 1 inch apart, on ungreased cooky sheets.
4. Bake in hot oven (400°) 30 minutes, or until puffed and lightly golden. Remove at once from cooky sheets; cool completely on wire racks.
5. Prepare pudding mix with skim milk, following label directions; chill. **(Pudding will be very thick.)**
6. Cut a slice across top of each eclair and lift off. Scoop out any bits of soft dough from bottoms with tip of teaspoon. Fill each with 1 rounded tablespoon pudding. Cut each top in half crosswise; push pieces into pudding in shell, butterfly style. Garnish each with half a fresh strawberry, if you wish.

Calorie-counter's serving: 2 eclairs.

CINNAMON PEARS

Makes 8 servings, **50 calories each**

- 4 medium-size firm ripe pears
- ½ cup water
  Granulated, liquid, or tablet no-calorie sweetener
- 1 two-inch piece stick cinnamon

1. Pare pears, then halve and core; place, cut sides down, in a large frying pan.
2. Sweeten water with your favorite no-calorie sweetener, using the equivalent of 12 teaspoons (¼ cup) sugar in a cup; pour over pears; add cinnamon stick to pan; cover.
3. Heat to boiling, then simmer 10 minutes, or just until pears are tender. Spoon into serving dishes; pour sauce over. Serve warm or chilled.

Calorie-counter's serving: ½ pear with syrup.

COCONUT CUP CUSTARDS

Bake at 325° for 40 minutes.
Makes 6 servings, 81 calories each

3 eggs
½ teaspoon grated lemon rind
⅛ teaspoon salt
2¼ cups skim milk
½ teaspoon vanilla
 Granulated, liquid, or tablet
 no-calorie sweetener
2 tablespoons flaked coconut

1. Beat eggs slightly with lemon rind and salt in a medium-size bowl. Stir in milk, vanilla, and your favorite no-calorie sweetener, using the equivalent of 12 teaspoons sugar. Strain into 6 ungreased 5-ounce custard cups, using about ½ cup for each.
2. Set cups in a shallow pan; place on oven shelf; pour boiling water into pan to depth of about an inch.
3. Bake in slow oven (325°) 40 minutes, or until centers are almost set but still soft. (Custard will set as it cools.) Remove at once from pan of water.
4. Serve warm or chilled, in cups, or to unmold: Loosen custards around edges with a thin-blade knife, then invert into serving dishes. Sprinkle tops with coconut.

Calorie-counter's serving: 1 custard with 1 teaspoon coconut.

HONEY GLAZED APPLES

Bake at 400° for 45 minutes.
Makes 6 servings, 98 calories each

3 large baking apples
½ cup water
¼ cup honey
½ teaspoon grated lemon rind
 Few drops red food coloring

1. Pare apples, then halve and core; place, cut sides down, in a shallow baking dish.
2. Mix water, honey, lemon rind, and food coloring in a 1-cup measure; pour over apples; cover.
3. Bake in hot oven (400°), basting once or twice with syrup in dish, 30 minutes; uncover. Baste apples again; bake 15 minutes longer, or until tender but still firm enough to hold their shape.
4. Cool apples in baking dish, basting once or twice to make a rich glaze. Garnish with a sprig of mint, if you wish. Serve warm.

Calorie-counter's serving: ½ apple.

CHEERY CHERRY ROLL

Bake at 400° for 8 minutes.
Makes 10 servings, 135 calories each

½ cup sifted cake flour
¾ teaspoon baking powder
¼ teaspoon salt
3 eggs
½ cup sugar
1 teaspoon vanilla
2 tablespoons 10X (confectioners' powdered) sugar
1 cup cherry pie filling (from an about-1-pound can)

1. Grease a jelly-roll pan, 15x10x1; line with waxed paper cut ½ inch smaller than pan; grease paper.
2. Measure flour, baking powder, and salt into sifter.
3. Beat eggs until foamy-light and double in volume in a medium-size bowl; beat in sugar, 1 tablespoon at a time, until mixture is thick; stir in **vanilla just to blend.**
4. Sift flour mixture over and fold in until no streaks of white remain. Spread evenly into prepared pan.
5. Bake in hot oven (400°) 8 minutes, or until center springs back when lightly pressed with fingertip.
6. Cut around cake about ½ inch in from edge of pan with a sharp knife; invert cake onto a clean towel dusted with 1 tablespoon of the 10X sugar; peel off waxed paper. Starting at one short end of cake, roll up; wrap in towel; cool completely.
7. Unroll cake carefully; spread evenly with filling; reroll; dust top with remaining 1 tablespoon 10X sugar.
8. To serve, cut crosswise into 10 slices.

Calorie-counter's serving: 1 slice.

ICED FRUITS

Makes 4 servings, 63 calories each

1 can (about 9 ounces) diet-pack pineapple tidbits
⅛ teaspoon ground ginger
1 can (about 11 ounces) diet-pack mandarin-orange segments
12 purple grapes

1. Drain syrup from pineapple tidbits into a cup; stir in ginger. Drain mandarin-orange segments, discarding the syrup.
2. Crush a tray of ice cubes finely; pile in a cone shape on a serving plate. Place a small cup on top; fill with the pineapple-ginger syrup. Arrange pineapple tidbits, mandarin-orange segments, and grapes in rows on ice cone.
3. Serve with wooden picks to spear fruits, then dip into sauce.

Calorie-counter's serving: ¼ of the fruits and sauce.

CHOCOLATE-ORANGE TORTE

Bake at 325° for 30 minutes.
Makes 12 servings, 104 calories each

¼ cup sifted regular flour
¼ cup dry cocoa powder (not a mix)
¼ teaspoon baking powder
¼ teaspoon salt
4 eggs
½ cup sugar (for cake)
1½ teaspoons vanilla
 Liquid no-calorie sweetener
½ cup instant nonfat dry milk
½ cup orange juice, well-chilled
1 tablespoon lemon juice
2 tablespoons sugar (for filling)

1. Grease a jelly-roll pan, 15x10x1; line with waxed paper cut ½ inch smaller than pan; grease paper.
2. Measure flour, cocoa powder, baking powder, and salt into sifter.
3. Beat eggs until foamy in a medium-size bowl; gradually beat in the ½ cup sugar until mixture is thick. Stir in ½ teaspoon of the vanilla and your favorite liquid no-calorie sweetener, using the equivalent of 12 teaspoons sugar. (Remaining vanilla is for filling in Step 7.)
4. Sift flour mixture over egg mixture and fold in until no streaks of white remain. Spread evenly into prepared pan.
5. Bake in slow oven (325°) 30 minutes, or until top springs back when lightly pressed with fingertip.
6. Cut around cake about ½ inch in from edge of pan with a sharp knife; invert cake onto a large wire rack; peel off waxed paper; cool cake completely.
7. Sprinkle nonfat dry milk powder over chilled orange juice in a chilled large bowl; beat with an electric beater at high speed 3 minutes, or until soft peaks form. Add lemon juice and remaining 1 teaspoon vanilla; continue beating 5 minutes, or until mixture stands in firm peaks; carefully fold in the 2 tablespoons sugar.
8. Cut cake crosswise into three even pieces. Spread each to edges with about 1 cup of the whipped orange mixture; stack layers on a serving plate. Chill at least 15 minutes, but not longer than 2 hours, for filling-topping loses its fluffiness. Just before serving, garnish with orange slices, if you wish. Cut crosswise into 12 even slices.

Calorie-counter's serving: 1 slice.

Cake lovers can cater to their sweet tooth for surprisingly few calories—and here's proof. Diet-light Spongecake (recipe on page 144) is the lacy old-fashioned water-type sprinkled lightly with confectioners' sugar for extra sweetness. For an additional 25 calories, you can serve each big wedge with one-half cup plump juicy strawberries

Total calories per serving for cake: 125

WHITECAP CHEESECAKE

Makes 10 servings, 130 calories each

2 eggs
1 cup water
¼ teaspoon salt
  Granulated or liquid no-calorie
    sweetener
2 envelopes unflavored gelatin
⅓ cup instant nonfat dry milk
1 teaspoon grated lemon rind
3 tablespoons lemon juice
1 teaspoon vanilla
3 cups (1½ pounds) cream-style
    cottage cheese
1 cup evaporated milk, well-chilled
3 tablespoons graham-cracker crumbs
    (2 crackers)

1. Separate eggs, putting whites in a small bowl and yolks in a second small bowl. Beat egg yolks slightly; beat in water and salt; sweeten with your favorite no-calorie sweetener, using the equivalent of 48 teaspoons (1 cup) sugar.
2. Mix gelatin and dry milk in the top of a double boiler; stir in egg-yolk mixture.
3. Cook over simmering water, stirring constantly, 5 minutes, or until gelatin dissolves completely and mixture coats a metal spoon. Strain into a large bowl; stir in lemon rind, 2 tablespoons of the lemon juice, and vanilla. (Set remaining lemon juice aside for Step 5.) Chill 30 minutes, or just until mixture is as thick as unbeaten egg white.
4. Press cottage cheese through a sieve; stir into gelatin mixture until blended.
5. Beat egg whites until they stand in firm peaks. Beat chilled evaporated milk with remaining 1 tablespoon lemon juice until stiff in a small bowl.
6. Fold beaten egg whites, then whipped milk into cheese mixture; pour into an 8-cup mold. Chill at least 4 hours, or until softly set.
7. Unmold onto a serving plate; press graham-cracker crumbs around the edge. Slice into 10 wedges. (If you wish, garnish with a ring of fresh red raspberries or strawberries.)
Calorie-counter's serving: 1 wedge.

LEMON TAPIOCA

Makes 6 servings, 73 calories each

1 egg
2¾ cups skim milk
3 tablespoons quick-cooking
    tapioca
⅛ teaspoon salt
½ teaspoon vanilla
  Grated rind of ½ lemon
  Granulated, liquid, or tablet
    no-calorie sweetener

1. Beat egg with milk in a medium-size saucepan; stir in tapioca and salt; let stand about 5 minutes.
2. Cook, stirring constantly, 5 to 8 minutes, or until mixture comes to a full rolling boil. Remove from heat.
3. Stir in vanilla, lemon rind, and your favorite no-calorie sweetener, using the equivalent of 8 teaspoons sugar; cool.
4. Spoon into 6 sherbet glasses, dividing evenly. Serve warm or chilled.
Calorie-counter's serving: 1 sherbet glassful.

MAPLE-CHIFFON MOLD

Makes 6 servings, 100 calories each

1 envelope unflavored gelatin
6 tablespoons sugar
⅛ teaspoon salt
2 eggs, separated
1½ cups skim milk
1 teaspoon vanilla
¼ teaspoon maple extract

1. Mix gelatin, 2 tablespoons of the sugar, and salt in a small saucepan; beat in egg yolks and milk. Cook, stirring constantly, over low heat 5 minutes, or until gelatin dissolves and custard coats a metal spoon; remove from heat.
2. Strain into a small bowl; stir in vanilla and maple extract. Chill 1 hour, or until as thick as unbeaten egg white.
3. Beat egg whites until foamy-white and double in volume in a medium-size bowl; beat in remaining 4 tablespoons sugar until meringue forms soft peaks. Fold in thickened gelatin mixture until no streaks of yellow remain. Pour into a 4-cup mold. Chill several hours, or until firm.
4. When ready to serve, unmold onto a serving plate; cut in 6 equal wedges.
Calorie-counter's serving: 1/6 of mold.

BANANA BOUNTY PIE

Bake at 425° for 15 minutes.
Makes 8 servings, 173 calories each

  Low-calorie Pastry *(recipe on
    page 154)*
2 tablespoons flaked coconut
3 eggs, separated
1 cup skim milk
1 envelope unflavored gelatin
1 teaspoon vanilla
  Granulated or liquid no-calorie
    sweetener
2 tablespoons sugar
1 small banana, peeled and sliced
    thin

1. Make LOW-CALORIE PASTRY. Roll out to a 12-inch round between two sheets of waxed paper (no flour needed); fit into a 9-inch pie plate. Trim overhang to ½ inch; turn under, flush with rim; flute. Prick well all over with a fork.
2. Bake in hot oven (425°) 15 minutes, or until golden; cool completely on a wire rack. Turn off oven heat.
3. Spread coconut in a pie plate; toast in heated oven 5 minutes, or until golden. (Watch it, for it browns quickly.) Set aside for Step 9.
4. Beat egg yolks with milk until blended in the top of a double boiler; sprinkle gelatin over top.
5. Cook, stirring constantly, over simmering water 5 minutes, or until gelatin dissolves completely and mixture coats a metal spoon; remove from heat.
6. Stir in vanilla and your favorite no-calorie sweetener, using the equivalent of 12 teaspoons (¼ cup) sugar. Chill 30 minutes, or until as thick as unbeaten egg white.
7. Beat egg whites until foamy-white and double in volume in a medium-size bowl; beat in sugar, 1 tablespoon at a time, beating all the time until meringue forms soft peaks. Gradually fold in thickened gelatin mixture until no streaks of white remain.
8. Spoon into cooled pastry shell. Chill several hours, or until firm.
9. When ready to serve, arrange banana slices in a ring on top; mound coconut in center. Cut into 8 wedges.
Calorie-counter's serving: 1 wedge or ⅛ of pie.

Your calorie counter

FOOD COUNT AMOUNT

A

Food	Count	Amount
Almonds, shelled,	850	1 cup
salted	83	10 nuts
Anchovies, canned fillets	28	4
Apple	70	1 med.
Apple butter	33	1 tbsp.
Apple juice	120	1 cup
Applesauce, canned,		
sweetened	230	1 cup
diet-pack	100	1 cup
Apricots		
fresh	55	3
canned in heavy syrup	110	½ cup
canned, diet-pack	56	½ cup
dried	90	10
Apricot nectar, canned	140	1 cup
Artichokes, fresh, cooked	30	1 med.
frozen, hearts, cooked	22	½ cup
Asparagus, fresh, cooked	20	6 spears
canned	20	6 spears
frozen, spears, cooked	23	5
Avocado	245	½ med.
	186	½ cup

B

Food	Count	Amount
Bacon, broiled or fried	100	2 slices
Canadian, lean, broiled	50	3 slices
Bamboo shoots, canned	41	1 cup
Banana	85	1
Barley, pearl, cooked	142	1 cup
Bean Sprouts, canned	20	½ cup
Beans, baked, with pork		
and molasses	325	1 cup
with pork in tomato sauce	295	1 cup
Beans, green or wax		
fresh cut, cooked	15	½ cup
canned, cut	14	½ cup
frozen, cut, cooked	18	½ cup
kidney, canned	230	1 cup
lima, fresh, cooked	180	1 cup
frozen, cooked	94	½ cup
dried, large, cooked	260	1 cup
Beef, brisket, fresh	266	1 slice
corned	266	1 slice
pot roast, blade	506	1 slice
rib roast	243	1 slice
rump	235	1 slice
sirloin	186	1 slice
steak, cubed, raw	793	12 oz.
steak, club, raw	305	6 oz.
steak, flank	200	3 slices
porterhouse	412	1 piece
round	406	1 piece
ground, round, raw	271	6 oz.
sirloin	353	1 piece
stew meat, chuck,		
boneless, raw	421	4 oz.
Beef and vegetable stew		
canned	210	1 cup
Beef broth canned,		
condensed	66	1 can
cubes instant	8	1 env.
canned corned beef	185	3 oz.
canned corned beef hash	155	3 oz.
Beef potpie, frozen	436	8 oz.
Beef TV Dinner	350	1
Beer	100	1 cup
Beets, fresh, cooked,		
diced	50	1 cup
Biscuits, baking powder	129	1
Blackberries, fresh	43	½ cup
frozen, unsweetened	55	½ cup
Blueberries, fresh	43	½ cup
frozen, sweetened	129	½ cup
frozen, unsweetened	45	½ cup
Bologna	87	1 slice
Bran flakes, 40%	95	¾ cup
Brandy	100	2 oz.
Brazil nuts, shelled	100	4
Bread		
Boston brown	100	1 slice
cracked-wheat	60	1 slice
French	108	1 piece
Italian	108	1 piece
pumpernickel	65	1 slice
raisin, unfrosted	60	1 slice
rye	55	1 slice
white, enriched	60	1 slice
whole-wheat	55	1 slice
Bread crumbs, dry	345	1 cup
soft	120	1 cup
Broccoli, fresh, spears,		
cooked	40	4
frozen, chopped, cooked	25	½ cup
frozen, spears, cooked	26	3
Brownies	120	1
Brussels sprout, fresh,		
cooked	45	1 cup
frozen, cooked	29	½ cup
Butter	100	1 tbsp.
Buttermilk	90	1 cup

C

Food	Count	Amount
Cabbage, raw, finely		
shredded	25	1 cup
cooked, finely shredded	35	1 cup
Cabbage, Chinese, raw,		
chopped	15	1 cup
cooked, chopped	20	1 cup
Cakes		
angel	110	1 wedge
chocolate with icing	445	1 wedge
cupcake with icing	185	1
plain cake, without		
icing	200	1 slice
poundcake	140	1 slice
spongecake	120	1 wedge
Candy		
caramels	42	1
chocolate creams	47	1
chocolate fudge	66	1
chocolate-mint patty	40	1
marshmallows	26	1 large
peanut brittle	125	1
Cantaloupe	60	½ med.
balls	20	½ cup
Carbonated beverages	90	8 oz.
Carrots, raw, whole	20	1
raw, grated	45	1 cup
cooked, diced	45	1 cup
Cashew nuts, roasted	164	8
Catsup	15	1 tbsp.
Cauliflower, raw		
flowerets	25	1 cup
cooked, flowerets	25	1 cup
frozen, flowerets, cooked	15	½ cup
Celery, raw, diced	15	1 cup
raw, stalk	5	1
Cheese		
blue or Roquefort	105	1 oz.
Camembert	86	1 oz.
Cheddar or American,		
grated	445	1 cup
grated	30	1 tbsp.
process	105	1 oz.
cottage, skim milk		
cream-style	240	1 cup
cottage, dry	195	1 cup
cream	55	1 tbsp.
Parmesan, grated	31	1 tbsp.
Swiss, natural	120	1 oz.
Swiss, process	105	1 oz.
Cheese foods, Cheddar	90	1 oz.
Cheese spreads	35	1 tbsp.
Cherries, sour, red, canned	230	1 cup
Cherries, sweet, fresh	80	1 cup
canned, sweetened	112	½ cup
canned, diet-pack	57	½ cup
Chicken, broiled,		
quartered	248	1 piece
roast	200	3 slices
roast	101	1 leg
roast	147	1 thigh
Chicken broth, canned		
condensed	74	10 oz.
cubes	6	1
instant	10	1 env.
Chicken livers	146	¼ lb.

Food	Calories	Amount
Chicken potpie, frozen	482	8 oz.
Chicken TV Dinner	489	1
Chili con carne, canned		
with beans	335	1 cup
without beans	510	1 cup
Chili sauce	17	1 tbsp.
Chocolate, unsweetened	145	1 oz.
semisweet pieces	906	6 oz.
Chocolate bar, milk, plain	150	1 oz.
Chocolate malted milk		
shake with ice cream	500	1½ cups
Chocolate milk	205	1 cup
Chocolate syrup, thin	50	1 tbsp.
Clams, raw	65	6 large
canned, clams and liquid	45	½ cup
Clam juice	35	1 cup
Cocoa, with whole milk	235	1 cup
Cocoa powder	21	1 tbsp.
Coconut, shredded	335	1 cup
Cod, fresh, poached	84	4 oz.
frozen, fillets, poached	84	4 oz.
frozen, sticks, breaded	276	5
Cola	95	8 oz.
Cookies		
chocolate wafer	36	1
creme sandwich, chocolate	54	1
fig bars, small	55	1
gingersnaps	52	1
sugar wafer	10	1
vanilla wafer	18	1
Corn flakes, plain	100	1 cup
presweetened	110	¾ cup
Corn, sweet		
fresh, cooked	70	1 ear
canned, cream-style	92	½ cup
canned, whole-kernel	70	½ cup
frozen, whole-kernel	73	½ cup
Corn meal, dry	420	1 cup
Corn muffins	150	1
Corn oil	125	1 tbsp.
Corn syrup, light or dark	60	1 tbsp.
Cornstarch	30	1 tbsp.
Cornstarch pudding with		
whole milk chocolate	67	½ cup
vanilla or butterscotch	72	½ cup
low-calorie, with skim		
milk chocolate	57	½ cup
vanilla or butterscotch	55	½ cup
instant chocolate	183	½ cup
vanilla or butterscotch	170	½ cup
Cottonseed oil	125	1 tbsp.
Crab meat	89	3 oz.
Cracker meal	45	1 tbsp.
Crackers		
cheese	34	10
graham, plain	30	1
chocolate graham	56	1
oyster	60	20
peanut-butter sandwich	45	1
pretzels	7	5 sticks
rye wafers	21	1
saltines	14	1
soda	23	1
Cranberry juice, bottled	160	1 cup
Cranberry sauce,		
sweetened, canned,		
jellied or whole-berry	26	1 tbsp.
Cream, half-and-half	20	1 tbsp.
heavy or whipping	55	1 tbsp.
light, coffee, or table	30	1 tbsp.
sour, dairy	29	1 tbsp.
Cucumber, raw, whole	30	1
raw, sliced	5	6 slices
Custard baked with		
whole milk	285	1 cup

D

Food	Calories	Amount
Dates, dry, whole	100	5
Doughnuts, cake type	125	1
Duck, roast	165	3 slices

E

Food	Calories	Amount
Egg, whole	80	1
white	15	1
yolk	60	1
Eggplant, fried	139	1 slice

Food	Calories	Amount
Endive, Belgian	10	1 stalk
curly or chickory, broken	5	1 cup
Escarole	5	2 leaves

F

Food	Calories	Amount
Farina, cooked	100	1 cup
Figs, fresh	90	3 small
canned, in syrup	150	½ cup
canned, diet pack	68	½ cup
dried	100	2 med.
Flounder, fillet, fresh,		
poached	170	8 oz.
frozen, poached	76	4 oz.
Flour, all-purpose	400	1 cup
cake or pastry, sifted	365	1 cup
self-rising, enriched	385	1 cup
whole-wheat	400	1 cup
Frankfurter (10 per lb.)	120	1
French dressing, low		
calorie	9	1 tbsp.
regular	65	1 tbsp.
Fruitcake, dark	115	1 sliver
Fruit cocktail canned,		
in syrup	195	1 cup
canned, diet-pack	60	½ cup

G

Food	Calories	Amount
Gelatin, unflavored	35	1 tbsp.
Gelatin dessert, flavored		
ready-to-eat, regular	81	½ cup
low calorie	9	½ cup
Gin	105	2 oz.
Ginger ale	80	8 oz.
Gingerbread	175	1 piece
Grapefruit fresh	55	½ med.
fresh sections	75	1 cup
canned, sections	175	1 cup
canned, diet-pack	70	1 cup
Grapefruit juice, fresh	95	1 cup
canned, sweetened	130	1 cup
canned, unsweetened	100	1 cup
frozen concentrate,		
sweetened reconstituted	115	1 cup
unsweetened reconstituted	100	1 cup
Grapes, fresh, Niagara,		
Concord, Delaware,		
Catawaba, Scuppernong	65	1 cup
Malaga, Muscat,		
Thompson seedless,		
Emperor, Flame, Tokay	95	1 cup
Grape juice, bottled		
or canned	165	1 cup

H

Food	Calories	Amount
Haddock, fresh, broiled	100	6 oz.
frozen, broiled	88	4 oz.
frozen, fish-sticks,		
breaded	280	5
Halibut, fresh, broiled	217	8 oz.
frozen, broiled	144	4 oz.
Ham, baked	253	1 slice
boiled sliced	135	2 oz.
Herring, pickled	127	2 oz.
Hominy grits, cooked	120	1 cup
Honey, strained	65	1 tbsp.
Honeydew melon	73	⅛ med.
cubes	58	1 cup

I

Food	Calories	Amount
Ice cream, commercial		
chocolate	200	⅔ cup
vanilla	193	⅔ cup
Ice cream, brick	145	1 slice
Ice milk, chocolate	144	⅔ cup
vanilla	136	⅔ cup

J and K

Food	Calories	Amount
Jams, jellies, preserves	55	1 tbsp.
Kale, cooked	30	1 cup
Kidney, cooked, beef	118	3 oz.
lamb	111	3 oz.
pork	130	3 oz.

L

Food	Calories	Amount
Lamb chop, loin, raw	223	6 oz.

Food	Calories	Amount
rib, raw	240	5 oz.
shoulder, raw	252	5 oz.
Lamb roast, leg	165	1 slice
Lamb shank, raw	275	10 oz.
Lard	125	1 tbsp.
Leeks, chopped, cooked	25	½ cup
Lettuce, head	47	1 lb.
Lemon	20	1 med.
Lemonade concentrate,		
reconstituted	110	1 cup
Lemon juice, fresh	5	1 tbsp.
	60	1 cup
Limeade concentrate,		
reconstituted	105	1 cup
Lime juice, fresh	4	1 tbsp.
	65	1 cup
Liqueurs	165	1 oz.
Liver, cooked beef	117	3 oz.
calf's	136	3 oz.
lamb	171	3 oz.
pork	115	3 oz.
Liverwurst	100	1 slice
Lobster, fresh, boiled	108	¾ lb.
canned, meat	80	½ cup
frozen tails, boiled	81	3 small

M

Food	Calories	Amount
Macaroni, cooked	155	1 cup
Macaroni and cheese,		
baked	470	1 cup
Mandarin oranges canned,		
in syrup	55	⅓ cup
canned, diet-pack	29	⅓ cup
Mango	133	1 med.
Manhattan	165	2½ oz.
Margarine	100	1 tbsp.
Martini	145	2½ oz.
Mayonnaise	100	1 tbsp.
imitation	55	1 tbsp.
Melba toast	17	1 slice
Milk,		
buttermilk	90	1 cup
condensed, sweetened	980	1 cup
dry, instant nonfat	250	1 cup
evaporated	345	1 cup
skim	90	1 cup
whole	160	1 cup
Mixed vegetables,		
frozen, cooked	55	½ cup
Molasses	50	1 tbsp.
Muffins, plain	140	1
Mushrooms, fresh	14	6
canned, with liquid	40	1 cup
Mustard, prepared	4	1 tsp.

N

Food	Calories	Amount
Nectarines	50	1 med.
Noodles, egg, cooked	200	1 cup

O

Food	Calories	Amount
Oat cereal, ready-to-eat	100	1 cup
Oatmeal	130	1 cup
Okra, fresh, cooked	25	8 pods
frozen, sliced, cooked	26	½ cup
Olives, green unpitted	15	4 med.
ripe, unpitted	15	2 large
Olive oil	125	1 tbsp.
Onion, green	20	6 small
raw, whole	40	1 med.
raw, chopped	60	1 cup
Onion soup mix, dry	150	1 env.
Orange, fresh	70	1 med.
sections	50	½ cup
Orange juice, fresh	110	1 cup
canned, unsweetened	120	1 cup
frozen concentrate,		
reconstituted	110	1 cup
Oysters, raw	160	15 med.
Oyster stew	200	1 cup

P

Food	Calories	Amount
Pancakes, buckwheat	55	1 cake
plain, home recipe	60	1 cake
Papaya, fresh, cubed	70	1 cup
Parsley, fresh, chopped	1	1 tbsp.
Parsnips, cooked, diced	100	1 cup

Food	Value	Measure
Peaches, fresh, whole	35	1 med.
fresh, sliced	65	1 cup
canned, in syrup	90	2 halves
canned, diet-pack	54	2 halves
dried, uncooked	420	1 cup
cooked, unsweetened	220	1 cup
frozen, sweetened	99	1/3 cup
Peach nectar, canned	120	1 cup
Peanuts, roasted, salted	100	20 med.
chopped	55	1 tbsp.
dry-roasted	170	1/4 cup
Peanut butter	95	1 tbsp.
Pears, fresh, whole	100	1 med.
canned, in syrup	58	2 halves
canned, diet-pack	62	2 halves
Pear nectar, canned	130	1 cup
Peas, blackeye, frozen, cooked	95	1/2 cup
Peas, green, fresh, cooked	115	1 cup
canned	146	1 cup
frozen, cooked	60	1/2 cup
Pecans, halves	100	12
	376	1/2 cup
Peppers, sweet, green, raw	15	1 med.
green, raw, diced	16	1/2 cup
red, raw	20	1 med.
Persimmons	75	1 med.
Pickles, dill	15	1 (5")
sweet	30	1 (3")
Pies, apple	290	1/8
blueberry	255	1/8
cherry	299	1/8
custard	233	1/8
lemon meringue	264	1/8
mince	298	1/8
pecan	479	1/8
pumpkin	230	1/8
Pimientos, canned	10	1 med.
Pine nuts (pignolias)	671	1/2 cup
Pineapple, fresh, diced	75	1 cup
canned, crushed, in syrup	195	1 cup
canned, sliced, in syrup	90	2 slices
canned, cubes, juice-pack	57	1/2 cup
Pineapple juice, canned	135	1 cup
frozen, reconstituted	125	1 cup
Plums, fresh, whole	25	1 med.
canned, in syrup	100	3 plums
canned, diet-pack	75	3 plums
Pork, chop, rib, raw	250	6 oz.
chop, loin, raw	283	6 oz.
roast, loin	330	1 chop
luncheon meat	165	2 oz.
Popcorn, popped, with oil and salt	40	1 cup
plain	24	1 cup
sugar-coated	135	1 cup
Potatoes, baked, without skin	90	1 med.
boiled, without skin	80	1 med.
French fried, frozen	125	10 pcs.
mashed, with milk only	70	1/2 cup
Potato chips	115	10
Pretzels, small sticks	10	10
Prunes	70	4 med.
cooked, unsweetened	295	18 med.
Prune juice	200	1 cup
Pumpkin, canned	75	1 cup

R

Food	Value	Measure
Radishes	5	4
Raisins	460	1 cup
Raspberries, red, fresh	70	1 cup
canned, in syrup	100	1/2 cup
frozen, sweetened	115	1/2 cup
Rhubarb, cooked with sugar	385	1 cup
Rice, cooked, brown	100	2/3 cup
precooked, cooked	140	2/3 cup
long-grain, white	185	1 cup
wild	73	1/2 cup
Rice cereal, ready to eat	115	1 cup
puffed	55	1 cup
Rolls, frankfurter	120	1

Food	Value	Measure
French	118	1
hamburger	123	1
Parker house	114	1
Rum	105	2 oz.
Rutabagas, cubed, cooked	25	1/2 cup
Rye wafers	63	3

S

Food	Value	Measure
Salad dressings, blue cheese, low-calorie	15	1 tbsp.
regular	65	1 tbsp.
French, low-calorie	9	1 tbsp.
regular	65	1 tbsp.
mayonnaise, imitation	55	1 tbsp.
regular	100	1 tbsp.
salad dressing	65	1 tbsp.
Thousand Island, low-calorie	33	1 tbsp.
regular	75	1 tbsp.
Salad oil	125	1 tbsp.
Salami	130	3 slices
Salmon, fresh, steak, broiled	430	6 oz.
canned	120	1/2 cup
Sardines, canned, in oil	100	4
Sauerkraut, canned	32	1 cup
Scallops, sea, fresh, steamed	105	6 med.
frozen, steamed	210	1 cup
Sesame seeds	10	1 tbsp.
Sherbet, orange, milk	260	1 cup
Shortening, vegetable	110	1 tbsp.
Shredded wheat biscuit	94	1
Shrimps, fresh, poached	100	7 med.
canned	167	5 oz.
frozen, poached	100	9 med.
cocktail, tiny, canned	33	15
Sole, fillet, fresh, poached	177	1 piece
Sole, fillet, frozen, poached	88	4 oz.
Soups, canned condensed, prepared with water, following label directions,		
asparagus, cream of	51	1 cup
bean with bacon	130	1 cup
beef broth	22	1 cup
beef noodle	55	1 cup
black bean	80	1 cup
celery, cream of	75	1 cup
cheese	142	1 cup
chicken broth	85	1 cup
chicken, cream of	85	1 cup
chicken gumbo	48	1 cup
chicken noodle	54	1 cup
chicken vegetable	60	1 cup
chicken with rice	44	1 cup
chili beef	133	1 cup
clam chowder	60	1 cup
consomme	25	1 cup
green pea, cream of	110	1 cup
madrilene	27	1 cup
minestrone	85	1 cup
mushroom, cream of	113	1 cup
onion	52	1 cup
pepper pot	83	1 cup
potato, cream of	59	1 cup
Scotch broth	74	1 cup
split pea	130	1 cup
tomato	73	1 cup
tomato rice	82	1 cup
turkey noodle	65	1 cup
turkey vegetable	58	1 cup
vegetable	63	1 cup
vegetable beef	61	1 cup
Soups, packaged mix prepared with water, following label directions,		
beef	87	1 cup
chicken noodle	60	1 cup
chicken rice	55	1 cup
green pea	128	1 cup
mushroom, cream of	46	1 cup
onion	40	1 cup
potato, cream of	90	1 cup
tomato vegetable	69	1 cup
vegetable	69	1 cup

Food	Value	Measure
Soy sauce	10	1 tbsp.
Soybean oil	125	1 tbsp.
Spaghetti, cooked	155	1 cup
Spinach, fresh, cooked	40	1 cup
canned	45	1 cup
frozen	24	1/2 cup
Squash, yellow, zucchini, crookneck, patty pan, sliced, cooked	30	1 cup
frozen, cooked	20	1/2 cup
Squash, acorn, banana, hubbard, baked, mashed	130	1 cup
frozen, cooked	50	1/2 cup
Strawberries, fresh	55	1 cup
Strawberries, frozen, whole, unsweetened	55	1 cup
sliced, sweetened	140	1/2 cup
Succotash, frozen, cooked	87	1/2 cup
Sugars, brown, firmly packed	820	1 cup
	51	1 tbsp.
granulated	770	1 cup
	45	1 tbsp.
lump	25	1
10X (confectioners' powdered)	495	1 cup
	30	1 tbsp.
Sweet potatoes, baked or boiled	170	1 med.
canned, without syrup	235	1 cup
Syrup, corn, light, or dark	60	1 tbsp.
maple	61	1 tbsp.
maple-blended, low-calorie	21	1 tbsp.
maple-blended, regular	54	1 tbsp.
pancake	55	1 tbsp.
sorghum	55	1 tbsp.

T

Food	Value	Measure
Tangerine	40	1 large
Tangerine juice, canned unsweetened	105	1 cup
Tapioca, quick-cooking, uncooked	35	1 tbsp.
Tomatoes, fresh	35	1 med.
canned	50	1 cup
Tomato juice, canned	45	1 cup
Tuna, canned, in oil, drained	170	1/2 cup
canned, in water	109	1/2 cup
Turnips, yellow, cooked, diced	50	1 cup
white, cooked, diced	35	1 cup
Turkey, roast	134	1 slice
Turkey potpie, frozen	429	8 oz.
Turkey TV dinner	325	1 pkg.

V

Food	Value	Measure
Veal, chop, loin, raw	251	8 oz.
chop, rib, raw	240	6 oz.
roast, leg	159	1 slice
scallopini, sauteed	172	3 pieces
Vinegar	2	1 tbsp.

W

Food	Value	Measure
Walnuts, chopped	50	1 tbsp.
halves	650	1 cup
Watermelon, fresh	115	1 wedge
cubed	40	1 cup
Wheat cereal, cooked	175	1 cup
flakes, ready-to-eat	100	1 cup
puffed	83	1 cup
puffed, presweetened	105	3/4 cup
shredded	94	1 biscuit
Wheat germ	27	1 tbsp.
Whiskey	105	2 oz.
Wine, dry	85	3 oz.
sweet	160	3 oz.

Y and Z

Food	Value	Measure
Yams, pared, cubed, cooked	90	1/2 cup
Yogurt, skim milk	120	1 cup
whole milk	176	1 cup
Zwieback	31	1 slice

Index of recipes

General index

See also Index of Recipes, page 157

ACKNOWLEDGEMENTS

OUR thanks go to American Medical Association consultants who reviewed the health material in this guide; to Dr. Orrea Florence Pye, professor of nutrition, Teachers College, Columbia University, for background material on diet and weight loss and nutrition and the reducing diet; to John E. Eichenlaub, M.D. *("Ten Tested Ways To Control Your Weight," pages 68-71)*; YWCA, National Board *(Physical-fitness Test, pages 16-17)*; Sara Mildred Strauss *(alignment and exercises, pages 20-39)*; Evelyn Loewendahl *(exercises, pages 42-63)*; Adele Kenyon *(exercises, pages 64-65)*. All leotards by Danskin; robe, page 18, from Edith Lances, New York.

"Desirable Weights for Women" and "Average Weights for Women" from *Statistical Bulletin* (November-December 1959) Metropolitan Life Insurance Company. "Predicted Daily Calorie Needs for Women" from *Quarterly Bulletin* (1952) Department of Health, City of New York. "Relative Change in Weight with Age" from *Weight, Height, and Selected Body Dimensions of Adults* (1965) Public Health Service Publication No. 1000-Series 11-No. 8, United States Department of Health, Education, and Welfare. "Calorie Equivalents of Activities" by Dr. Frank Konishi, Chairman, Department of Food and Nutrition, Southern Illinois University. "The Energy Cost of Activities" adapted, with permission of The Macmillan Company, from *Foundations of Nutrition,* 6th edition, by Clara Mae Taylor and Orrea Florence Pye, Copyright © 1966, The Macmillan Company. "Major-Vitamin Chart" adapted from *Vitamins and Your Body* (1971) Vitamin Information Bureau, Inc. and *Recommended Dietary Allowances.** "Recommended Daily Dietary Allowances" adapted from *Recommended Dietary Allowances.** "Foods High in Calcium" and "Foods High in Iron" adapted from *Nutritive Value of Foods* (revised 1971) Home and Garden Bulletin No. 72, United States Department of Agriculture and *Recommended Dietary Allowances.**

Recommended Dietary Allowances, seventh edition (1968). A Report of the Food and Nutrition Board, National Research Council, Publication 1694, National Academy of Sciences.

PHOTOS:
Page 12 by Roger Prigent; pages 54-55, 56 by Flip Schulke; page 66 by Luis Lemus; all others by FAMILY CIRCLE STUDIO.